Team-Based
Strategic
Planning

TEAM-BASED STRATEGIC PLANNING

A Complete Guide to Structuring, Facilitating, and Implementing the Process

C. Davis Fogg

This publication may not be reproduced, stored in a retrieval system, or transmitted in whole or in part, in any form or by any means, electronic, mechanical, photocopying, recording or otherwise without the prior written permission of C. Davis Fogg.

Contents

List of Figures

Preface

This book is about how to make the conventional strategic planning process work—to bend it, shape it, and modify it to meet your unique needs. It's about:

▲ *Structure.* We explain how to structure an efficient strategic planning process that uniquely fits your company, selecting the minimum steps needed from the conventional process to fit your company's size, financial and strategic situation, planning history, time constraints, culture, and your staff's abilities and personalities.

▲ *Facilitation.* We review the practical organizational, behavioral, and interpersonal techniques and skills needed: how to structure and run the many different types of meetings required; how to achieve consensus and intervene with dysfunctional individuals and teams; how to document the process and the plan; how to present the plan and communicate effectively with the organization about strategy; how to train staff members in planning skills; how to review plans and results.

▲ *Teams and teamwork.* We describe how to use teams from the top team down to gather needed information; develop, coordinate, and implement plans; place and accept accountability; resolve team conflicts; develop the team's self-sustaining facilitation skills; and get results.

▲ *Management and leadership.* We describe your role—when and why you need to be involved and when to stay away.

▲ *Organization involvement.* We discuss when and how to involve the various layers and functions in the organization in information-gathering, planning, and implementation tasks.

▲ *Information-gathering and analytical techniques.* We describe the precious few techniques that are truly useful, from diagnosing the organization's health through market, financial, and competitive analysis.

This book is not a rehash of the steps in the conventional strategic planning process. Though we cover the conventional and the tried-and-true process in Chapter 1, we leave detailed coverage of the planning process and its steps to others . . . if you don't already know it.

This book is real. Every example in it is taken from a real company. It's based on my twenty-five years as an executive, my dozen years as a consultant, and my work with dozens of clients.

Every technique and process covered has been used and proved by my company time and time again. They work. No theory or academic stuff.

The techniques and processes have been applied successfully in a wide variety of industries: manufacturing, healthcare, professional and financial services, publishing, distribution, packaged goods, chemicals, electronics, retail, food, not-for-profits, and consumer products, to name a few.

This is a practical book. It's meant to be used as you plow through and evolve the strategic planning process over the years. It's aimed at your company's top planning-team members—the chief executive officer (CEO), the president, and the key officers—who must develop strategic direction for the company. It's aimed at departmental managers who must develop their lower-level plans in alignment with the corporate plan. It's aimed at internal planners and facilitators as well as consultants who design and facilitate strategic planning processes.

The book is designed for active use during the planning process.

▲ First, the text presents the *principles* applicable to each stage of the process, always with examples of how the principles have been applied.
▲ Second, *facilitation guides* are set up for easy reference on the fly as you design pre-work for planning meetings and as you actually facilitate them. They describe the technique used for each step and discuss when to apply it, how to apply it, how long it takes, and who does it.
▲ Third, *real examples* are inserted at appropriate places in the facilitation guides so that you can see what your output should look like.
▲ Fourth, *key facilitation techniques and meeting agendas* are presented in the form of "cue cards" and graphic flowcharts for easy reference during meetings.

The book is written predominantly from the perspective of a single business with multiple related markets and products, managed through a number of functional departments and organization layers (e.g., a moderate-size bank serving the residential and commercial real estate market and the big business and small commercial markets with transaction, loan, and investment products. The principles, however, are applicable to both more and less complicated businesses.

Holding companies and companies with multiple businesses or strategic business units (SBUs) will obviously need several layers and levels of strategic plans—a corporate plan, a plan for each SBU, plans for corporate functions, and plans for functional departments within the SBUs. The slight complications caused by these more complex, multibusiness structures are not covered here, but the principles and process we discuss apply to all of them.

Reference to a product means either a tangible product (such as soap) or a service (such as on-line databases) that is offered to the target customer. *Product* should always be read as *product or service*.

This is not a "scholarly" book. I did no library research. There aren't vast citations. Everything in here I've learned or invented and applied over the years.

The book is divided into four sections.

Part One, *The Strategic Planning and Change Process*, covers, as a reminder, the steps in the conventional strategic planning process. It then goes on to the critical organization and human issues that must be addressed to make the process work: understanding the change process itself; deciding who does what during the process; determining the job of the facilitator; structuring the general planning process to meet your organization's exact needs; and getting buy-in from planning participants.

Part Two, *The Nuts and Bolts: Facilitating the Process Step by Step*, is a hands-on guide to facilitating planning process analyses and meetings. You can use this section to design your own process, meeting agendas, timing, and business analyses. You can refer to it during meetings as a reminder of facilitation techniques to use at each stage of the meeting and the process.

Part Three, *Implementing the Plan*, deals with the important but often overlooked or botched issue of how the plan should be put into action. The section covers how to cascade the plan down into the organization, place accountabilities, and review the plan effectively. It tells how to update the plan annually, a far simpler task than developing the first plan. The section concludes with the history of planning at two companies to illustrate how the planning process and its actual results evolve over time.

Part Four, *Team Processes*, covers how to form and use productive teams to develop and implement plans. It explains in detail the twelve core facilitation and intervention techniques needed by every facilitator and team leader. It provides a facilitation technique guide for use during meetings. It concludes with a discussion of how to remove the most common personnel, team, and process blockages impeding the strategic planning success.

Enjoy the book. And make it happen.

Acknowledgments

I want to acknowledge and thank the many people who gave me the knowledge and experience that enabled me to write this book.

First and foremost, the two men who started me thinking about the crucial importance of cultural and behavioral factors and "process" in determining organization performance and change: Professor Edgar H. Schein, my thesis adviser at MIT and currently on the faculty of that institution's Sloan School; and the late Professor Donald Marquis, who headed MIT's early efforts in what was then called industrial psychology.

Second, Professor Michael Beer, now professor of business at Harvard Business School, who, during our years as colleagues and friends at Corning, Inc., showed me how to apply behavioral change techniques in the real world.

Third, my clients over the years, whose problems and opportunities let me invent some of the techniques used in this book—and practice all of them. Without those thousands of hours of real-world experience, this book would have been neither possible nor practical.

Fourth, those companies, both named and disguised, who generously let me use real examples taken from their experiences.

And finally, the many universities and institutions that gave me the privilege of teaching strategic planning—and, coincidentally, of honing my material. I would particularly like to thank Vanderbilt University's Owen School of Management and Deans Sam Richmond and Martin Geisel, as well as the American Management Association's Presidents' Association and its director, Ed McCarthy.

Heartfelt thanks also go to those who helped me prepare the manuscript. Mary Burton, my virtuoso assistant, who helped me juggle the deadlines of a hefty manuscript and running a business; Barbara Brooks, a close friend and consultant in my firm, who worked with me over the years to develop the client and proprietary planning manuals on which many of the graphics and techniques presented in this book are based; Donna Deeprose, who helped me edit and wordcraft the final manuscript; Donna Pritchett, who ably designed the illustrations; and Adrienne Hickey, my editor at AMACOM, who had infinite patience and provided exceptional support. Finally, special thanks go to my wife, Mary, who served as my "editor in residence."

Thank you all.

Part One

The Strategic Planning and Change Process

Chapter 1

The Traditional
Strategic Planning Process

If you don't know where you're going, any path will take you there.
—Sioux proverb

Every moment spent planning saves three or four in execution.
—Crawford Greenwalt, former president, E. I. du Pont de Nemours

There is a classic and proven strategic planning process that works for businesses both large and small, whether they are manufacturing, professional, or service companies. Although this book draws most of its examples from business, the same process is readily adapted to not-for-profit and governmental organizations.

This chapter summarizes that process. It briefly describes the steps, how they are accomplished, and the outcome of each. The process flow is shown in Figure 1-1, and the key concepts used in the process are defined in Figure 1-2. (A glossary of terms appears at the end of this book.)

Although strategic planning may seem a sterile, intellectual analytical process, it's not. As we'll see later in this book, the human element is critically important. Strategic planning requires the organization's intimate and enthusiastic involvement, often using formal and informal teams, in providing information, making decisions, and successfully implementing them.

Content of the Strategic Plan

First plans typically follow the sequence presented here: situation analysis (external assessment, internal assessment), priority issues, mission,

Figure 1-1. Planning process flow.

PLANNING BASE	RESULTS REQUIRED	HOW	IMPLEMEN- TATION	REVIEW
INTERNAL ASSESSMENT EXTERNAL ASSESSMENT ASSUMPTIONS PRIORITY ISSUES	VISION/ MISSION OBJECTIVES	STRATEGIES PROGRAMS	DELEGATED OBJECTIVES DELEGATED PROGRAMS	REVIEWS
WHERE ARE WE NOW?	WHERE DO WE WANT TO BE?	HOW WILL WE GET THERE?	WHO MUST DO WHAT?	HOW ARE WE DOING?

objectives, strategies, program development, delegation, and account-ability and review. More experienced planners should view the steps as pieces in a jigsaw puzzle, to be selected and pieced together into a com-plete picture that addresses the organization's specific situation. Such planners may accomplish some steps in parallel, shorten or expand steps, and even omit some, depending on the organization's business situation, priorities, and capabilities.

Organizations with an existing plan, however good or poor, should preface a plan update or total ground-up revision with an up-front step: a review of the existing mission, plan, and accomplishments.

External Assessment

The outside world can be hostile, difficult to understand, and some-times impossible to influence. It exists in an ever-changing economic, regulatory, political, and social environment. Nonetheless, it contains the customers you must win and the competitors you must beat. To plan successfully, you must learn as much as you can about the outside factors and trends that will affect your future.

Your customers may buy your products or services in a multina-tional, national, or city market. They may be a specific population for which you provide entitlements (e.g., social services within a city), or they may be other departments or individuals within your own organi-zation. If you work in human resources, for example, your customers are all the people in your company served by your department. Whether your "outside world" is global or just down the hall, an exter-nal assessment is necessary.

A typical external analysis looks at relevant trends in each of the seven external areas listed in Figure 1-2.1, watching for trends that can help and those that can hurt. Which are potential opportunities to capi-talize on? Which are potential threats to avoid or somehow mitigate? The external analysis also identifies possible strategic responses to each high-impact trend. The external analysis typically involves three activ-ities:

1. Evaluating and reporting on key data and trends in each of the seven external areas, paying particular attention to your markets, cus-tomers, competitive moves, and product and service innovation. Most companies assign this activity to an analyst or a department, often the marketing department.

2. Identifying your business's two to four critical success factors— those areas and capabilities in which you must excel if you are to win with your customer and beat out competitors. For example, one of Rolex's critical success factors is its advertising and promotion, which

(text continues on page 8)

Figure 1-2. Key elements of the strategic planning process.

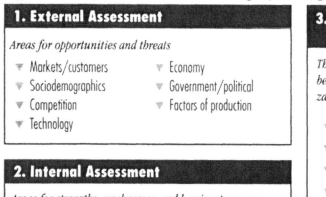

1. External Assessment

Areas for opportunities and threats

- ▼ Markets/customers
- ▼ Sociodemographics
- ▼ Competition
- ▼ Technology
- ▼ Economy
- ▼ Government/political
- ▼ Factors of production

2. Internal Assessment

Areas for strengths, weaknesses, and barriers to success

ORGANIZATION DIMENSIONS

- ▼ Culture
- ▼ Organization structure
- ▼ Systems
- ▼ People
- ▼ Management practices

OTHER KEY DIMENSIONS

- ▼ Cost-efficiency
- ▼ Financial structure performance
- ▼ Quality
- ▼ Service
- ▼ Technology
- ▼ Market segments/ performance
- ▼ Innovation/new products
- ▼ Asset condition/productivity

3. Source of Priority Strategic Issues

The critical issues that must be addressed if the organization is to succeed

- ▼ **S**trengths
- ▼ **W**eaknesses
- ▼ **O**pportunities
- ▼ **T**hreats

SWOTs

▼

Priority Issues

▼

Strategic Programs

4. Mission Contents

▼ **VISION:**
Your purpose in life. Where and what you want to be in the future. Key numbers; core markets; core values; strategic thrusts.

▼ **BUSINESS DEFINITION:**
The arena of products, services, customers, technologies, distribution methods, and geography in which you'll compete to get results.

▼ **VALUES:**
Desired attitudes and behavior toward internal and external stakeholders that will yield the culture and business results you want and that you will execute and turn into action through policy, programs, procedures, personnel selection.

5. Source of Strategic Objectives and Programs

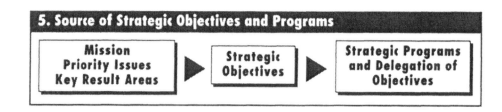

Mission
Priority Issues
Key Result Areas
▶
Strategic
Objectives
▶
Strategic Programs
and Delegation of
Objectives

6. The Strategic Pyramid

Levels and tiers of strategies

TOP LEVEL

▼ **OVERALL FINANCIAL POSTURE**
Grow; hold; milk; get out

▼ **PRIORITIES AND POSTURES**
(Grow; hold; milk)
Markets; business units; products/services

▼ **ROUTES**

Acquire	Internal development
Joint venture	Divest
Shut down	Restructure

▼ **COMPETITIVE ADVANTAGE**

Cost	Value	Differentiation

EXECUTIONAL

▼ **EXTERNAL STRATEGIES**

Product	Convenience
Service	Image
Target customer	Geography
Distribution	Product design
Delivery	Quality
Value	Reliability
Pricing	Advertising/promotion

▼ **INTERNAL STRATEGIES**

People/skills	Facilities
Organizational structure	Product development
Management style	Incentives/rewards
Training	Spending
Equipment	Sourcing/ manufacturing
Technology	Systems
R & D	Service
Financing	Quality

7. Strategy Statement Content

▼ Priorities and Posture
 Business unit
 Market
 Product

▼ Strategic thrust/competitive advantage

▼ External strategies

▼ Internal strategic thrust

▼ Internal strategies

▼ Strategic fixes

8. Strategic Program Content

▼ **LEADERSHIP:** who

▼ **OBJECTIVES**

▼ **KEY STEPS:** who, what, when

▼ **FINANCIAL AND STRATEGIC GAIN AND COST**

▼ **PEOPLE:** numbers and skills

▼ **COORDINATION REQUIREMENTS:** People and organizational units outside your control who must contribute

▼ **LEVERAGE:** the high leverage individuals and units who must contribute at lower levels

9. Strategic Accountability/Reviews

▼ **QUARTERLY:** Programs and strategic numbers' progress

▼ **INDIVIDUAL OBJECTIVES:** Performance appraisal

▼ **REWARDS AND CONSEQUENCES:** Based on strategic performance of teams and individuals

▼ **INFORMAL VIGILANCE**

maintain the watch's elite, masculine "I've made it and I have it" image. Physical and electronic information distribution systems are critical success factors for Federal Express. Determine how well you perform on each of your critical success factors compared to your competition.

3. Conducting a market needs assessment, an analysis of the organization's market and competitive position. To do a needs assessment, you'll need to:

▲ *Segment the market.* Divide your company's current and potential markets into clusters of buyers whose needs are similar to one another but distinctly different from those of buyers in other clusters in the same general market. For example, the luxury car market contains a younger, performance-oriented segment typified by BMW and a more conservative, older, image-oriented segment typified by Mercedes. Market segmentation lets you develop incisive competitive strategies that address the unique needs of each segment you subsequently target for emphasis.

▲ *Rank, order the product, service, pricing, technological, psychological, and other needs of customers within each key market segment.* Many companies identify customer needs in customer focus groups and personal interviews, then quantify their conclusions through telephone and mail surveys.

▲ *Appraise the company's strengths and weaknesses against those of the competition in meeting customer needs.* This competitive assessment points out where you are underperforming against the competition, requiring strategic fixes. It also identifies where you do or can outperform the competition. These areas are fertile ground for potential strategic thrusts or key competitive strategies. Companies commonly present the results of the needs assessment on a standard Importance/Performance matrix. One axis rates the importance of each customer need, and the other indicates the company's and the competition's perceived performance. This allows easy graphic representation of where the company is outperforming and where it is underperforming the competition.

The output of the external analysis is a list of four to five opportunities and four to five threats derived from the trend analysis, the critical success factor analysis, and the market needs assessment, along with potential strategic responses to each.

Internal Assessment

The most brilliant competitive strategy will fail unless your internal organization is well honed to support it. You therefore need to identify your organization's strengths and weaknesses, particularly those that affect performance in the company's critical success factors, since these are your keystones to future success.

Strengths are capabilities that can be used to get an advantage over competition. They may be technical skills, consumer franchises, or low-cost production capabilities, but usually they are directly involved in delivering what the customer wants in highly ranked areas of need. At Wal-Mart, for example, a key strength is delivering branded and pri-vate-label merchandise to customers at a total unit cost far below that of the competition.

Weaknesses, on the other hand, are barriers to strategic success. If your capability of delivering to the customer trails your competition's, that's a weakness. Weaknesses also show up in ineffective critical sup-port functions, such as advertising and promotion or human resources. One of General Motors' key weaknesses in the 1980s was its inability to produce consistent consumer-acceptable quality, the result of flaws in the company's labor force, management, and production processes and in the design of its cars.

Strengths and weaknesses begin to emerge in the external analysis as market and competitive research point them out from the all-im-portant customers' point of view. Equally important, however, are the views of employees and associates, who have valuable insights into the functioning of the organization. For strategy implementation to suc-ceed, the internal organization must be suitably configured, staffed, motivated, and well lubricated.

You can identify key organization strengths and weaknesses through a combination of diagnostic questionnaires, confidential inter-views, and internal focus groups with employees. Figure 1-2.2 lists the overall key areas to probe, including culture, organization structure, systems, people and management practices, costs, quality, service, and technology.

Finally, many companies perform specialized analyses of internal capabilities in critical areas, such as financial performance, structure, and forecasts; current versus state-of-the-art technology; production costs, wastes, quality, yields, and supervision; market segmentation, position, and performance; potential new products and markets; and organization skills, competence, and succession.

Out of the internal assessment should emerge four or five strengths and four or five weaknesses or barriers to success, along with prelimi-nary recommendations for bolstering the strengths and fixing the weak-nesses.

Remember, as you prepare your external assessment, to be on the lookout for assumptions—your projections concerning future uncon-trollable key external factors on which the success of the plan rests, for example, future market size and growth, pricing, competitive activity, and the cost or availability of critical raw materials. The plan must change if your assumptions prove false.

Priority Issues

Most organizations develop far more strengths, weaknesses, opportunities, and threats (SWOTs) than they can address effectively, profitably, and with the available resources. They therefore boil down their long lists of SWOTs to three to five priority strategic issues they must confront if the organization is to have a healthy future (Figure 1-2.3). Successful companies develop detailed strategic programs to address these issues later in the planning process.

A priority issue is a broad area that (1) affects the fundamental way a business approaches its markets and internal organization and (2) has strategic and long-term performance significance. Typical priority issues are cost of production, service levels and delivery, organization and managerial effectiveness, customer service and friendliness, corporate direction, new product/service innovation, and quality.

The broad issues change little from year to year, although the programs designed to address them do change and normally get more sophisticated over time. For example, one supermarket chain for years designated customer service and friendliness as a priority issue. Its initial programs to address the area were primitive, focusing on "smile training" for customer interface personnel that taught them to acknowledge and to deal with customers in a friendly, supportive manner. Later programs evolved into more sophisticated and expensive efforts. The store trained personnel in product benefits, provided video carts to help customers locate merchandise and bargains, and installed computer systems to manage inventory and to prevent product shortages annoying to their customers.

Eventually, successful organizations deal so effectively with priority issues that handling them becomes routine and they are dropped from the priority list.

Mission

A mission statement portrays what the company is to become over the long haul. It is the navigational star toward which the organization aligns the bow of the corporate ship in order to reach its desired destination.

Technically, a mission statement's function is to define the business's purpose, direction, and future thrust. A company that plans effectively communicates its mission to employees, ensures that everyone in the organization understands his or her part in fulfilling the mission, and helps employees bring their thinking, planning, and actions into alignment with the corporate direction.

Mission statements typically contain three parts (Figure 1-2.4):

1. *Vision.* A succinct statement of the corporate vision, describing how management envisions the business in the future and answering the quesitons, "Why do we exist?" "What do we want to become in the future?" and "How will we get there?" The vision usually includes desired financial performance, desired market position compared to the competition, core products/services to be offered, key competitive advantages (strategic thrusts), and a few pivotal values for which the company hopes to be known among internal and external constituencies and customers (such as superiority of customer-measured quality and service, technical innovation, and high-quality, motivated people).

2. *Business definition.* A detailed definition of the business, describing targeted end markets, customers, customer needs to be met, and key competitive advantage, as well as technologies, distribution methods, and geographic thrusts to be emphasized.

3. *Values.* A complete list of key values, defining both external values (e.g., superior customer service and community involvement) and internal values (e.g., management by teamwork, promotion and compensation based on contribution, and maintenance of a highly productive, motivated work force with ever-growing skills).

Needless to say, to prevent your mission statement from becoming "Mom, Honda, and apple pie," you need to ensure that every word and intent turns into results. This means that you must delegate objectives, programs, policies, procedures, spending, and management actions and decisions. Otherwise, mission statements become meaningless documents, creating cynical rather than motivated employees.

Objectives

Strategic objectives are what the organization commits to accomplish in the long term. Companies set three- to five-year directional objectives and detailed first-year objectives that serve as stepping stones in the long-term plan.

Strategic objectives usually establish (Figure 1-2.5):

▲ Performance levels to be achieved on priority issues, such as cost reduction

▲ Measures of success in fulfilling critical mission statement elements, such as "delivering superior customer service"
▲ Expected performance in key result areas (those additional areas in which you must get measurable results if you are to succeed), including:
—Expected financial performance standards such as profitability, sales revenue, growth, and cost/expense levels
—Targets for performance on strategic measures that drive future financial performance, such as market share, customer-perceived quality and service, employee satisfaction, organization skills and succession, and innovation

Once you have set strategic objectives, you need to break down the overall organization objectives into components and delegate these to high-leverage individual work units and people, giving them the responsibility, resources, and authority they need to achieve the objectives for which they are to be held accountable

Strategies

Strategies are the means, the ways, the hows, the devilishly detailed methods by which organizations accomplish their objectives. You'll need to formulate and carry out a number of different levels and types of strategies, from competitive, financial, product, and market through organization, capital spending, quality, and service.

Some strategies will be broad and grand and originate at the highest levels of the organization. Only top people can choose between growing by acquisition or by internal development, for example, or decide to emphasize certain businesses and deemphasize others. Other strategies, such as long-term media, promotion, and communications strategy, may be relatively narrow and specialized. Figure 1-2.6, describing the strategic pyramid, illustrates types of business strategy and the various levels in the organization at which they are formulated and implemented.

It helps to differentiate between external and internal strategies. The critical external strategies are the one to three key competitive strategies or strategic thrusts that will achieve pervasive customer-perceived advantages over targeted competition. For many companies, competitive strategy revolves around the decision to compete on price and therefore become a low-cost producer; by differentiation on some other factor, such as product features, technology, service, or quality; or on "value," positioned between price and strong differentiation.

Once you've selected your strategic thrusts, you'll need to define all the other subsidiary external strategies that are important to success, including distribution, advertising, promotion, and selling methods.

To succeed, external strategies require supporting internal strategies. The internal thrusts are the one to three key internal strategies that are most important for implementing the external strategic thrust. For example, if the strategic thrust is customer service, the key internal strategies may focus on selection and training of customer interface personnel; computer, telephone, and other systems to support them; and working capital to sustain customer credit and inventories.

When you have defined your internal thrusts, you should generate subsidiary internal strategies in other support areas, such as capital facilities and equipment or compensation and benefits.

Note that strategies can be as broad as "grow by acquisition and joint venture" and as narrow as "expand distribution into three additional cities." But few businesses are built on grand-stroke-of-genius strategies, such as "invent the light bulb." Most successful strategies are a collection of key directions and actions, often with an infinite number of detailed steps, discharged at many levels in the company.

Strategies are often summarized in a succinct statement covering the topics shown in Figure 1-2.7.

Program Development

Action plans breathe life into strategy. Companies need to develop strategic program action plans for all priority strategic issues, designated mission elements, strategic objectives, and overall strategies. Each program should include a measurable program objective; a few key action steps, defining who, what, and when; an estimate of the financial and strategic gains from the program; its capital and spending costs; and the human resources required to implement it (Figure 1-2.8). Each program also requires leadership, a person or team leaders who will be responsible for its implementation and for the coordination of all of the resources necessary to achieve targeted results.

This process typically produces more potential programs than the organization has time, people, and resources to effectively implement. Of the programs developed, the top team selects a few, perhaps five to seven, high-priority strategic programs on the basis of their long-term financial and strategic impact, their alignment with the company's mission, and the organization's ability to implement them.

Delegation

Implementation starts when management delegates overall strategic objectives, program objectives, and action steps to people with the skill, power, resources, and authority to act.

Delegation takes place at several levels:

▲ Overall strategic objectives, or parts of them, become the responsibility of the units in the company most capable of carrying them out. For example, a company might delegate a sales objective of $100 million in incremental sales of existing products to its marketing organization, leaving it up to the marketing group to achieve the objective through its ongoing sales and marketing efforts.

▲ Responsibility for strategic program action plans or key action steps goes to functional departments, teams, or individuals.

▲ Every key objective and step in a strategic action plan becomes part of someone's personal objectives.

A key responsibility of management is to identify the handful of "leverage" individuals and organization units who will be charged with achieving strategic objectives and implementing programs. Management is responsible for ensuring that adequate resources are allocated to these individuals and units and that accountabilities are established and accepted.

Accountability and Review

"What you *inspect* gets accomplished, not what you *expect*." That's an old saw, but it's still true.

Companies need to review all plans and objectives and to hold accountable all those responsible for carrying out programs and meeting objectives. Timely review allows organizations to take corrective action when plans are heading off track, change priorities as the external environment and the internal situation change, and reallocate financial and human resources as necessary.

Plan review is an ongoing process, both formal and informal, that takes place at every level.

▲ Senior management reviews key programs and long-term strategic numbers at least quarterly.

▲ Those responsible for program objectives and action plans review major steps before or as they come due.

▲ In performance reviews or in reviews scheduled in management-by-objective (MBO) systems, individuals and their managers assess progress toward the objectives and the action steps incorporated into individuals' personal performance objectives.

To strengthen accountability, some portion of individual rewards, including bonuses, salary increases, and personal recognition, should be based on each employee's contribution to the achievement of the company's strategic objectives and programs.

Finally, management by wandering around, keeping in touch, and being ever vigilant among those executing plans really pays. In the heat of day-to-day battles, it's a deadly mistake to ignore the long-term programs and actions.

Integrated Planning: Where the Strategic Plan Fits in the Annual Planning Cycle

Strategic planning is a fundamental management tool that should fit smoothly into an organization's annual planning cycle. This may not happen the first year. First and sometimes second plans often require extraordinary efforts in external, organizational, financial, and especially market and competitive analysis. Once the initial plan is developed, however, the planning process becomes a way of life. Companies become adept at questioning and at quickly and efficiently updating the situation analysis, assumptions, priority issues, and strategic programs in their existing strategic plans. They create annual operating plans and budgets that integrate strategic tasks and spending.

Annual operating plans, distinct from strategic plans, contain detailed objectives and supporting programs to be achieved in the coming year in functional areas such as sales, marketing, manufacturing operations, research and development (R&D), and human resources. A sales and marketing plan, for example, might address sales budgets, key customer objectives, pricing, promotions, advertising, profit margins, service levels, and new product releases. Operating plans also incorporate those parts of strategic plan programs and objectives that are to be accomplished in the coming year. Such programs may include major market penetration campaigns, cost reduction programs, organization restructurings, and development of new products. The operating plans lead to final capital and expense budgets.

Most companies develop operating plans and strategic plan updates in parallel, starting their operating plans slightly later. Ultimately, they often consolidate strategic and operating budgets and programs into one document called the annual business plan. At the individual level, performance objectives of accountable individuals combine objectives and tasks from both the strategic and the operating plans.

The multilevel review process keeps both the strategic and the operating plans on track. The compensation system links annual op-

Figure 1-3. Initial strategic and annual operating planning process.

M	A	M	J	J	A	S	O	N	D	J	F

Strategic Plan

ANALYSIS
- Situation analysis
- Market and competitive analysis
- Financial history and forecast

INPUT
- Input on priority issues from lower levels

PRIORITY SETTING MEETING
- Priority issues
- Internal and external strategies

PROGRAMS
- Strategic program development

STRATEGIC PLANNING MEETING
- Vision/mission
- Objectives
- Strategies
- Final programs
- Resource allocation

DELEGATION
- Delegation of objectives and programs
- Final written plan

FUNCTIONAL PLANS
- Funtional strategic plans completed

BUDGETING
- Budgeting of strategic spending

FINAL BUDGET

INDIVIDUAL OBJECTIVES

START FISCAL YEAR

PLAN PERFORMANCE REVIEWS — Corp./Func./Indiv.

Budget and Operating Plan

CORPORATE DIRECTION
- Budget
- One-year priorities

START ANNUAL BUDGET
- Sales
- Price
- Capacity
- Capital
- People

Annual sales/marketing plan completed

Annual manufacturing plan completed

Other annual functional plans completed

erating, strategic, and program performance to the company's reward plan.

Figure 1-3 shows the steps in a typical initial strategic and annual operating planning process and the relationships among actions at the corporate and the functional department levels. It assumes a relatively large and complex organization.

Revising the Strategic Plan Annually

Annual revision and continuing review of the strategic plan are not herculean efforts. Indeed, if the process is carefully conceived, it's relatively simple, motivational, and welcomed by organizations. Here are typical steps (see Figure 1-4):

1. Gathering input from all levels of the organization on priority strategic and operating issues to be addressed in the coming year. This requires a structured process with clear how-to's for soliciting lower-level information and for conducting meetings to arrive at consensus. It helps to have standard formats for recording information and for preparing summaries to send upstairs.

Issues that can be addressed at each level "stick" (are delegated back to that level). Issues that affect the entire company or that have high impact on resources or results move up to the top for consolidation and review.

2. Reviewing the prior year's plan and results. The top team and staff analysts determine if there have been significant changes in the external environment, assumptions, or internal performance or capabilities that might affect the company's strategic situation. A new financial forecast is produced.

3. Reviewing the prior year's and the newly submitted priority issues to establish new priorities and means of addressing them. The top team usually concludes this step at a one- to two-day meeting after members have reviewed inputs from the organization and results of the prior strategic plan.

4. Delegating the development of strategic program action plans, addressing the new priorities, to accountable individuals or functional departments.

5. Reviewing, massaging, and getting consensus on final strategic programs and updated strategic objectives, as well as on allocation of resources for budgeting purposes. Companies often accomplish this step at an annual two- to three-day strategic planning retreat.

6. Delegating objectives to individuals and functional departments for execution to be followed up by performance reviews.

Figure 1-4. Annual revision and review of the strategic plan.

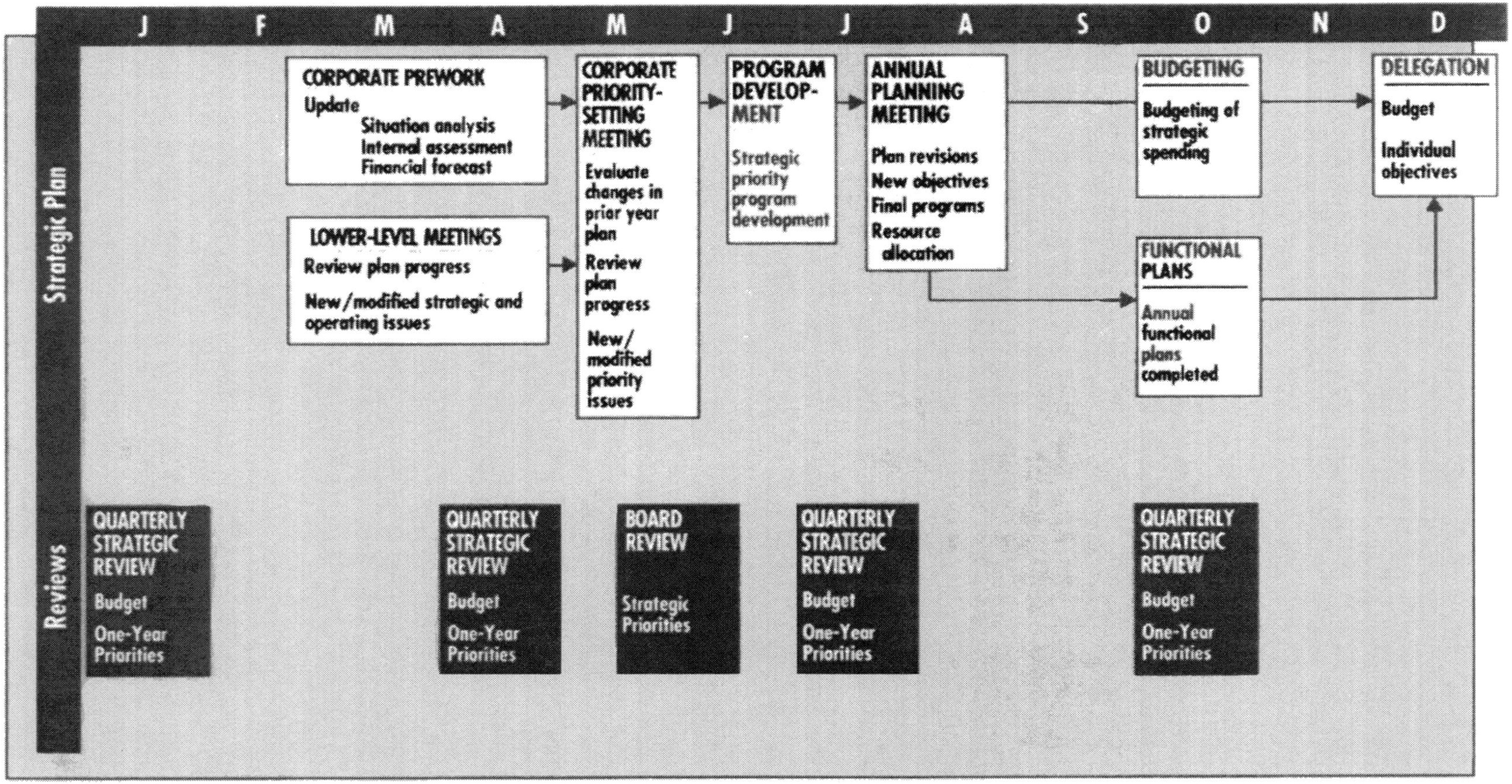

When to Redo the Plan

Businesses usually go through the complete planning process every three to five years. This keeps the plan and strategies fresh and helps management stay in touch with internal and external realities.

Sometimes drastic changes in outside circumstances or internal performance or new leadership warrant starting over from the ground up. When confronted by strong competition from food discounters such as Wal-Mart, for example, many supermarkets had to rethink their target customer, store format, products, pricing, warehousing, and sourcing.

The remainder of this book examines in greater detail each of the steps summarized in this chapter.

DO'S AND DON'TS

DO

- *Minimize time* demands on busy executives with a carefully thought-out planning process.
- *Maximize coordination* and consensus among involved individuals and organization units.
- *Think.* Thoughtful, fact-based plans work; those based on a wish and a promise or on superficial assumptions fail. Remember Du Pont's entry into the footwear material market with Corfam, the man-made product that promised breathability, good looks, and long wear but failed to meet customer expectations on any of those counts, or Xerox's failure to anticipate and to combat the Japanese onslaught into the copier market with low-price, plain-paper copiers.
- *Involve* those who must execute the plan. Making them responsible for planning as well as for execution wins their commitment and produces realistic plans.
- *Simplify.* Don't complicate. The purpose of planning is to focus management's efforts. A clear, unacademic process that sticks to the basics works; cumbersome, complex, arcane planning processes don't. In truth, most good plans come from the gut, depending on analysis only to uncover basic flaws and underlying external trends and to document what instinct already knows.
- *Communicate* the plan to all levels, highlighting overall mission, objectives, and priority issues, tailoring the message and making it relevant to each organization unit and level to emphasize its contribution.
- *Allocate resources* in line with your mission and strategic priorities. Remember, when boiled down to its essence, strategic planning simply sets strategic priorities and allocates scarce dollar, time, and skill resources to the most important.
- *Pace* the process prudently. In the early years of planning, you may be trying to make significant changes in strategy and direction with the same staff needed to run the base business. You'll also be allocating limited resources to more programs.
- *Establish accountabilities.* If you don't have an accountability/MBO system and

culture, *get them first,* as part of the plan. Hold people's feet to the fire. Reward only those who get results, and ultimately get rid of or relocate those who don't. Passing on nonperformers to future generations is corporate strategic suicide.

- *Review and revise* as major changes in circumstances dictate. Don't get rigid. In this fast-moving, accelerating, competitive world, rewards go to the fleet of foot. This is not to advocate change for change's sake or change because people haven't met their commitments. Quite the contrary; switching direction, waffling, and letting people off the hook confuse organizations and spawn underachievement or failure. Just recognize the need for significant structural change, and act on it.
- *Stick* with it. It takes three years to get significant results.
- *Lead* the process from the top. No organization succeeds strategically without strong leadership, direction from the top, and a strong top-down commitment to planning.

DON'T

- *Rush.* Resist the temptation to do it all in one year or, indeed, in a few short months. Plan your planning. Structure a workable process. Give your organization lots of advance notice on what's required and time to prepare and participate.
- *Dictate.* Plans dictated from the top down don't work. Nor do staff-prepared plans. Successful plans require the involvement, commitment, and realistic, workable input of the lower-level people who have to carry them out.
- *Overdo it.* Don't do any more analysis or segments of the plan than is necessary to address your strategic situation and priority issues. Focus on the important stuff.
- *Overwrite.* Don't confuse paper with effective thought. Thick plans often reflect thick thinking. A good plan can be summarized in a few pages with a handful of attached action plans.
- *Pay lip service.* Talking about planning without doing it effectively makes the organization cynical. Do it right or not at all.

Chapter 2

Whose Job Is It?
An Overview of Roles
and Responsibilities

Clarity, clarity, surely clarity is the most beautiful thing in the world.
—George Oppen, American poet

Top management work is work for a team rather than one man.
—Peter Drucker, management consultant and writer

In principle, planning is everybody's job. It permeates every nook, corner, and cranny of the organization. In reality, however, involving everyone directly in the strategic planning process would make it too cumbersome to get off the ground.

Whose job is planning? When you answer that question in your organization, start with this basic principle: Developing a plan is the job of the people responsible for executing it. Line executives produce better plans than do staff planners for several reasons.

1. *They have the information needed.* They are in touch with both the market and the resources needed to generate a company's products, services, and competitive advantage.
2. *They know what internal resources and capabilities are available.* They can tap the resources they need to execute a plan.
3. *They have the power, authority, and influence to get results.* They can delegate plan tasks, enforce accountabilities, and enlist needed help from others. What they want to accomplish can get done.
4. *Most important, they are in the best position to make the corporate mission meaningful to the layers below them.* It's up to them to earn

Figure 2-1. Planning information flow.

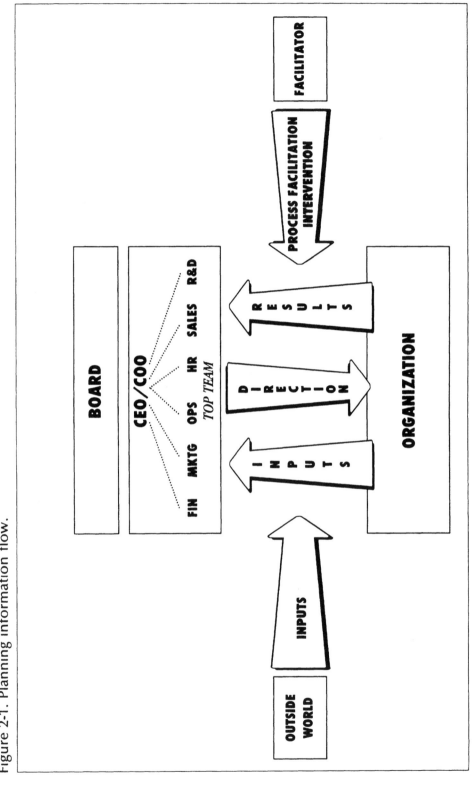

the commitment and to direct the actions of all the people who are needed to make the strategy work.

Figure 2-1 illustrates, in broad terms, who does what in planning. It traces typical information flows in a successful strategic planning process. The top management team develops the plan, taking inputs from the organization and the outside world. The board gives its input and approves policy and direction. The top team delegates the plan to the organization for execution. The organization carries out the actions needed to achieve specified (or better) results. Accountability for results resides with every function and at every layer, accumulating at each higher level until it winds up back with the top team, ensuring that the plan's objectives are met or exceeded. Simple in concept. Hellish in execution. And the bigger and more complex the business, the more devilish the process can get.

Taming the complexity requires clearly defined roles and carefully delineated responsibilities for getting information and making decisions. Here is the classic planning cast.

The Chief Executive Officer

Driving the Vision, Owning the Plan

The buck stops here—with a Harry Truman, an Alfred Sloan, a Stanley Gault (Rubbermaid), a Bill Gates (Microsoft), a Bob Crandell (AMR)—with the chief executive officer (CEO), who is ultimately responsible for developing the plan and for making it happen. Every strategically successful organization has a strong leader who drives the plan, pushing, shoving, and prodding to bring it to reality. At the same time, these leaders model and demand the high standards, contribute the long-term focus, and provide the inspired vision that distinguishes their organizations from the legions of companies bogged down in the flurry of day-to-day activities.

Steering the Process

To render forceful strategic leadership, the CEO should:

▲ *Make planning important.* Insist that it be treated as a critical management responsibility and used as a business tool at all levels in the organization. Constantly reinforce its importance and herald good strategic results.

▲ *Provide an inspired, broad, and "stretch" vision* of the organization's direction. Communicate it frequently throughout the organization.

▲ *Look for the unlikely or not-so-obvious.* Champion creative moves that make $2+2=10$. Apple looked past the obvious when it took the Xerox iconic PC interface and created the Macintosh computer; Corning did it when it embarked on a strategy of rapid international growth through worldwide strategic investments and alliances.

▲ *Install an integrated planning process and planning infrastructure,* an annual system that starts with strategic plan development early in the fiscal year and carries through to the final operating plan and budget approval. See to it that everyone involved is trained to participate effectively.

▲ *Provide staff support* to shuffle the onerous paperwork, arrange and facilitate meetings, summarize and publish plans and plan results, and provide management with information needed for reviews. In short, take much of the detail work off the backs of busy executives.

▲ *Allocate time, money, and personal support.* Give busy executives time to plan and financial resources to get the training, staff, or consultant assistance they need. Be a stimulating sounding board and an asker of penetrating questions. Hold their hands during critical decisions.

▲ *Deal with the outside world.* Translate the plan for investors, the financial community, the board of directors, or others who have a stake in the organization's future or who can help or hurt its progress. Keep a finger on the pulse of the industry, interpreting competitive moves, market trends, government influences, and technological advances. Watch for new management and competitive tools that offer a business edge.

▲ *Make, push, or affirm timely decisions.* Although team planning usually results in workable strategic decisions derived by consensus, the planning team is not a democracy. The CEO must affirm or, in the absence of timely consensus, make key strategic decisions.

▲ *Set high standards.* Hold out for strategic performance standards that surpass those of the competition. Make sure to keep planning from slipping into the status of a second-class activity. You must at all times make it the axis around which the business pivots.

▲ *Hold people accountable* for long-term results.

▲ *Reward them* accordingly.

The Top Team

Although the CEO is the visionary and the steward of strategic planning, it takes a team to forge the plan and to oversee its execution. Good planning requires the cross-functional perspective and the cross-fertilization of ideas that only a team can bring to the task. Teams produce superior plans because they bring more inputs, generate more ideas, and broaden the commitment to planning and the ownership of the process. Team planning results in better coordination of actions between functions, a practical pace, and peer accountability. (Characteristics of effective teams are explored in detail in Part Four.)

Making the Team: Membership in an Exclusive Group

Two guidelines govern membership in the top planning team. First, include those who have the information to plan and the power to execute, wherever they are in the organization hierarchy. Second, keep the team small, optimally five to seven people. Mandatory members include the CEO and direct reports (these may include the chief operating officer, the chief financial officer, and the vice presidents of operations, marketing and sales, and human resources). Lower-level personnel with critical specific expertise can supplement this permanent team.

WESTERN SUPERMARKETS, INC., a real company disguised here to protect proprietary information, is one of America's most successful regional supermarket chains. Western's top management team consists of the chairman, the chief financial officer, the chief operating officer, the vice president of human resources, the vice president of merchandising, the vice president of administration, and the vice president of operations. Supplementing this group on the planning team are lower-level officers, including the three vice presidents of merchandising (general merchandise, perishables, and grocery/dairy/frozen), the vice president of warehousing and manufacturing, and the vice president of real estate. Without in-depth knowledge of these important supplemental functions, the company could not make effective strategic decisions.

Limiting the size of the top planning team permits good discussion and interplay and allows adequate "air time" for each function represented. It also affords opportunities for developing an open, supportive, and consensus-oriented culture; encourages a growing understanding of each member's strengths, weaknesses, and management styles; and fosters expeditious decision making.

Large, complex companies with many different businesses and geographic operations often do use bigger teams, some as large as

twenty-five to thirty members. These usually break into subteams to
deal with specific issues, such as service or cost-reduction strategies.
An executive committee of from five to seven top managers and staff
then consolidates the plan before presenting it to the large group for critiquing.

Playing a Dual Role

Members of the top team wear two hats. As a team, operating by consensus, they set corporate priorities, define competitive strategy, allocate resources to programs with the highest strategic impact, review
programs and strategic results, and take corrective action when needed.
They participate in key team decision-making meetings, including the
priority-setting meetings, the strategic plan meeting, and all key reviews.

As individuals, each team member also wears a functional hat. In
addition to being a team player, each is also the marketing person or
the finance person or the manufacturing person, who provides functional input into the plan's development and who has a functional strategic vision that contributes to the corporation's long-term competitive
advantage.

This dual role for top-team members requires that they set aside
turfdoms and look at what is best for the future of the overall business
and also that they be ready to flip-flop perspective and strongly represent their specific functions when appropriate. The vice president of
manufacturing, for example, needs to point out the impact of an increase in sales on manufacturing costs, service, capacity, and capital
spending. To achieve a corporate goal of increased market share, a plan
must recognize manufacturing's need for orderly and cost-effective increases in staffing and production capacity.

Functional challenges may feel territorial at first, but over time team
members get to understand one another's special concerns, easing the
development and the implementation of closely coordinated plans.

Linking With the Organization

There's no ivory tower for the top planning team. It depends on the
rest of the organization for information and implementation. To get results, the team needs to:

1. *Install systems* throughout the organization that establish and enforce strategic accountabilities and feed information on plan perfor-

mance and changes in the external world back to the top team. The business and functional level requires systems for budgeting, program action planning, and program and strategic plan review. At the individual level, systems are needed for setting objectives (MBO) and for performance appraisal. Compensation systems that reward strategic performance are necessary at both levels.

2. *Listen.* Although getting information for planning is a continuous, iterative process, there are several key listening points, or "dipdowns." These are the best opportunities to hear what's right and wrong, what has high potential and what doesn't, what is implementable and what isn't. They include:

▲ Situation analysis, in which marketing and finance uncover the state of your competition, markets, finances, opportunities, and problems.

▲ Priority issue development, in which the company identifies the key strategic and operating issues and potential ways of responding to them at all levels and in all functional areas. The most important organizational, functional, and competitive issues seen in the depths of the organization "bubble up" to the top for prioritization and action. Issues that can be resolved at lower levels become part of lower-level plans. Most of this information emerges through questionnaires and at lower-level meetings. Additional information comes from staff reports on markets, competition, and financial condition.

▲ Program action plan development, in which managers tell you what, in reality, you can or can't accomplish and how much it will cost to implement your plans.

▲ Implementation reviews, in which the early signs of success, failure, or a need to readjust strategy and programs often appear as a faint glimmer on the horizon.

▲ Annual plan revision.

▲ Changes in the plan resulting from changes in the outside world.

3. *Encourage lower-level teams.* Project or ongoing work teams can accomplish many of the important, complicated, multifunctional tasks that go into developing and executing parts of the corporate plan. Once overall direction was established at Western Supermarkets, for example, lower-level teams, sometimes chaired by a top-team member, fleshed out and implemented plans in priority-issue areas such as cost reduction, customer service and friendliness, and geographic expansion and acquisition.

After top management at UNITED STATES TOBACCO COMPANY (USTC) for the first time delegated a new product's development to a multifunctional team, it found that the time needed to get the product to market had been slashed dramatically. The company's critical path computer program, considering only individual inputs from uncoordinated functional areas, had predicted development time of two and one-half years. The team, consisting of members from manufacturing, engineering, marketing, finance, and R&D, was able to cut that time to ten months.

Another kind of lower-level team replicates the top planning team in individual departments and business units. Each of these teams develops the unit's own annual and strategic plans.

4. *Communicate* the plan throughout the organization so that all personnel can bring their activities into alignment with its objectives. Tailor communications to the businesses, functions, and levels to which you are communicating.

5. *Isolate the 'leverage points,'* those few individuals and organization units whose actions will be critical to the success of the plan, who are highly visible, and who will be held accountable.

6. *Delegate to the leverage points* the pivotal objectives, programs, tasks, and implementation benchmarks whose accomplishment means winning and achieving your strategic objectives.

7. *Ensure adequate "strategic linkages,"* the fanning out and cascading down of leverage strategic objectives and tasks until they have permeated the width and depth of the organization. Insist on detailed program action plans and individual performance objectives for each pressure point. Remember, it isn't just the managers who implement. Everyone with a key task must acknowledge it and be held accountable.

For example, examine the impact on the entire organization of an objective to build a new production facility and have it running at specified costs and production rates within a capital spending constraint. Achieving this goal will require a complex series of subobjectives and actions over several years. The key pressure point will be the vice president of manufacturing. But the linkage of objectives will involve engineering, as well as outside designers and architects, for the equipment and building design; human resources for aid in recruitment, selection, training, and labor negotiations; and R&D for process development and improvement.

The top team can monitor linkage through "alignment" meetings on audits that trace key objectives and action programs throughout the organization. (Alignment is explored further in Chapter 12.)

The Organization

Two types of planning activity take place throughout the organization: implementation of the top-level strategic direction and development of unit plans.

Lower-Level Alignment

Business units, functional areas, and individuals who must implement key plan tasks are responsible for bringing their objectives and activities into alignment with the overall plan. They develop the programs to address the corporation's priority strategic issues. After all, only those who must ultimately execute know the infinite number of detailed activities and the exact resources needed to generate and execute workable programs. Only they can detail programs costs, estimate financial and strategic gain, and calculate human and other resource requirements.

Departmental Planning

In addition, each business unit and functional department is also responsible for developing its own strategic plan. Self-contained business units within a company generally follow the strategic planning process for an overall business that we described in Chapter 1. Functional areas and departments are different. They each require a strategic plan that includes a situation analysis, priority issues, mission, objectives, strategies, and programs. For example, manufacturing might be charged with carrying out the corporate priority of designing and building new facilities that will provide strategically needed capacity five to seven years from now. At the same time, however, manufacturing must develop its own strategies to address its own priority issues. These might be in the areas of quality improvement, cost reduction, improved service, and organization department.

The perspective of functional departments differs from that of strategic business units in three ways. For one thing, the functions are responsible for feeding key issues up to senior management to aid in the development of the corporate plan. Early in the process and before the development of either the corporate or the subsequent departmental plans, functional teams meet to determine both strategic priority issues and operating issues that need to be dealt with at either the departmental or the corporate level.

It's important to define both strategic and operating issues and to deal with them together in order to strike a balance between short- and long-term allocation of corporate resources. This is the difference between making structural improvements and just "fixing the ship" as cracks occur.

Defined departmental issues stay at the departmental level, to be dealt with there. Issues that can be dealt with only by senior management or that require significant coordination and devotion of resources across organization units are passed up for resolution. Ultimately, new or key issues that are passed up will be returned to departments for inclusion in their plans and for execution.

A second major difference between functional/department planning and corporate planning lies in the stakeholders. Functional departments have to consider both internal and external customers.

Finally, each function narrows the strategic focus of the overall business. Individual departments take general direction from the corporate strategic plan (defined or anticipated), identify the components that affect them, and extract the pieces they must execute. Then each department must address how it will:

▲ *Support corporate strategy.* This involves identifying the key strategy drivers under functional control, the priority strategy issues within those functional drivers, and programs to address those drivers. For example, if business strategy dictates superior customer service, a driver within management information systems (MIS) may be order entry and processing systems. Programs may be needed to address the speed of processing and to monitor the reporting back to customers, focusing on detail and quality.

▲ *Develop strategy and programs for its initiator functions* (those functions and activities for which it has primary responsibility within the company). For example, one initiator function of a human resources department is usually compensation and benefit policy.

▲ *Support the plans and react to the needs of other functions and businesses.* For example, human resources may need to maintain or improve its labor negotiating and recruiting capabilities to support corporate expansion.

▲ *Support its internal growth and competencies (infrastructure).* For example, the manufacturing function might embark on a three-year effort to establish self-directed quality and cost improvement teams.

The extent to which each function effectively fulfills these challenging and complicated roles, shown in Figure 2-2, largely determines how well long-term corporate strategy will be implemented. These roles em-

Figure 2-2. Elements of departmental planning.

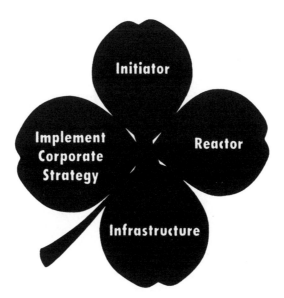

phasize the necessity of teamwork, coordination, and cooperation if the organization is to achieve its objectives.

In addition to fleshing out the corporate plan and developing its own unit plans, the entire organization must:

▲ *Encourage individual accountability* by establishing a culture that says "winners make their objectives" and by rewarding sufficiently and appropriately. If key strategic actions are not incorporated within individuals' performance objectives and appraisals, the plan won't work. Instead, these key actions will get buried in the myriad day-to-day activities that seem invented to distract from a long-term focus.

▲ *Close the information loop* by feeding information on performance-to-plan and changes in the external environment back to the top team quickly enough for timely modification of the plan and reallocation of resources if needed.

The Facilitator

Most CEOs depend upon a skilled, objective strategic planning facilitator to jump-start the organization into strategic planning and to shepherd the process during the early years of implementation. A good facilitator helps the organization design and install an effective planning and review process, trains the planning team and the organization in facilitation techniques, intervenes when key organizational or strategic blockages occur, and exits once the team is self-sustaining and self-facilitating. This takes from two to four years, starting with intense early involvement and tapering off to "touch-up" tasks during the final years. Chapter 4 details the multiple roles played by facilitators, the skills required, and how to locate facilitators.

DO'S AND DON'TS

DO

- *Establish a top-level planning team* that includes key individuals who have the information, power, and influence to think out and to implement a comprehensive strategy.
- *Involve in your planning process* the many individuals, teams, levels, and functions that may have key insights into strategic matters. They have the information you need, and you need their commitment.
- *Identify, involve, and make accountable* to both planning and execution the 'leverage points', those individuals, functional areas, and teams whose actions will have the greatest impact on your strategic future.

DON'T

- *Attempt to involve everyone* because "it's the right or the nice thing to do." A limited number of people have the knowledge and the vision of the battlefield to give strategic input. Involve them. Inform the others—the foot soldiers who must implement—once the grand strategy is clear.

Chapter 3

Demystifying the Process:
The Four Phases of Change

Change alone is eternal, perpetual, immortal.
— Arthur Schopenhauer, German philosopher

Change is disturbing when it is done to us, exhilarating when it is done *by* us.
— Rosabeth Moss Kanter, professor of business, consultant, and writer

Strategic planning is not an end in and of itself. It is a framework for continuous, productive, strategic change within an organization. The framework supports the surfacing of issues and provides a structure for their effective and profitable resolution.

Planning as a Change Process

Like any change process, strategic planning is most likely to succeed in an organization that prepares itself in advance by gaining the support of those affected and by equipping them with the skills they need to make it happen.

Before you embark on a course of strategic planning, you need to understand why and how organizations change, what barriers and resistance to expect, and how to overcome the barriers and convert the resistance into support.

The Pressure to Change

Companies embark on change for one or more of the following six reasons:

Figure 3-1. Strategic change model.

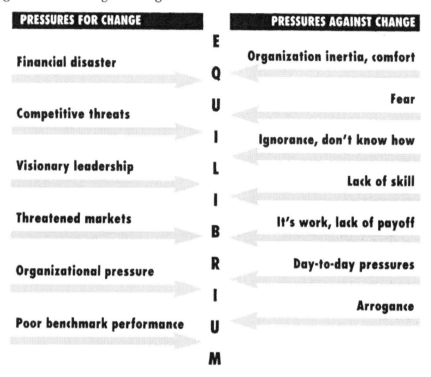

1. *Financial disaster*, impending or current, that forces a rethinking of the business's structure.
2. *Competitive threats*, either immediate or anticipated.
3. *Visionary leadership* that intuitively, objectively, or analytically "sees" the wave of the future and is determined to spearhead it.
4. *Pressure from below*, which is usually focused on specific issues such as lack of direction, management failure, shortage of capital, or inadequate opportunities for personal progress. Submarine levels of the organization can force change up.
5. *Recognition of poor performance*, impelling leadership to seek reasons and solutions.
6. *Threatened markets*, which must be recognized and dealt with if the organization is to survive.

These threats are illustrated in Figure 3-1.

Resistance to Change and to Planning

People have to feel discomfort, pressure, and pain for an extended period of time before they will abandon the comfort of the familiar and struggle through the stressful change process. There are numerous reasons why employees at all levels resist change of any kind and planning in particular, including:

▲ *Organization inertia,* which keeps us doing what we've always done and what we are comfortable with. Change disrupts the standing order—what and how people do things. It's always uncomfortable and distrusted, at least to some extent, by both human beings and organizations.

▲ *Fear* of being held accountable for results, of failure, of being fired or demoted, of losing personal prestige.

▲ *Ignorance* of the outside pressures that are making change necessary and of how long it takes to get results; lack of information about what management expects, how to do what is necessary, and each individual's role in the process.

▲ *Resistance* to the extra paperwork, analysis, and thinking involved, all of which are hated by everyone, particularly low-energy people and organizations. Always required, these tasks add to the day-to-day burden of running the business.

▲ *Perceived lack of payoff,* immediate or future, in terms of monetary, psychological, or promotional rewards.

▲ *Time* taken from day-to-day responsibilities. Planning and enacting change are usually burdens added to an already crowded schedule. They are also usually undertaken during periods of stress and in reaction to problems that already have the organization stretched thin.

▲ *Arrogance or cynicism* (the GM syndrome), particularly on the part of an insular top management; usually manifested as "We've tried it before and (1) it never worked or (2) management didn't follow through." Alternative excuses are "We're already doing it" (however incorrectly or ineptly) and, worst of all, "We're king of the mountain and unassailable in our business."

Unfortunately, barring extreme pressure to change, resistance often wins out. When that happens, the organization maintains the status quo, fostering over the long term the decay of the business.

The Change Process

When an organization decides to confront the external or internal pressures that are dictating change, the organization and the individuals within it will go through the four-stage change process shown in Figure

Figure 3-2. The phases of strategic change.

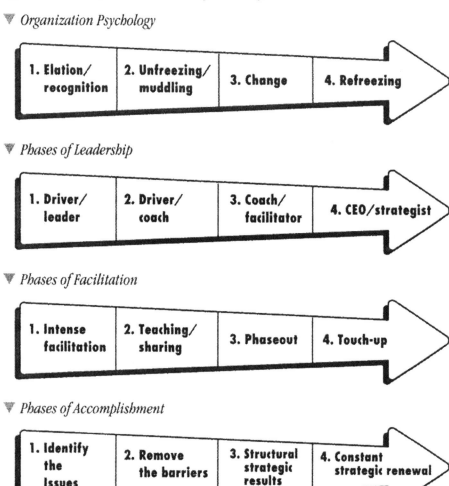

▼ *Organization Psychology*

| 1. Elation/ recognition | 2. Unfreezing/ muddling | 3. Change | 4. Refreezing |

▼ *Phases of Leadership*

| 1. Driver/ leader | 2. Driver/ coach | 3. Coach/ facilitator | 4. CEO/strategist |

▼ *Phases of Facilitation*

| 1. Intense facilitation | 2. Teaching/ sharing | 3. Phaseout | 4. Touch-up |

▼ *Phases of Accomplishment*

| 1. Identify the Issues | 2. Remove the barriers | 3. Structural strategic results | 4. Constant strategic renewal |

3-2. The dimensions describing, measuring, and governing change over time are (1) organization psychology, (2) leadership style, (3) facilitation style, and (4) the strategic results achieved.

Organization psychology usually moves through four predictable phases as change occurs.[1] It takes three to five years for the average organization to go through this four-phase process, significantly change its behaviors and business practices, and achieve substantial strategic

1. The basic model of attitude change used to describe organization psychology was developed in the 1950s by Edgar H. Schein at MIT in association with others (Kelman, Lewin, and Goffman). It was developed to model and describe major attitude changes during military brainwashing and the management development process. I previously used the model to describe attitude changes during bicultural contact between American expatriates and other nationalities in Africa.

results—that is, to put strategic planning in place and to institutionalize an emphasis on teamwork, high performance standards, introspection, and innovation. A culture that develops these characteristics can accommodate future changes much faster and with less trauma.

Phase 1: Recognition/Elation

During phase 1, which lasts from three months to one year, the organization experiences elation, challenge, or at least relief that the company is finally going to develop a vision, a direction, and an understandable future. Positive energy flows when key members of the organization recognize and articulate the need for change, identify the issues around which change will revolve, and commit to make change happen. Not that there aren't fearful, resistant people; there often are, but the leaders prevail.

Alternatively, as is often the case in turnaround situations, the organization may be shocked, angered, depressed, bewildered, and fearful of its future as people, products, and businesses are threatened, cut, or put on the block.

Phase 1 is the period when formal planning, as a catalyst of change, usually starts. People begin to face up to the reality that they must accept new attitudes and behaviors and change, and the "unfreezing" of the organization that is described in phase 2 makes its first tentative and discomforting appearance.

The CEO, COO, and key leaders drive the process, exhibiting strong content and process leadership—developing, driving, and communicating the mission; supporting and highlighting the importance of the planning process; making key decisions if they aren't quickly developed by consensus; being directive and driving when necessary to get the job done; making the tough decisions about people and resources; and carefully modeling the new organization behaviors prescribed by the strategic value statement.

Because the CEO, the top team, and the organization probably do not yet have the required skills, professional facilitators play an intense, key role in designing and implementing the planning process—up front, very visibly, and often in the limelight. The facilitator's phase 1 responsibilities often include:

▲ Conducting strategic and organization audits and diagnoses
▲ Designing, documenting, installing, and debugging planning processes
▲ Training the organization in strategic planning, strategy development, facilitation, and implementation skills

▲ Leading meetings and retreats

▲ Writing planning manuals, mission statements, and plans derived from planning-team and meeting input

▲ Intervening in key business and organization decisions that are going awry

▲ Locating outside consultants or trainers when the organization needs specific expertise in specialties such as manufacturing methods, organization behavior, and team building; compensation, sales management, and selling skills; and financial control systems

▲ Consulting personally with the CEO and with managers on tough decisions and on the executives' own growth needs and managerial styles

▲ Sharing planning process leadership with the CEO/COO

▲ However subtly or pointedly, holding the top team's feet to the fire to hold reviews, account for results, and make tough decisions

Tangible accomplishments during phase 1 include setting strategic direction, removing strategic barriers, addressing fix-the-ship actions such as organization cleansing and rebuilding, reducing the work force, and "getting to par" in service, quality, products and services, cost, profitability, and productivity.

Phase 2: Unfreezing/Muddling

During phase 2, which lasts for one or two years, the organization becomes—reluctantly, unevenly, and in fits and starts—receptive and adaptive to change.

Collectively and individually, people are forced to face the reality that old performance, behaviors, and management practices are inadequate. They find that new, unfamiliar, and difficult business issues and problems must be confronted and resolved, often by new, different, and untried methods. Management makes it clear that change and performance demands will not go away. The resulting discomfort causes a psychological "unfreezing"—the questioning of old behaviors and practices and the search for new ones that will succeed in the new environment.

Unfreezing is accompanied by some degree of organizational stress, depression, anxiety, and conflict. This stress is particularly intense when wrenching decisions are made to cut personnel, reorganize, prune expenses, or slash product lines. The demands of simultaneously running the ongoing business and executing strategic change with the same or reduced resources produces additional strain.

Will people make the changes, survive the transition? In our experience, and to varying degrees, yes. About 85 percent of those affected will adapt. A precious few will rise to the occasion and become true leaders in the new environment. Many will change sufficiently to be able to meet the new demands on their old jobs. Others will move to positions that do not involve high stress or significant change, often positions that carry less responsibility but in which they can cope and perform adequately. Still others—the hard core who can't make it—will opt out or be opted out of the system.

It's during this unfreezing period that all of the organization's managerial, skill, and competence warts become obvious and that most needed key personnel changes are planned or made.

It's also during this phase that the change process can be derailed by the old culture and by key individuals with a vested interest in the past. Two phenomena have been observed in this regard. The first is obstructionism and sabotage by workers who agree to accomplish move-forward tasks but do not do them, reverting instead to traditional behavior while hoping and waiting for the latest management snake oil to go away. The second phenomenon is the rejection of competence. This takes place at two levels: first, the rejection of permanent outside personnel brought in with needed new skills and a charter to change the business, often as replacements for familiar but poorly performing insiders; second, the rejection, skirting, or attempted discrediting of alien concepts as well as outside facilitators, consultants, or other temporary change agents brought in to precipitate and help manage the change process.

One CEO, as well as a number of people that he brought to a troubled Fortune 500 company, resigned in disgust after the stodgy and tradition-bound culture that he inherited refused to change. The old management won in the short term, but the company, which suffered two more management upheavals over eight years until the resisters were ousted and worn down, lost big time. In other instances, existing management may reject advice from outside consultants. Another company went through three very expensive consultants and studies over several years; all recommended the same changes—that the CEO step aside and install a new leader. When this finally happened, forced in part by concerned bankers, the company started to implement significant and recommended changes.

The CEO's phase 2 role, managing the change process, has three components. The first is to ensure that the results envisioned by the strategic plan are achieved. This requires carefully managing the balance of activity devoted to and the transition from resolving fix-the-ship issues to addressing move-strategically-forward issues. Second, the CEO must become more of a coach, facilitator, questioner, prober, supporter, and intervener and less of a directive leader for those changing successfully. This leadership style change should be possible as the top team and lower-level teams take more responsibility for the strategic health of the business, become adept at planning and making strategic decisions, and prove their ability to sustain results. The CEO will continue some driver/leader behavior in parts of the organization that are new to planning or that are performing poorly. Third, the CEO must begin to focus less on day-to-day, short-term concerns and more on long-term creative strategies.

The facilitator refines the change and strategic planning process, shares leadership, and moves leadership operationally into the organization's hands by:

▲ Fine-tuning the strategic planning process—changing the information required, revising the method by which it is obtained, and altering the timing of the next plan's development and implementation based on experience with the first plan
▲ Sharing meeting facilitation and meeting leadership with the CEO and top-team members, critiquing their facilitation styles, and helping them improve
▲ Extending the change process and the facilitation techniques to many levels and functions—applying them to departmental planning or planning in problem areas, for example
▲ Conducting audits to get the pulse of the organization and intervening when the process becomes stalled or results are not being achieved
▲ Making other personal interventions as needed

Tangible accomplishments in phase 2 often include continued improvement in fix-the-ship areas and the beginnings of true structural strategic progress. Positive change is seen in improved profitability, quality, and service. There may be the beginning of tangible strategic progress toward marketing new products, moving into new markets, increasing organization skills and capacity, and using new technologies and assets. There is evidence that desired new organization values and attitudes are taking hold. During this period, the employees, individually and collectively, begin to emerge from muddling, depression, and confusion as they see concrete results, gain confidence in themselves, buy into the vision, and relate the overall vision to their own particular jobs.

Phase 3: Structural Change

Phase 3 is a period of structural change. The organization finds solutions to the problems and pressures that caused pain. Members experience business, personal, and organizational successes. Victories such as improved profitability, greater market share, and new product introductions reinforce the new culture and validate the practices and behaviors that have produced positive change. Teamwork and coordination of strategy across organization boundaries improve, and the organization becomes more confident that it can continue these changes. The new skills needed to ensure future success are imbedded in areas key to future successes.

The CEO continues to shift his style from that of directive, supportive leader to that of coach, facilitator, questioner, prober, supporter, mission communicator, and intervener. This change is possible as the top and lower-level teams take more responsibility for fostering the strategic health of the business and as they are able to sustain promised results and become adept at planning and making strategic decisions.

The facilitator, whether an insider or an outside consultant, phases out and turns the process completely over to the planning group. This requires:

▲ Observing meetings from the back of the room, making occasional interventions, supporting, and reinforcing good facilitative behavior
▲ Ensuring that planning is documented and "seated" at lower levels
▲ Verifying that training is completed and institutionalized

During phase 3 the organization makes significant strategic strides Typical tangible results include significant new products, entry into new markets, new industry leadership, innovative production and service technologies, and a well-trained organization that is performing at high levels in key strategic areas.

Phase 4: Refreezing

In phase 4 there is a refreezing of organizational behavior and business practices, it is to be hoped on a higher plane of performance and organizational satisfaction. The organization has acquired skills, organization, planning processes, and culture that emphasize and lead to continuous self-renewal and positive strategic change. If they do not, the organization risks becoming once again threatened and unstable.

By phase 4 the CEO should be firmly in a predominantly strategic role, having become a true CEO, removed for the most part from day-to-day involvement in operations. Instead, the CEO now concentrates on developing and implementing strategy, planning organization succession, and being "keeper of the culture."

For the facilitator, this last phase calls for helping to fine-tune the process. Typical actions include:

▲ Occasionally meeting with the planning team and reentering the organization to audit its effectiveness and the execution of the plan
▲ Serving as a sounding board for the CEO and the top team
▲ Conducting a strategic and organization audit after two to four years of planning to ensure that no barriers to success have developed and that the business's strategic position is on target

Tangible results in phase 4 often include a succession of strategic successes, such as improved and stabilized high levels of profitability, innovative new products, increases in market share, admiration and kudos from industry peers, state-of-the-art operations, and the ability to attract the best people.

DO'S AND DON'TS

DO

- *Recognize that you are involved in a complex and long-term change process.* Communicate the process to your people. Indicate your willingness to manage the organization through it—if workers are willing to undertake the painful transformation as well. Hold out the light at the end of the tunnel for your people.
- *Compress the process* in time through careful, visible, decisive, supportive, but forceful leadership and resource reallocation—from the unproductive to the strategically productive.
- *Be patient.* It takes time. Behaviors, attitudes, and skills have to change. Only then will strategic results ensue.
- *Imbed continuous change skills,* behaviors and processes that will lead to sustained strategic improvement in the future.
- *Focus on structural change,* those seminal changes in the underlying architecture of the business that will propel you into fulfilling your future vision.

DON'T

- *Try to preach results,* and assume that change will take place through communication of a fancy mission statement. Change is based on identifying, tackling, and resolving tough issues.

- *Avoid the tough decisions* as your organization tries to maintain the old, ineffective status quo. To get your employees through muddling you'll have to make the tough people choices, enforce accountability, cause stress as you cut the unproductive, and overload the areas singled out for positive change.
- *Confuse cosmetic change with structural change*—and dote on the superficial organization changes, reductions in force, and lopping off of a few losing businesses that at best save money only in the short term. These steps don't cause true structural changes that result in a better future.

Chapter 4

What Facilitators Do

The new leader is a facilitator, not an order giver.

—John Naisbett, *Megatrends*

What Is Facilitation?

Facilitation is the ardent skill of moving a team to a consensus on workable directions for an organization and on solutions to problems, and then nudging it to effective and timely execution of these solutions.

Who Does It?

Everybody involved in team management is a facilitator—professional facilitators, team leaders, team members, and most good managers as a matter of course.

What Facilitators Do: The Types and Levels of Facilitation

Organizations undergoing strategic change need the following three types and levels of facilitator skills, as illustrated in Figure 4-1:

Process:	Putting the planning process together and making it work
Content:	Giving specific solutions to business and strategic problems
Intervention:	Breaking personal, organization, and business decision blockages

Figure 4-1. The levels of facilitation skills.

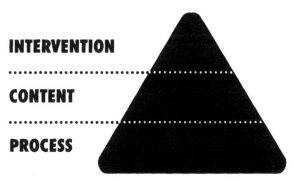

Figure 4-2 shows an ideal detailed job description for a facilitator, embracing all three skill levels.

Note that:

▲ All needed skills don't have to, and in fact rarely do, reside in one person; they can come from many sources, within and outside the organization.
▲ At one time or another during the strategic change process, all three types of skills will be needed to some extent.
▲ The skills needed are situational and brought to bear only when needed, although it's important to ensure continuity throughout the entire strategic planning process by having one overall process facilitator and administrator.
▲ The more of the three skills that are offered by one person, particularly an outside facilitator, the more effective and efficient that person and your process will be—and the more expensive, albeit cost-effective, your facilitator.

Process Skills

As a minimum, a facilitator must have the following "process" skills:

▲ *Process/structure*—intimate and practical knowledge of all pieces of the planning and implementation process. The facilitator must know how to knit them into a lean strategic planning process adapted to your business situation and to the complexity and the specific needs of your industry and organization.

▲ *Understanding of organization behavior and the change process*—the skill to determine how best to introduce and implement planning, change, and accountability. These skills come from experience in three areas: first, a thorough grounding in organization diagnostic tools, such

Figure 4-2. Facilitator's job description.

What the Facilitator Does

I. Process

▼ **STRUCTURE**
   Structures the process
   Defines key analyses
   Produces the manual
   Handles documentation

▼ **TRAINING**
   Trains in planning and process

▼ **FACILITATION**
   Facilitates major meetings
   Teaches others to facilitate
   Gives private advice on process
   Schedules meetings

▼ **RESOURCING**
   Training
   Outside facilitators
   Content specialists

II. Content

   Solutions to specific strategic issues

III. Intervention

▼ Diagnostic interviewing
     Initial
     In process
▼ Private counsel — particularly CEO
▼ Team interventions
▼ Keeps process on time

What the Facilitator Doesn't Do

▼ Develop the plan

▼ Write the plan

▼ Make decisions

▼ Become a power point

▼ Play politics

▼ Execute the plan

When the Boss Facilitates; Is Part of the Team

▼ Be a member of the group

▼ Speak last

▼ Use good facilitator skills

▼ Be neutral

▼ Let the team come to consensus

▼ Don't dominate or be authoritarian

▼ You always have the deciding
   vote — use it sparingly

as surveys of culture, climate, leadership, and attitude; second, a track record of having introduced planning and lived with its results in a variety of different business and market situations; and third, a history of successfully installing or at least living with the results of the im-

Figure 4-3. Key facilitation and meeting management techniques.

T-1 ▼	Meeting rules
T-2 ▼	Round-robin idea generation
T-3 ▼	Brainstorming
T-4 ▼	Consensus
T-5 ▼	Storyboarding
T-6 ▼	Problem identification/solving
T-7 ▼	Open discussion
T-8 ▼	Small groups
T-9 ▼	Solution development
T-10 ▼	Fishbowling
T-11 ▼	Process meetings/feedback
T-12 ▼	Personal Intervention

portant implementation tools of personal objective setting (MBO) and performance appraisal systems, action planning programs, and systems for reviewing strategic plan and program team performance.

▲ *Leadership*—the competence, credibility, and presence to run and control the overall process and to facilitate large and small meetings and retreats, as a "stand up" leader and facilitator when necessary.

Figure 4-4. Facilitator's personal skills.

▼ Stand-up, flexible meeting facilitation

▼ Building rapport

▼ Listening

▼ Probing/questioning for information/clarifying

▼ Framing concepts/issues

▼ Framing/resolving conflicts

▼ Restating/clarifying issues

▼ Summarizing concepts/meeting segments

▼ Giving and receiving supportive feedback

▼ Observing/commenting on/processing
   team and individual's effectiveness

▲ *Technical facilitation skills*—mastery of the techniques required to run effective meetings for a multitude of purposes. (These techniques are listed in Figure 4-3 and are detailed in Chapter 17.)

▲ *Personal skills*—the personal and communications skills listed in Figure 4-4, which make delivery of the technical skills and the planning process smooth and effective. The facilitator must also have the personal presence and the chemistry to relate well to your organization.

▲ *Administrative sense*—a good feeling for how the minimal paperwork should flow; how to design a readable, effective planning manual; and how to pace the entire planning process over time.

▲ *Analytical skills*—the ability to structure and conduct key business, market, customer, competitive, business/product portfolio, product, cost, and financial analyses. He or she should also be adept at picking the techniques germane to your situation.

▲ *Resources*—a network of resources from which to tap needed outside help, particularly in market and competitive research and analysis, training of various types, team building, organization and executive assessment, and financial analysis and control systems, as well as in manufacturing, service, and quality systems and planning.

▲ *Training*—the ability to train the organization in the planning process and in facilitation skills. Most good facilitators are excellent trainers.

A superior facilitator is not only fluent in all of these skills but is quick on her feet and fluid in adapting and applying these techniques, quickly and seamlessly fitting the correct technique to the situation, the emotion, and the mentality of the moment. Although you can generally plan which techniques to use in each part of the planning process or at meetings, the best facilitators cut and fit as the process or the meetings unfold.

Process Administration vs. Facilitation

Although the facilitator's job is to design and implement the planning process, someone, typically an inside member of the planning team, has to do or arrange for the dog work: arranging meetings, publishing schedules, nagging people to get assignments finished, answering routine questions from the planning team, and summarizing meeting results not handled by the facilitator.

Content Skills

The three types of content skills often found and sought in a facilitator are (1) knowledge of effective competitive strategies, (2) knowledge of functional strategies, and (3) general knowledge of the industry. The first two skills are particularly necessary to help management quickly make business decisions during strategic planning and are often sought in a facilitator.

The Three Types of Content Skills

1. *Knowledge of strategy:* knowing which competitive strategies work and which don't in a variety of market and competitive circumstances; being able to identify which internal departments and functions should be the drivers of market-oriented strategy; having experience in helping these drivers develop their subsidiary plans and configure their objectives, plans, and organization to deliver the desired competitive advantage.

2. *Functional expertise:* practical managerial experience and expertise in specific functional areas such as marketing, sales, technology, operations, or general management, as well as knowledge of advanced analytical and planning techniques, such as market research, acquisition planning and searches, total quality program installation, cost and overhead reduction methods, management succession, and compensation systems. Functional expertise gives the facilitator the ability to suggest specific solutions to specific strategic problems, such as how to market a new product, what distribution systems might or might not work,

what the best sales force structure might be, and what counterstrategy to use to thwart a competitor's thrust.

3. *Industry expertise:* specific industry expertise that, although rarely imperative, sometimes helps a facilitator get quickly up to speed on the company's situation and suggest industry-specific solutions to strategic issues. If you use an industry specialist, be sure to pick one with broad experience and an open mind focused on the future. Avoid people who appear wedded to traditional solutions to historical problems and to the old ways of doing things. Recognize that most needed industry-specific inputs and detailed knowledge of your business should, with facilitator prompting, come from your organization.

Rarely will you find in one person or facilitator all the content skills required to make the broad range of strategic decisions that will face you. Seasoned facilitators, particularly those with general management experience, can usually suggest specific solutions to specific problems within their experience base; for example, one facilitator used by a Fortune 500 company was especially adept at suggesting new consumer marketing, distribution, selling, and new-product development systems and strategies while expertly facilitating the entire planning process.

A good facilitator and, indeed, a good planning team will recognize when to call in inside or outside expert opinion for advice on key strategies and decisions. It's rare that a facilitator has specific industry knowledge in more than one or two industries. Often the facilitator's functional expertise will be skewed toward, for example, marketing or manufacturing or human resources. One planning team called in compensation experts to design a compensation, bonus, and performance appraisal system to fit the company's new strategies. Another, recognizing its weak knowledge in a new market selected for development, brought in consultants expert in that market for affirmation of its strategies and for help with implementation plans.

Good, experienced facilitators usually have a wide range of experts to recommend; if they don't, they know how to find and qualify them.

Intervention Skills

One of the most valuable facilitation services is helping individuals or teams overcome strategic, organizational, personnel, or personal blockages. Pointed, timely interventions by the facilitator can expedite key decisions and significantly compress the change process.

Most managers, particularly often isolated CEOs, need and appreciate candid advice from facilitators who are effective confidential

Figure 4-5. Individual interventions.

▼ Identification of key strategic and organization issues

▼ Feedback on organization morale, attitudes, key issues

▼ Assessment of quality of plan implementation

▼ Personal managerial style

▼ Organization structure

▼ Competence, relationship of individuals and functions

▼ Specific business and strategic decisions

▼ Outside perspective on business performance; benchmarking versus other companies' performance and managerial practices

sounding boards and who have experience with a wide variety of businesses. The two types of individual interventions are:

1. *Personal and personnel:* helping an executive with his or her managerial style and with interpersonal, personnel, and organizational issues
2. *Business:* offering advice on key strategic and business issues

One CEO, for example, sought advice on how to handle a conflict over strategy with his board; another, on the structure of his future organization and on the facilitator's reading of who within the organization should play what part; a third, on what businesses should be emphasized for growth and why; and a fourth, on whether to acquire two strategically attractive but troubled companies in light of turmoil in the CEO's current business and markets (the answer was no).

Typical individual interventions are listed in Figure 4-5.

Business and project teams can be exceptionally effective in developing and implementing strategy. They have complicated interpersonal dynamics, however, and often require intervention from facilitators or team members to keep them on track, particularly during the team's formative stages. Typical team interventions are listed in Figure 4-6.

There are four types of team interventions:

1. *Process:* Making interventions with team members as a group to help them define their team mission and their individual roles,

Figure 4-6. Team interventions.

PROCESS

▼ Facilitate team mission;
roles/job description/processes used

▼ Process checks during and at end of meetings —
what's good and bad versus norms

▼ Redirect process when off track

▼ Point out dysfunctional team behavior

MEETING

▼ Off agenda/subject—get team back on track

▼ Summarize/crystallize key points; transitions

▼ Offer stand-up facilitation when team is bogged down

▼ Crystallize/facilitate/resolve conflicts

▼ Missing the point—suggest it

CONTENT

▼ Wrong decision — point out correct options/process to define
correct decision

▼ Suggest expert outsiders

▼ Give specific content solutions

INDIVIDUAL

▼ Point out dysfunctional individual behavior
or interactions

▼ Offer individual/pair counseling

to clarify the decision-making and planning processes they'll use, and to train members in facilitation and team behaviors.

2. *Meeting:* Helping to keep meetings on track by summarizing and clarifying key points, facilitating personally when necessary, and

intervening when participation is inappropriate, points are being missed, or the pace is wrong or the agenda aborted.

3. *Content:* Suggesting specific solutions to specific problems.
4. *Individual:* Counseling individuals or conflicting pairs of team members when personal style or functional contribution is inhibiting team effectiveness. Interventions involving individuals' personal styles are sometimes difficult and require either private or direct public confrontation on sensitive issues; but when they are used as a matter of course, they improve both individual and team effectiveness and help build an atmosphere of trust and honesty.

In addition, facilitators sometimes make diagnostic interventions at the beginning of and periodically throughout the planning process. Here, the facilitator interviews and administers instruments to the organization, identifying whether the organization is functioning properly and what key issues are to be resolved and then helping the planning team understand and develop solutions to those issues.

Intervention skills are the most difficult facilitation abilities to obtain and apply. Successful interventionists are good interviewers, have personalities that encourage people to share confidences, and are well grounded in individual and organization psychology. Most of all, they know how to intervene, when to intervene, and when to stay out of a situation (when organization members must "work it through for themselves"), and they have workable solutions to offer when they do intervene.

Ideally, one facilitator will bring all three facilitation skills to planning. If an organization cannot find all these qualities in one individual, it may require the services of several facilitators to get all the talents it needs.

Where Do You Find Facilitators? What Do You Look For?

Should you serve as facilitator yourself or get someone outside the executive ranks? It's virtually impossible, initially, for a CEO to facilitate. CEOs often invoke undue deference to their power and authority and frequently dominate meetings—behaviors that are counterproductive to surfacing, discussing, and resolving crucial issues and conflicts in the team-planning context. In addition, most first-time planners and team members don't have the needed technical facilitation skills. Without question, therefore, get a professional facilitator who has the requisite skills, can keep confidences, is viewed positively, and is perceived as being objective by your organization.

Good facilitators may be external or internal consultants and usually have one of two backgrounds. Some facilitators with all three facilitation skills have a minimum of four to five years of full-time experience in facilitating strategic planning, in addition to five to twenty years of practical managerial experience. Others have degrees in psychology or organization behavior, usually Ph.D.s, with a minimum of five to seven years of practical experience. They are normally strong in process and intervention skills but not in content skills.

Large organizations sometimes have professional facilitators available for loan to operating divisions or members. Corning, Inc., once maintained a loanable cadre of facilitators at its corporate offices; the Credit Union National Association does the same. But most companies engage outside consultants as facilitators because of their expertise in dealing with a wide variety of industries, competitive situations, and organizational circumstances and because they are a variable expense; the company does not have to train them or keep them on the payroll once the planning system is running smoothly.

Where and How? The best ways to find qualified facilitators are: (1) through recommendations of other companies with problems similar to yours that have successfully used a facilitator, (2) through consulting firms specializing in strategic planning or organization behavior and psychology, (3) through industry associations, which sometimes have their own facilitators or else can recommend them.

Who? Look for a facilitator with lots of experience along the following lines:

▲ *Facilitation experience.* Look for people with three to five years in the business, at least ten complete plans under their belts, and at least a three- to four-year track record with several companies so that they understand the glitches that take place during implementation and have solutions to implementation problems. Make sure that your choice has superb process skills as well as the all-important personal chemistry and the ability to deal with your people and culture.

▲ *Business experience.* Lots of it. The best facilitators have had significant business experience as line or staff managers. If you're looking for someone to facilitate a top-level strategic plan, you want a person with significant general management experience. Plans with narrower scope can be handled by facilitators with narrower backgrounds.

▲ *Industry experience.* Nice to have but not a necessity. Put your emphasis on facilitation skills and general business knowledge, rather than on specific industry experience. A good facilitator will quickly pick up the specifics of your industry—believe it or not, most businesses have the same general problems and solutions and differ only in the implementation details. Indeed, some companies feel that industry specialists are at a disadvantage because they think in terms of one industry, its "common wisdom," and its sometimes trite solutions to problems.

▲ *Academic background.* Far less important than the other qualifications mentioned so far. It does help to have some academic background relevant to your industry or situation. You might seek, for example, a facilitator with a technical degree for a manufacturing or technically based business or one with training in organization behavior if your problems are principally organizational.

▲ *Range of facilitation skills.* If your facilitation job is limited in scope, say, running a three-day retreat or facilitating a functional plan, or if the job is expected to be short-term, a facilitator with only strong process skills will do. If you're dealing with broad, weighty strategic problems that will involve a facilitator over a long period of time and that need content advice and interventions, go for a heavy with all of the skills. The latter are expensive, but, in the long pull, the good facilitators with all three skills are extremely effective in aiding long-term change.

The cost for outside facilitators? You get what you pay for. Expect to pay per hour or per day at least what you would pay for a first-class lawyer. Senior experienced consultants who have all three facilitating skills are quite expensive. They often work with less expensive partners and associates who handle much of the consulting burden.

In-House Facilitation

When do you do the facilitation yourself? How do you phase out the "hired gun"? Where can you get training?

Using In-house Facilitators

Your organization's objective should be to learn and to become self-sufficient in the core process facilitation skills. You can do this in the following ways:

▲ *Training your own facilitators.* The best way to get a thorough grounding in the facilitation art is by observing experts and by experiencing facilitation yourself. Books such as this one, commercial videos, and public facilitation training courses will give you the theoretical framework, but only practice will make you a good facilitator. You can get excellent interactive training in the personal communication skills required for facilitation from a variety of universities, training companies, consultants, and personal communication coaches.

When you bring in an outside facilitator, your expressed objectives should therefore be twofold: first, to develop your plan and to start its implementation; and second, to get a facilitator to train you, your organization, and perhaps a designated inside facilitator in facilitation.

It generally takes three planning cycles to learn facilitation and to phase the facilitator out. During the first cycle, watch the pro deliver as he or she does the bulk of the work of structuring the process and facilitating meetings and begins to train your staff members in facilitation, giving them practice where appropriate. During the second cycle, team members cofacilitate the process with the pro. During the third planning cycle, often the third year, the facilitator observes and critiques the facilitation and process management handled by team members or inside facilitators.

▲ *Using team members to facilitate.* Not everyone can become a completely skilled facilitator. Indeed, few people have the personality, skills, or time to train to learn to be one. That's why there are people who make a profession of facilitation. But everyone can and should do some facilitation: Share facilitation of team meetings, facilitate his or her own staff and team meetings, and facilitate parts of meetings in which his or her own expertise is particularly important. Indeed, rotating meeting facilitation teaches valuable skills useful in the day-to-day job, and putting each individual up front increases commitment to the team's job.

▲ *Using internal technical experts.* Internal technical experts and managers often participate in top-planning-team meetings when highly technical areas are being discussed—subjects such as new manufacturing processes, computer systems, new product technologies, or marketing methods. These technical experts, if also skilled in facilitation, can efficiently lead those parts of the planning process that deal with their areas of expertise. They can conduct shorter, crisper meetings by avoiding discussion of technically fruitless topics, directing the discussion toward fruitful technical areas, quickly arriving at technically correct solutions, and pointing out the areas where coordination is needed from indirectly involved functions. They are often good at suggesting specific solutions to problems, although they have to be careful not to dominate and to suggest only, not demand.

The same functional and technical leaders, of course, often facilitate strategic project teams at lower levels in their areas of expertise.

When the CEO/Boss Facilitates

Contrary to popular myth, some CEOs and bosses make excellent facilitators and should share the facilitation burden. Although they should generally be the last to speak or render an opinion on key issues, lest they prejudice the discussion or the resulting consensus, they can and should learn neutral facilitation skills and model them for the organization. Some CEOs appropriately prefer to stay out of the facilitation role in discussions of important decisions on which they are known to have strong opinions. Some, also appropriately, want to facilitate in areas that are key to the CEO's performance, such as vision, mission, criteria for new ventures, and corporate performance standards. See Figure 4-2 for the boss's meeting and facilitation roles.

DO'S AND DON'TS

DO

- *Start with professional facilitation*—it pays.
- *Stick with pros until your people are trained* and you are getting strategic results.
- *Get the right facilitator* for the specific job to be done—if it's a narrow job, you can use a facilitator with limited skills; if it's "reinvent the corporation," pick a heavy.
- *Train internal people* who must lead teams in facilitation. It's a learned skill.
- *Have your people facilitate.* Letting staff members facilitate your planning meetings and process, as well as the planning for their teams, creates involvement and commitment and builds skills useful in day-to-day management.

DON'T

- *Confuse the three types of facilitation*—process, content, and intervention. They're used to address different situations and require distinctive experience and skills.
- *Think that facilitation can be taught academically*—it can't. Good facilitators learn only by experience—lots of it.
- *Try to structure and facilitate your own first plan* or diagnose your own organization's ills. An outsider or an inside pro will get you there faster and more objectively, with results superior to those that can be achieved on your own.

Chapter 5

Tailoring the Process to Your Organization

Successful generals make plans to fit circumstances but do not try to create circumstances to fit plans.

—George S. Patton, Jr., U.S. Army general

Form follows function.

—Louis Sullivan, architect

Less is more.

—Ludwig Mies van der Rohe, architect

Designing a strategic planning process is like putting together a jigsaw puzzle whose parts can yield more than one picture. Using all the pieces produces a strategic landscape that is broad, deep, and detailed. But fewer pieces, carefully chosen, also create a smaller but complete and beautiful picture, a focused portrait of a few key issues framed with workable programs to address them.

Although you have all of the parts at your disposal, your job is to pick only those needed to develop and implement an efficient plan relevant to your company's size and stage of growth, its competitive situation, the maturity of its markets, whether public or private, and its culture. Another critical factor is your company's business situation: Is it profitable and well positioned for change or in a desperate turn-around situation?

In developing its first plan, every company must address each of the steps in the strategic planning process. But which steps are emphasized, how much information is developed, what information-gathering processes are used, and how long it takes to develop and implement the plan can vary from company to company.

The "Typical" Process

Before exploring these variations, we need to define a "typical" process to use as a basis for comparison. Figure 5-1 outlines a complete strategic planning process and timetable for a moderate to large company in good condition that wants to plan a better future. It breaks the planning steps presented in Chapter 1 into logical sequences and bite-size increments that build on each other and can be handled by most organizations.

Figure 5-1 contains all the steps for a first plan, including extensive market research at the beginning, which is often omitted by companies during their first effort. The process also allows for a number of dip-downs, points at which the organization reaches into its lower levels to gather information and ideas, develop commitment, and encourage collaborative fleshing out of strategic actions. These dip-downs help keep the plan practical and doable.

Deviating From the Typical Process: Company Types

Because every company is different, you will have to tailor the planning process to your individual situation. The profiles of company types and cultures given in this chapter illustrate how planning changes from one situation to another. Even if your company falls within the typical range—medium to large size, in good condition, and wanting to plan a better future—you'll probably identify some variables that will affect your choice of what steps to emphasize, as well as your timing and your selection of facilitation methods. You need to establish which characteristics and culture describe your company, and design your process accordingly.

Big Companies

Characteristics: Revenues of $50 million to billions of dollars, multiple businesses, often multinational, multitiered, thousands of employees, formal control systems, well-established culture, typically a bit bureaucratic and slow to make decisions. Probably has some type of planning system, effective or not.

Planning focus: Because big companies move slowly, they are often better off restricting first-year planning to the corporate level with only limited, essential input from below. They need to develop the overall corporate mission; set financial and other strategic objectives for most business units; establish guiding

Figure 5-1. Flowchart of planning events.

I. PREWORK I

A. Departmental/ Functional Area Input	B. Individual	C. Assigned and Circulated
Cover level input on SWOTs and priority issues	▼ Strengths ▼ Weaknesses ▼ Opportunities ▼ Threats ▼ Priority issues ▼ Programs	▼ Environmental analysis ▼ Financial: baseline history & forecast ▼ Market and competitive analysis; strategy ▼ Strategy statement ▼ Assumptions ▼ Organization audit

II. PRIORITY-SETTING MEETING

A. Discussion	B. Consensus
▼ Environmental analysis ▼ Assumptions ▼ Market & competitive analysis; strategy ▼ Strategy statement ▼ Financial history/forecast ▼ Organization audit	▼ Strengths, weaknesses, opportunities, threats ▼ Strategic alternatives ▼ Priority issues ▼ Strategic programs ▼ Key result areas ▼ Summary ▼ Assignments for planning meeting

III. PREWORK II

A. Individual	B. Assigned/Circulated
▼ Programs to address priority issues	▼ Draft mission statement ▼ Draft objectives ▼ Final strategy statement ▼ Resource balance

IV. STRATEGIC PLANNING MEETING

Consensus on:	▼ Strategy	▼ Resource allocation
▼ Mission	▼ Key programs	▼ Communications
▼ Objectives	▼ Action plans	▼ Review structure

V. POSTMEETING WORK

▼ Completion of action plans	▼ Delegation of objectives/steps
▼ Coordination of programs	▼ Final strategic plan

strategies, including which businesses, products, and markets to emphasize; and identify burning, corporatewide, priority strategic issues to address immediately. This top-down direction will guide subsequent downstream planning and action as lower-level teams bring their strategies and actions into alignment with corporate direction. In addition, the company needs to begin installing a planning process that will eventually work throughout a large, complicated structure.

Priority issues tend to be broad and oriented toward improving the internal environment and creating conditions in which individual businesses can effectively plan and operate. Such issues include allocating financial resources, encouraging growth in certain businesses and cutting it back in others, and making key personnel and structure changes. Big companies' first-year plans also often address corporate-level issues that will change the long-term character of the company, such as acquisitions, investment in new business directions, and major R&D initiatives.

Keys to success: First, make sure that the corporate mission, strategic priority issues, and businesses priorities are well grounded and then communicated.

Getting the process right the first year is also critical, because changing it later, after diffusion into a large, complex organization, is difficult, embarrassing, and costly in both time and money. Once the battleship is going in one direction, it is very hard to turn around.

Finally, large companies should take advantage of their extensive resources to move quickly into sophisticated techniques for researching the market, studying competition and its competitive positioning, and measuring customer satisfaction. They can also afford the luxury of organization change techniques such as team building and training in team management and facilitation.

Dangers: Moving too slowly in making key decisions. Focusing too much on process and paperwork rather than on decisions. Courting paralysis by trying to involve the organization too much in gathering information and in making decisions and relying too much on consensus decision making, which can result in fuzzy compromise decisions or no decisions at all.

Time to develop and to implement the plan: Slower than average because of the size of the organization and the high need for coordination.

Cost: Above average, because big companies tend to involve more people in planning and diagnostics and to use more outside research.

Facilitation requirements: Emphasis on designing the process and on leading meetings. Ability to recommend strategies and solutions is desirable but secondary. Keys are developing the process, forms, procedures, and timetables; orchestrating input of accurate information from varied groups and condensing it for effective decision making; and leading key planning and information meetings.

Small Companies

Characteristics: Typically $5 million–$100 million in revenues, 30–2,000 employees. Often dominated by a family or a single entrepreneur used to making seat-of-the-pants decisions. Informal, sometimes loose systems. Often minimal financial control systems, usually few if any market-oriented systems except those necessary to support sales. Not a lot of planning structure. Time, money, and talent to implement sophisticated change strategies are in short supply.

Planning focus: Initial emphasis is on identifying priority issues, usually short-term fix-the-ship actions and changes needed to position the company for future strategic growth. Typical issues are removing people, systems, and resource barriers; increasing market penetration; and improving profitability of existing businesses. With these issues targeted, the focus is on quick implementation.

Keys to success: Overcoming inertia and the tendency to run the day-to-day business "the way we've always done it." Convincing the organization to apply its limited resources to planning and strategic efforts.

Despite their limited resources, small companies have several advantages to bring to planning. Their size and style lend themselves to a process that is informal, with a minimum of paperwork and analysis. Information on what's working and what's not is relatively easy to get because top-level planners are often close to the marketplace and the customer. Communicating priorities is relatively easy. CEO is very much in touch and involved in directing the process. Rewards and results are quicker in coming. Can be a lot more fun.

Dangers: Spending too much time addressing superficial or operational issues, rather than dealing with the tough fundamentals of strategy. Leaping right to solutions without gathering the minimum internal and external data necessary for good decisions.

Time: Faster than average to develop and to implement plan. Gets through whole process in first year.

Cost: Below average. Tends not to use outside research, and minimizes outside facilitation.

Facilitation requirements: A multitalented facilitator who is well versed in the planning process, knows which strategies work and which don't, and can recommend specific solutions to organization, marketing, leadership, and control problems. The facilitator needs to be able to condense the process into a series of small, informal meetings after minimal pre-work by the planning team and inputs from below.

The facilitator has to be particularly adept at giving personal counsel to the CEO/COO, who may run the company on a very personalized basis with limited industry, strategic, and organizational experience.

Rapid-Growth Companies

Characteristics: Often start-ups or in the second (seeking additional venture capital) or third (going public) stage of growth and financing; may be a high-growth, high-tech division within a larger company. Has grown opportunistically by making quick decisions in a narrow market, product, or technical area. To sustain growth, needs planning and structure, as well as professional management.

Planning focus: Strategies focus on consolidating and gaining market share and winning competitive advantage and technological position in existing, evolving, and related market segments. Companies begin thinking about leveraging strengths and core competencies into new markets and businesses for the future. All this requires segmenting markets, developing key new products/ services, and expanding distribution.

Another emphasis is improving operations—controlling costs and raising performance and quality to levels necessary for the business to win in the long run.

Independent, underfinanced companies focus on the few things that will keep them alive, attempting to find the market and the technology niche where they can either survive and eventually win or else build marketable value and sell out. Well-financed companies scramble for market position while laying the groundwork to broaden their market/product base before the competition beats them to it.

Keys to success: Picking technologies and market segments that play to the company's core strengths and competencies; thinking two market/product evolution steps ahead.

Dangers: Fragmenting limited resources on too many product and market opportunities; focusing on technology and products to the detriment of marketing, sales, competitive, and cost management strategies.

Time and cost: Same as for small companies.

Facilitation requirements: Quick, informal, and to the point. The facilitator must be able to develop competitive strategies that work in highly competitive growth situations and to apply them to the company.

Stable, Mature Companies

Characteristics: Large, ponderous, multilayered, bureaucratic, set in their ways, often smug and insensitive to a changing outside world, likely to be serving maturing markets.

Planning focus: What these companies should do is shake off their lethargy, protect existing profits and markets, and decide how to grow profitably or, if growth is not appropriate, sustain high profitability. Their plans should focus on: (1) fine-tuning the existing business to make more money and be more efficient; (2) fending off new (perhaps overseas) competitors and maintaining market position; (3) beating the competition to new market niches; and (4) using its cash throw-off to enter into new businesses, move into new geographic/international markets, and diversify.

Unless they are troubled, however, these companies tend not to plan, making them highly vulnerable to travails like those of General Motors, IBM, the U.S. footwear and optical industries, and the German camera companies.

Keys to success: Instilling a "blank sheet of paper" mentality. Bringing in outside ideas, market research, competitive information, and key managers to shake up conventional thinking, while realistically assessing the organization's internal competencies.

Dangers: Not dealing with incompetence within the organization, which creates an inability to engineer change. Continuing to believe in its own insular wisdom.

Cost: High for a large organization because of the need to overcome resistance, build up momentum, and redo false starts.

Time: Usually long. Such organizations move at a sluggish pace and make decisions slowly.

Facilitation requirements: Strong process and diagnostic skills to get organization and market input, identify strategic priorities and barriers to change, and design an effective planning process. The facilitator needs to challenge the organization and get it moving by generating and resolving conflict, then keep it on track by holding the leaders' feet to the fire.

Troubled Companies

Characteristics: In deep market, financial, or organizational trouble, usually fueled by years of poor management, lack of a jugular instinct, internal complacency, and outmoded skills.

Planning focus: Survival, accompanied by strategic repositioning for future growth and profitability.

Survival depends on a blitzkrieg diagnosis of organization, operations, financial, and marketplace problems. Step one is to identify potentially fatal problems and to apply immediate "staunch the bleeding" fixes. Stabilizing the ship in the tempest requires short-term, tough, and heroic actions.

It's cost-efficient to cut fat—strategic and operational deadwood—at this time, taking care not to slice into the muscle, such as core skills, technologies, and growth assets. The resulting assets, organization, and structure should be positioned for growth once the patient is out of the hospital.

Keys to success: Targeting future market segments, services, products, and needed strengths and ensuring that all fix-the-ship moves are consistent with long-term objectives.

Dangers: Unwillingness to do the tough things necessary to reposition the company, such as firing unproductive retainers, cutting costs, eliminating product lines, and restructuring management.

Time: Very fast to staunch the bleeding, cut the gangrene, and rescue the patient.

Cost: Average. Initial planning costs may be reduced by going right to priorities and minimizing early organization involvement. But troubled companies often require extra analysis to diagnose afflictions such as manufacturing inefficiencies and other internal and external problems.

Facilitation requirements: Content-oriented, very directive. A troubled company needs an experienced facilitator who can counter the company's specific problems with solutions that work and who can quickly instill accountability in the organization. The facilitator needs skills to ferret out and to deal with problems and barriers at all levels.

New Planners

Characteristics: Any size company that senses a need to change but doesn't understand how to get a grip on planning. Its problems are like a vaguely defined ache that requires an M.D. to diagnose it and to prescribe a cure.

Managers typically turn to planning because of a business crisis that requires strategic solutions, frustration in achieving company goals, lack of a company vision, or doubt about the company's future. Sometimes they "get religion" at a planning seminar (seminars are the revival meetings of business).

Planning focus: Early emphasis is on education in planning, strategic and organization diagnostics, designing a planning system that will work now and in the future, and overcoming the cynicism of skeptics who can't see immediate results.

Keys to success: Educating people in the fundamentals of planning and competitive strategy and convincing them that planning will have an impact and is a fundamental management skill to be used year in and year out.

Dangers: Getting caught up in form rather than in substance, concentrating on process, meetings, and paperwork. Getting frustrated because planning takes time and doesn't get immediate results; giving up or assuming it isn't worth the time spent. Trying to design and implement a planning process without professional advice or facilitation is a little like teaching yourself to drive a car at age eight—even if you succeed, it may be at the expense of costly digs and dents in the vehicle and possible injury to yourself.

Cost and time: Average.

Facilitation requirements: Good diagnostic and process design skills.

Old Planners

Characteristics: Stale, smug, "we plan fine" attitude, locked into ways that worked fine the first time. The process and the paperwork are obsolete, routine, and too familiar, and planning has calcified into an exercise in dusting off the old plan and changing the numbers. The process no longer stimulates strategic thought and probably glosses over current internal and external issues. Old planners can be any size but tend to be medium to large companies.

Planning focus: Tough-minded strategic, external, internal, and organization audits. Companies need to examine thoroughly what the existing process has and hasn't achieved and then determine if and how the process needs to be changed.

Keys to success: Reexamination of the plan and process every four to five years or when the outside environment or competitive situation drastically changes. This planning exam can be life-saving.

A CEO who drives strategy, keeps it fresh, and refuses to let process stand in the way of good strategy.

Dangers: Simply plodding through the old ways of planning and confirming the old strategies without really taking an incisive look at either. Old planners are in danger of staying internally focused and believing the myths and rhythms that no longer apply.

Cost: Average. Even when the existing planning process requires only fine-tuning, money goes toward diagnostics, external research, and training to improve teamwork and coordination.

Time: Average.

Facilitation requirements: Good diagnostic skills and the ability to challenge and redirect outdated internal and external strategies. Process skills are important but secondary.

Family Companies

Characteristics: Internally oriented, paternalistic, dominated from the top, poor flow of upward information, slow to bring in outside people and ideas.

Keys to success: Using outside facilitators who can bring objectivity to the process, whose chemistry is compatible with the family's, and who understand the special subtleties affecting family businesses, such as inheritance and succession issues and parent, child, and sibling relationships. Facilitators must also be mentors to junior family members when a generation gap prevents parents, uncles, and aunts from playing that role. In addition, the facilitator must have the ability to deal with fear of family among nonfamily members in the organization.

Other factors: Planning's focus, cost, time, and facilitation requirements depend on previously noted business and cultural factors, rather than on whether the company is family-owned.

Cultural Issues

The quickest definition of corporate culture is "the values we hold and—we hope—practice; how we do things around here." "How we do things" covers a multitude of descriptors: bureaucratically, on the fly, by the book, on the sly, through endless channels, by end runs, quickly and opportunistically, slowly and steadily, with humor and a sense of fun, innovatively, with a customer orientation, looking inwardly, with all due gravity—and a score of other phrases you might use to describe cultures you've been part of.

It's up to the facilitator to design a planning process and to use techniques that tap into cultural characteristics that advance planning, rein in those that hinder it, and result in strategies and action plans that won't be zapped in their implementation by a deep-seated counter-productive culture. What follow are a few commonly observed cultural factors (two or more of which can exist simultaneously in the same organization) and their planning implications.

Entrepreneurial Cultures

These organizations tend toward an informal, seat-of-the-pants, deal-making style—meet, decide, and go do it. The planning process for such organizations needs to feel informal but be structured enough to keep the planners focused on key strategic issues and the long term. It needs to be disciplined enough to keep the impatient doers from acting before they collect the information on which they need to base their actions. And it needs to be pared down enough to be completed informally and in meetings because, outside of meetings, formal planning activity won't happen.

The output tends to be a minimum of paperwork and formal procedures—all to the good as long as the planners build in accountability systems.

Bureaucratic Cultures

Typically large, older companies, bureaucratic organizations wallow in paperwork and procedures, too often at the expense of creativity and the development of fresh strategies. A crisp, formal structure with tight timetables; formal, facilitated meetings; and standard paperwork schedules and formats is important. But the trick is to get more entrepreneurial and creative juices running. This means encouraging freewheeling sessions to generate ideas and to identify and solve problems. It means identifying the leverage managers who will lead change, replacing those who won't. It takes a shake-'em-up facilitator with a lot of credibility to make this happen. Sometimes it simply won't work without key personnel changes, often in the CEO/COO or in the marketing departments.

Authoritarian Cultures

Such companies recognize only one kind of leadership: top-down direction. Departments and functions are relatively isolated from one another, and they lack coordination of mutually dependent objectives. Delegation is poor, and people are not encouraged to make decisions, accept responsibility, or act independently. Planning in such organizations needs to have a joint purpose: to break down the barriers, develop communications laterally and vertically, loosen up the ideation process, and build a top team, as well as to develop the plan. This may require team building with professional organizational psychologists and significant amounts of training in communication and decision making. The facilitator must be good at personal counseling, opening up communications, and surfacing and resolving key issues and conflicts.

Unaccountables

These organizations are filled with people who won't risk bruising relationships by pointing fingers at nonaccomplishment. For them, a key element of planning has to be holding people's feet to the fire. The success of planning hinges on implementing formal accountability systems such as project planning, MBO, compensation tied to performance, plan reviews, and personal performance appraisals.

Nice-but-Incompetents

Ambition outruns skills in these companies—or else there simply isn't very much ambition. As in the "unaccountables," emphasis in "nice but incompetents" has been on maintaining relationships, not on performance. Old-line organizations seeking a turnaround and long-term change are often hamstrung by just such a culture. To overcome it requires diagnosis of personnel needs and skill assessment, organization planning, and the willingness to make tough organization moves.

Well-Glued-Together, Professional Cultures

Although rare, well-managed companies do exist. They delegate strong strategic and operations responsibility and accountability, and they emphasize performance and skills. As a result they have achieved significant strategic results and market position. The traditional planning process with normal facilitation and paperwork works well.

The time and the cost of planning increase when organizations are bureaucratic and rigid, lack accountability, and have poor knowledge of customers and markets. Extra effort must go into building team management skills, removing organization barriers, installing accountability systems, and learning to understand the outside world.

Figure 5-2. The three process types.

	ISSUE FOCUS	ENTREPRENEURIAL	BIG COMPANY/COMPLEX

CHARACTERISTICS	▼ Turnarounds
	▼ Obvious barriers/
	  problems
		▼ Small to moderate
		▼ At transition
		▼ Seeking management
		  professionalism
		▼ Sound but unfocused
		  business
			▼ Usually in transition
			▼ Needs to focus entire company
			  and drive strategy into
			  business units/functions

ELEMENTS	▼ Diagnostic ▼ SWOTs ▼ Priority issues ▼ Programs	▼ Diagnostic ▼ SWOTs ▼ Segmentation/strategy ▼ Mission ▼ Priority issues ▼ Programs	▼ Complete process ▼ Layered throughout organization
STYLE	▼ Driven ▼ Heavy facilitation ▼ Leadership ▼ Fast	▼ Informal	▼ Highly structured ▼ Complex ▼ Either initial top down/bottom up ▼ Process installation

Three General Approaches to Planning

Every company and every situation is different and unique. You'll likely find, however, as you pick and choose among the jigsaw pieces in your effort to tailor planning to your own strategic, organizational, and cultural needs, that the specific planning process you design will fall into one of three general approaches: issue-focused, entrepreneurial, or holistic/complex. (These approaches are illustrated in Figure 5-2.)

Issue-Focused Planning

Issue-focused planning is a search-and-destroy procedure geared to locating critical strategic (and operating) issues and resolving them fast. Growth companies and troubled companies, irrespective of size, use it effectively their first time around. They usually find more fix-the-ship issues than move-forward issues. Ideally, they follow up this rapid-fire planning by installing a formal planning process later, when the immediate crisis has been resolved.

The stress, and there is a lot of it, in issue-focused planning is on doing sufficient diagnosis to pinpoint the most pressing top-level strategic and operating issues, and determining how to address them. There is usually just enough organization involvement to identify problems, implement solutions, and get results.

Issue-focused processes are quick and driven from the top, and they require heavy, pervasive leadership and facilitation.

But issue-oriented planning is not always crisis-focused. After their first year of planning, smoothly running companies with stable competitive environments usually take an issue-oriented approach instead of doing a ground-up plan every year.

Entrepreneurial Planning

Entrepreneurial planning is typical of small to moderate-size companies, often companies in transition from being freewheeling one-man shows to being larger and more professionally run companies. They usually have sound but unfocused and inefficient businesses and are fumbling to figure out what the next steps are.

Their planning processes are very informal, involving a handful of people and a series of short and intense periods of analysis followed by meetings to discuss data, deal with priority issues, and make decisions.

These companies typically touch on all the key elements of the planning process and—usually for the first time—put a good deal of effort into segmenting and objectively understanding their markets.

Holistic/Complex Planning

Holistic planning is process-oriented and organizationally broad and deep in scope. It's typical of large, multilayered, multibusiness companies that are not facing immediate strategic crises and that are seeking continued incremental improvements or attempting transformation into a significantly different and more vital entity.

Sooner or later, holistic planners run through the entire planning process, taking the time necessary to complete most steps. They reach into many levels and functions to gather information and to identify strategic issues throughout the company. They address these issues and develop strategic plans in appropriate levels, functions, and businesses. It allows them to achieve the dual purpose of developing strategy and imbedding a formal planning process throughout, one that will continuously update and refresh strategy, allowing only the most critical strategic issues to bubble to the top for resolution.

To do holistic planning, companies rely on heavy organization involvement, training, and commitment. On the downside, holistic planning consumes time and money on the front end. Making it work requires extremely competent people at many levels, especially at leverage points, who will accept responsibility for both planning and implementation.

Scheduling Your Time

Planning takes time—time for data collection and analysis, rudimentary or in-depth, and time for meetings. There is no escaping the fact that planning invariably adds to the schedules of overburdened, operations-oriented executives, many of whom are not enthusiastic about planning in the first place. Winning their support starts with giving them plenty of advance warning on the timetable and the time commitment they are going to be asked to make.

Figure 5-3 shows typical time commitments for a CEO and staff for the first year of a complete planning process in a typical company. Your actual time will vary as you emphasize or downplay some steps in tailoring the process to your company's size and strategic situation.

CEO and Top Team

Developing and conducting quarterly reviews of the first plan requires about fifteen days from the CEO and twenty to twenty-four days from each of the other top-team members. (The other members' five to nine additional days are spent directing the work of the functional groups that produce the internal audits, external market research, financial analyses, summaries of plan inputs from lower levels, and, particularly, fleshed-out action plans.)

From start to finish, while you are running the business as usual, expect to take eight months to develop a first plan and ready it for implementation—five months in a pinch.

Facilitator

A typical first-year process for a typical company takes about twenty days of a skilled facilitator/trainer's time, assuming that the process is bare-bones and that the facilitator conducts an interview diagnostic (which personally asks a limited number of questions of a small sample of people in one- to two-hour interviews or focus groups, instead of administering a large-scale written questionnaire) with a small sample

Figure 5-3. Full-scale plan development timing.*

	ACTIVITIES	PEOPLE INVOLVED	TIME
JAN	▼ Diagnostic interviews	Select mid- to lower-level supervisors/managers	1 1/2 hours/person
	▼ Questionnaire diagnostic	Most nonexempts	1 hour/person
FEB			
MAR	▼ Diagnostic results	Top team	1 day
	▼ Market segmentation/ analysis	Marketing team	4 separate days plus individual analytical time
APRIL	▼ Planning manual delivery; manager training	Top team plus key managers	1 day
MAY	▼ Lower-level departmental input		3/4 day per dept. plus 1 – 2 hours prework
	▼ Individual prework I	Top team	2 hours
	▼ Financial analysis	CFO	2 days
	▼ Environmental analysis	VP Marketing	2 days
JUNE	▼ Priority-setting meeting	Top team off-site	2 days
JULY	▼ Pre-work II		
	▼ Mission/vision	CEO	1 day
	▼ Financials	CFO	1 day (varies; avg.
	▼ Programs	As assigned	2 days per program)
	▼ Objectives	CEO/CFO	1 day
AUG	▼ Strategic planning meeting	Top team off-site	2 days
SEPT	▼ Final plan		

* TYPICAL MEDIUM/LARGE COMPANY

of people, delivers the results, develops a process and a planning manual, trains the top team, and facilitates all key meetings. Half of the facilitator's time is spent on-site conducting interviews and facilitating meetings; the remainder is spent "at home" preparing analyses and presentations and doing the inevitable administrative chores for the client and engaging in phone conversations with him or her.

This time estimate excludes extensive market and competitive research, organization diagnostics, and analyses or training at multiple levels of the organization. The process will also require secretarial support and five to ten days of high-level support staff time to write and produce manuals, answer client requests, and summarize flipcharts from meetings.

DO'S AND DON'TS

DO

- *Carefully and consciously tailor the planning process* to your strategic situation, the corporate culture, and the size and complexity of your organization. Pick the right pieces of the puzzle. Sugarcoat the pieces and flavor them so that your organization and culture will like—or at least accept—them.
- *Pick a "matching" facilitator*—one who has handled the type of planning you've chosen and can deal effectively with your organization's personality.

DON'T

- *March serially through a "book" process,* assuming that any generic planning process fits all. It won't.
- *Assume that the same process will work year in and year out.* The process has to be changed as your strategic circumstances and accomplishments change.

Chapter 6

Preparing the Organization: Getting Buy-In and Developing Skills for Strategic Change

Model first, teach second.
>—Dennis C. Kinslaw, president, Development Products, Inc., and Donna Christensen, consultant

To communicate, put your thoughts in order, give them a purpose; use them to persuade, to instruct, to discover, to seduce.
>—William Safire, newspaper columnist

The sergeant is the army.
>—Dwight D. Eisenhower, while a U.S. Army general

Thomas Watson [IBM's founder] trained, and trained, and trained.
>—Peter F. Drucker, management consultant and writer

Now that you've decided to plan and have designed a culture-friendly process that fits your strategic situation, you have to make the pill easy to swallow. In short, you have to overcome people's natural resistance to planning and motivate them to do a superlative job.

What Motivates People to Plan

Most employees want to plan—or at least will accept the idea. They intellectually or intuitively understand the need for planning, the need for a structure to create a secure future. Without prompting, hundreds of seminar participants identified the following reasons for planning, the hooks you use to sell planning to your organization:

▲ *Secures the future* for the organization and the individual by crafting a viable future business.

▲ *Provides a roadmap*, direction, and focus for the organization's future—where it wants to go and the routes to get there. It lets the organization align its activities with the thrust of the corporation, a continuous process that most people and organizations subconsciously and inherently seek. People know that aimlessness gets you anywhere the winds of competition and serendipity take you, often to detours and dead ends.

▲ *Sets priorities* for the really important strategic tasks that must be accomplished, come hell or high water, including those hairy, burning issues, such as lack of direction and growth, lack of profitability, and organizational ineffectiveness, that everybody talks and knows about, while wondering why they aren't being addressed.

▲ *Allocates resources* available for growth and change to the programs and activities with the highest potential payoff.

▲ *Establishes measures* of success so that the progress of the organization and individuals can be measured. It's a fundamental business and human need to know where you stand.

▲ *Gets inputs and ideas* from all parts of the organization on what can be done to ensure future success and eliminate barriers to that success in accordance with the old adage that ten or one hundred or one thousand heads are better than one.

▲ *Gains commitment* to implement the plan by involving the organization in its development.

▲ *Coordinates* the actions of diverse and separated parts of the organization into unified programs to accomplish objectives.

When all is said and done, employees also recognize what's in it for them personally: the resources to do what they want if they plan; a more secure future if the organization plans well and does well; financial rewards if they make themselves heroes as a result of the process; recognition by their peers and superiors if they succeed; and, of course, the inverse of all the above if they fail.

Overcoming Resistance to Planning

Resistance to change eventually dissolves when people understand the reasons for it, have the skills and resources to make it happen, and feel confident of a successful outcome. These are the results you need to achieve by your preparation for planning. You will achieve them if you take the following eight-pronged approach:

1. *Initially communicate* the need for planning and the issues it will resolve.
2. *Train* key people in how to plan and effect change.
3. *Conduct team building* to establish and expand teamwork for both developing and implementing plans.
4. *Prepare and distribute planning manuals* that specify who does what and when.
5. *Remove barriers and provide resources* so that planning efforts bear fruit.
6. *Identify early tangible results* and publicize and reinforce these successes.
7. *Establish a tolerant climate* that accepts and learns from mistakes.
8. *Be persuasively persistent*, never letting up on the fact that there *will* be a plan, a vision, and subsequent results.

Our experience shows that if you diligently pursue all these efforts, which are explained in more detail later in this chapter, you will ultimately win over the majority of your employees. You can expect about 85 percent of employees eventually to embrace, or at least to accept, the need to plan. The other 15 percent will likely not be good, long-term contributors to the organization.

Communication Tasks

To reinforce employees' intuitive understanding of the need to plan and to spell out your organization's planning process, you need to:

▲ *Communicate to all participating levels* the basic reasons for planning. Supplement this general information, where possible, with objective results of internal organization audits and external market research that graphically point out significant internal or competitive barriers to progress, as well as opportunities to excel. Point out that the consequence of not planning is a poor, long-term financial future for the corporation, its stockholders, and its employees.

▲ *Respond quickly and tangibly to barriers.* Make planning time available, schedule training in the planning process for affected personnel, and announce rewards for planning and strategic successes.

▲ *Identify specific issues*, as you see them from your perspective, that the organization needs to address to provide a framework for lower-level plans.

▲ *Lay out a timetable and process* to be followed, specifying who will be involved and when.

▲ *Emphasize your commitment* to planning through communication, action, and leadership of the process.

▲ *Dip down into the organization* at random to see how well planning is understood and to judge the extent of commitment to the process.

One of the most effective tools for communicating planning needs and the process to be followed is the planning manual, discussed later in this chapter. Send it to planning participants for study, and then hold group meetings to explain the reasons for planning, the key elements in the manual, what planning information is required, when information is required and from whom, the schedule of meetings, and the due dates and timetables for parts of the plan. The impact of these presentations increases when they are followed by small-group sessions at which questions and surface concerns and problems can be addressed. Internal or externally contracted facilitators should be present at these sessions to help and to explain their roles.

In a moderate to large company, a series of meetings must be held with the key managers and supervisors who will implement the process throughout the company. The top managers meeting is usually chaired by the CEO/COO, whereas other line and staff personnel chair meetings at other levels.

Communication is only the first step in obtaining organization buy-in. Don't expect complete buy-in—or as complete as you ever get in a change process—until after you have finished training, assigned accountabilities, obtained significant results, rewarded heroes, slighted nonperformers, and proven management's continued commitment to the process. Accomplishing all this takes at least one and a half to three years for a small company.

Even after planning is under way, the need to communicate does not diminish. An organization needs to continue to emphasize its strategic direction, reinforce the need for and the effectiveness of planning, and broadcast its positive results throughout the organization. This is particularly important in the first three years, when the organization is experiencing unfreezing and muddling through the change process, often without current clear-cut gains and rewards.

Training

All managers responsible for preparing plans must be trained so that they can in turn train and coach subordinates, answer detailed questions, and lead their own planning teams through the process.

Carefully selected members of the organization need to be trained in the strategic planning process, the development of competitive strategies, the objective-setting-action, and planning-plan-and-program review process, and the art of facilitation and team leadership. Figure 6-1 gives brief outlines for typical courses designed to address these areas.

Training Needs

▲ *Understanding the strategic planning process.* The top-team members and key managers who must lead or facilitate planning for business units and key functional departments should attend a half- to two-day in-house program on strategic planning. (Courses with less verbal participation and fewer illustrative workshops can be held in one day, but they are far less effective in generating learning and getting commitment.) Internal seminars can usually accommodate twenty-five to thirty managers and as a rule are less expensive per person than external programs. The exercises and examples should be tailored to your industry, issues, and needs, and the planning process specifically designed for your company.

Participants might, for example, be asked to identify the company's strategic SWOTs and priority issues and to develop the company's key plan elements, including priority issues, vision, mission, objectives, and strategies. Such exercises are a useful way of gaining information and surfacing issues, getting buy-in to planning, and, perhaps most important, beginning to build consensus on issues to be addressed and on means of addressing them. Training in strategic planning can include an explanation of the company's process and planning manual as well as tips for participants on how to install and facilitate the process in their parts of the organization. After all, they have to make it work.

Although they lack the advantage of being company-specific, public seminars are probably the most cost-effective way for small companies to train key managers in strategic planning skills. Good seminars are run by organizations such as the American Management Association and by various universities.

One-half to one-day overview courses or briefings on strategic planning are adequate for participants in lower-level planning teams who are not expected to lead the process.

▲ *Developing competitive strategies.* Developing external competitive advantages and internal support strategies requires a good deal of information, thought, and work. Only key organization members such as chairpersons and presidents, vice presidents/directors/managers of marketing, key staff planners, and select team leaders or facilitators need to study detailed strategy development. Outside courses in competitive strategy are usually most cost-effective except in large companies, where it pays to hold one or two sessions in-house.

Figure 6-1. Key training topics.

STRATEGIC PLANNING

▼ **Planning Principles**
Why plan
Who plans
The overall process

▼ **External Assessment;**
Opportunities and Threats
Evaluating the external environment
Market segmentation
Assessing customer needs and
   competitive positioning
Identifying competitive advantage and
   strategic fixes

▼ **Internal Assessment;**
Strengths and Weaknesses
Internal diagnostic surveys
Key internal financial, product, market
   efficiency, and staffing analyses
Internal and external benchmarking

▼ **Developing Priority Issues**

▼ **Mission/Vision**

▼ **Key Result Areas; Objectives**

▼ **Internal and External Strategies**

▼ **Implementation Keys**
Delegation and alignment
Action plans
Plan and individual reviews
Accountability

▼ **Plan Revision**
When and how
The second-year process

COMPETITIVE STRATEGY

▼ **Analysis of Industry & Market Factors**
Industry competitive forces
Market segmentation
Critical success factors
Criteria for selecting profitable markets
Selecting profitable markets

▼ **The Bases for Competitive Advantage**
Cost
Value
Differentiation
Internal vs. external strategies

▼ **Characteristics of Successful**
Companies
Research data: keys to competitive success
Examples of companies and their strategies

▼ **External Research**
Market segment research
Tools for evaluating external data

▼ **Internal Research**
Organization diagnostic questionnaires & interviews
Key internal financial, product, market, efficiency,
   overhead, service cost, and staffing analyses

▼ **Developing External Strategic**
Alternatives
Selecting markets
Simulating strategic alternatives

▼ **Selecting Strategies**
Selecting external competitive strategies
Driving strategy inside: value chain analysis
Developing executional detail and programs at
   lower levels in the organization

SETTING OBJECTIVES	**TEAM MANAGEMENT**
▼ **Control Principles**	▼ **Why Teams?**
▼ **Writing Individual Objectives**	▼ **Types of Teams and When to Use Them**
Characteristics of good objectives	Business teams
Identifying key result areas	Project teams
Writing good objectives	Ongoing work teams
Examples	▼ **Team Roles and Development**
Practice	The roles of teams
▼ **Programs/Action Plans**	Principles of effective teams
Why action plans	Stages of team development
What's in an action plan	Establishing the team's mission and
Setting objectives	work pattern
Identifying key steps	Team membership
Resource estimates	Team leadership
Coordinating programs with "outside" resources	▼ **Facilitation and Behavior**
▼ **Reviews: Why and How**	Effective and ineffective team behavior
Reviewing individual objectives	Typical conflicts and behavioral problems
Reviewing action plans and reallocating resources	Running effective meetings
	Team facilitation and consensus techniques
	Facilitator's role

(continues)

▲ *Developing objectives and action plans.* It's amazing how many people, even top officers, can't write clear, measurable objectives and simple action plans. It's equally striking how few can break down senior-level objectives, delegate them throughout the organization, and gain lower-level task alignment and commitment. At a retreat for executives from one Fortune 500 company, a number of very senior officers undertook to write clear objectives and simple action plans for priority issues they would assign to subordinates who were not attending the retreat. After two hours of fumbling, they called on their facilitator for help. Recognizing that their lack of skills was replicated throughout the company, they decided not to delegate any assignments until recipients had completed a workshop in writing measurable program objectives, defining action steps, and identifying resource and coordination requirements.

Figure 6-1. (continued).

FACILITATION

▼ **Strategic Planning**

The strategic planning process overview

The strategic change process

▼ **What Facilitators Do**

The twelve key facilitation techniques

Where and how to apply them in the planning process

Personal and process intervention techniques

▼ **Designing a Planning Process
for Your Organization**

▼ **Infrastructure**

Planning manuals

The review process

Accountability systems

▼ **Holding Productive Retreats
and Meetings**

▼ **Monitoring and Improving
Meeting and Team Performance**

▼ **Core Interpersonal Skills Needed**

Gaining rapport

Effective influencing styles

Listening/sending skills

Problem solving

Team skills

If people in your organization don't know how to write measurable objectives and action plans, you need to train your key managers. Arrange for a seasoned instructor to teach them the principles and give them practice in writing a few realistic programs for their businesses or departments. These managers will in turn become instructors for the rest of the organization. They can provide on-the-job training as they go about the process of establishing programs in their own units.

Be sure your senior managers also understand how to break down objectives, delegate them to individuals and organization units, and hold people accountable. You can fold accountability for strategic planning into your MBO or performance management system, which requires managers to write personal performance objectives, review their own progress regularly with upper management, and be appraised on the basis of how well they achieve those objectives. Concurrently, they manage the same process for everyone in their units. Skills for personal objective setting, action planning, and performance review are similar to those required for strategic planning, and some companies combine training in both systems.

▲ *Learning facilitation and team leadership.* To develop the process skills we have described, planning-team members need both formal training and opportunities to learn by doing. Any planning team using a professional facilitator should receive facilitation training during the planning process. The facilitator's stated objective should be to teach facilitation principles to the top team, illustrate the principles as planning proceeds, and give each team member practice in facilitation and team leadership so that the top team becomes self-sufficient and each member is able to serve as both an example and an effective facilitator for his or her own organization.

Others in the organization who have been designated as resident facilitators, leaders of major planning efforts, or project team leaders also need considerable assistance. Like the top team, they should receive formal training in facilitation principles and skills. They will also require observation, assistance, and practical personal tutelage by a skilled facilitator as they begin to use their new skills within the organization.

Obviously, facilitation skills are applicable to more than the strategic planning process. They make any manager or employee more effective in running meetings, counseling employees or coworkers, and solving problems in groups. Indeed, Edgar Schein, professor of management at MIT's Sloan School of Management, maintains that managers increasingly require consultation skills, of which facilitation is a strong component.

Critical as it is up front, training shouldn't be ignored as strategic planning becomes a way of life. Don't forget that new people must be trained in planning as your organization grows and personnel turn over.

Team Skills and Team Building

Organizations with a team style of management develop better, more implementable plans than do companies that are organized hierarchically, and they accomplish strategic objectives in about half the time. That's because team-oriented organizations usually have:

▲ Better communication, horizontally, vertically, and between key functions whose efforts must be integrated to get strategic results
▲ Better coordination of plans and of implementation tasks
▲ Superior personal relationships, enhancing accomplishment on all fronts
▲ Greater ability to surface and resolve conflicts and key issues quickly
▲ Superior process skills
▲ The drawing power to bring recalcitrant team members into the fold and the will to throw them out if necessary
▲ Excellent peer accountability, the most effective way of holding people responsible for their commitments

Suffice it to say that a group of individuals put together to accomplish a task doesn't form a team. Some groups naturally gravitate to and use good team-management principles and behaviors. Others won't be effective without some formal training, coaching, and facilitation, and still others will require extensive and expensive "team building" in which team members first probe the effective and ineffective practices and behaviors of the team and its members and then commit themselves to improvement and continually work toward it with professional help.

Techniques for developing effective teams and team members are explored in detail in Chapter 16.

The Planning Manual

The planning manual succinctly details who does what and when to develop, implement, and review the plan.

Although some companies use short, outline-style manuals, others develop detailed "how to do it, paint by numbers" versions. I opt for the latter, particularly for people who are planning for the first time. They need to know in detail what information is required, how to get it, how to think out and facilitate the development of analyses and strategy, and what precise format will be used to present the plan. They also need instruction for writing the plan, for presenting it verbally, and for defending it in debate.

A good manual is instructive but not overly restrictive. Beyond defining basic plan requirements, it gives latitude to allow plans to conform to the idiosyncracies of individual businesses and departments and for lots of creative thought.

What's in the Manual?

A good manual contains seven basic sections:

1. *Summary and schedule,* a crisp, graphically presented overview of planning steps, timing, and responsibilities. The summary should show how the strategic planning cycle ties into the company's annual and operating plan, budget, personal MBO cycle, and personal performance reviews.

2. *Step-by-step instructions* for developing the initial plan, including for each step:

▲ Objective
▲ Requirements for analyses, thinking, information, and output
▲ Reasons why each step is important—decisions that will be made or actions that might be taken on the basis of the step
▲ Illustrations of various parts of the plan, for example, sample mission statements or objectives
▲ Instructions on how to carry out the step, including sources, methods, and involvement of experts, employees, and teams
▲ Formats to be followed in presenting data and qualitative analyses
▲ Information on when the step is to be completed and by whom

3. *Meeting agendas* for the priority-setting meeting and the final planning meeting.

4. *Facilitation guide* summarizing techniques for facilitating various types of planning meetings and teams at all levels.

5. *Action planning guide* containing standard formats for preparing strategic program action plans, including guidelines for sections on objectives, steps and accountabilities, resource and financial payback estimates, coordination with various external resource groups, and efforts required by those groups.

6. *Review procedures,* standard formats for preparing for periodic plan and program reviews and review meeting agendas, as well as a guide for facilitating reviews and ensuring follow-up and accountability for action.

The planning manual should also contain a section detailing the second-year process for updating the situation analysis, priority issues, and programs. This section can be added at a later date.

Figure 6-2. Contents of the planning manual.

OVERVIEW AND ASSIGNMENTS

Flow chart of the planning process   Time schedule

Chart of planning assignments   Definitions

PREWORK I

▼ **Lower-Level Inputs**
SWOTs
Priority operating and strategic issues
Facilitation guide for lower-level managers

▼ **Environmental Analysis**
Trend analysis
Planning assumptions

▼ **Market/Strategy Analysis**
Market and competitive analysis
Market strategy
Strategic alternatives

▼ **Financial Analysis**
Financial analysis
Financial benchmarking

▼ **Individual Preparation**
SWOTs
Priority issues
Potential strategic programs

▼ **Priority-Setting Meeting Agenda**

PREWORK II

▼ **President's Assignments**
Vision/mission
Strategy statement
Key result areas/objectives

▼ **Program Development**
Formats and procedures

▼ **Finance**
Investable cash forecast
Roll-up of program resources

▼ **Strategy Meeting Agenda**

▼ **Quarterly Reviews**
Procedure
Schedule

▼ **Appendix**
Process for developing departmental plans

---

7. *Guidelines for departmental planning.* The top-level team can't implement the entire plan. Ninety to 95 percent of implementation actions take place beneath the top team at the departmental, functional, business unit, or individual level. It's therefore critical that the

planning manual include procedures to: (1) get planning input from each lower-level unit and (2) direct the development of lower-level plans.

Typical contents of a corporate planning manual are summarized in Figure 6-2.

Mechanical Requirements

Planning manuals need not be fancy, but they must be well written, clear, and attractively composed, with good typography and graphics. Errors, misdirections, or irrelevant tasks multiply throughout the organization and have the potential for causing useless work or, worse, cynicism about the process and about management's intent. Figure 6-3 shows the format of typical planning manual pages.

Use a loose-leaf binder, tabbed by section and indexed so that it becomes a useful reference volume. You should be able to move pages easily and tailor the manual to a given team or organization level by incorporating only pertinent sections. It's helpful to color-key graphics and sections of the manual, which is easy to do in this day of desktop publishing and inexpensive color reproduction. Append extra copies of blank tables, in a different color from the body of the manual, so they can be easily copied for drafts and for circulating within the organization.

Revisions

Sometimes sections need to be changed, even during the first year. By the second year, you will be ready to correct errors and change steps that aren't productive, add other steps you incorporated during the first year, and insert instructions for the second year and for the continuing process for updating the plan annually.

Hints for Creating a Planning Manual

Some Do's:

▲ Make the manual concise and to the point. Although it should include all essential details, keep it to a minimum of pages, and use simple, readable, nonjargon language.
▲ Leave room for submission of "out of the format" ideas, analyses, charts, and so on.
▲ Test the readability and practicality of the draft manual before carving it in stone. If there is time, have one department or busi-

Figure 6-3. Typical planning manual page setup: financial analysis.

Financial Data

Business Unit, if applicable _____

	1 HISTORY Last Three Complete Fiscal Years			2 BUDGET Current Fiscal Year	3 BASELINE FORECAST Next Three Complete Fiscal Years			4 OBJECTIVES Next Three Complete Fiscal Years		
	19__	19__	19__	19__	19__	19__	19__	19__	19__	19__
Total market size ($'000)										
Sales ($'000)										
Market share (%)										
Sales growth (%)										
Gross margin %										
Gross margin $										
SG & A/										
Sales per										

Financial Data

Complete the following financial analysis on the organization overall and on any major business units. Record the data requested on the table, copying it as needed. Note: If any of the requested data are not currently available, complete the table to the extent possible and use estimates whe...

BASIC NUMBERS:

1. *History*— Collect data on the following key years and record it in Section 1 on the table: F...

Measure	Units	Def...
Total market size	$	Wher...
Sales	$'000	Total
Market share	%	Sales
Sales growth	%	Rate
Gross margin %	%	Sales
Gross margin $	$	Sales
SG & A/sales	%	SG &
Sales per employee	$	Sales
Sales per salesperson	$	Sales
Unit cost	$/KG	As de...
Return on total assets	%	Earni...
Net profit after taxes	%	Earni...
Capital/asset ratio	%	Net w...

2. *In Section 2*, record your best estimates or budget values for current fiscal

Industry Benchmarks

$____ $____ $____

1. | | |

| Measure | Poorest Industry Performer | Industry Average | Best Industr Perform... |

$____ $____ $____

2. | | |

| Measure | Poorest Industry Performer | Industry Average | Bes Indust Perform... |

ness unit prepare a plan using the manual as a trial to debug the process.

▲ Produce an exceptionally high-quality manual—as good as the quality of the strategy and the thinking you want.

▲ Train key managers and facilitators in the manual's use.

▲ Support the manual with live planning assistance from your facilitator or trained internal staff. Help individuals by explaining instructions and modifying the procedures to their particular situations. Suggest sources of data and methods of analysis.

▲ Get lots of feedback on the manual during planning. Find out which processes, analyses, and formats work and which don't so that you can make immediate and second-year revisions.

Some Don'ts:

▲ Don't overkill with "nice to have" analyses and information. Leave those for the ivory-tower types elsewhere.

▲ Don't require a lot of written reports and data. Keep them short and simple with lots of face-to-face interaction.

▲ Don't hesitate to correct mistakes in the process, manual, and instructions as they happen. You aren't perfect, and your first planning process won't be, either.

Setting the Stage for Early Success

If you want your planning process to be a success, there are a number of steps you can take to smooth the way:

▲ *Remove barriers, provide resources.* It is useless to espouse planning if you don't provide the needed time, people, skills, and money to implement needed strategic changes. Be prepared to divert funds and talent from strategically marginal activities and businesses to the new and potential winners. Otherwise, you'll need to add to your human and financial capital. But this takes time, particularly for integrating new people into the organization and making them effective.

Remove superfluous or unproductive people, cumbersome systems, cumbersome organization and decision-making structures, and inordinate paperwork and reporting requirements. Shut down losing operations or facilities; halt marginal activities. It's amazing how quick removal of deadwood can energize and grow the remaining branches of the organizational tree.

Finally, provide human resources to facilitate the process and to serve as objective and confidential coaches and counselors during the early years. This facilitative lubricant will pay huge dividends far out of proportion to its cost.

▲ *Show and reinforce tangible results.* Reward and herald early results from planning. One company established an annual planning conference for its thirty key business unit managers. At the first and subsequent conferences, the company gave significant travel awards for the most profitable plan, the most creative plan, and the most promising plan. In addition, experts educated the managers in industry trends, new methods of competing, and effective planning and management techniques.

Look for excuses to get early results. One company funded a number of strategic programs early in the planning process, skipping its usual lengthy and cumbersome approval procedures. By doing so, it gained two advantages. First, the planning process gathered enough coordinated information quickly to make early, reasonable risk decisions. Second, management sent out the signal to the organization that good programs in support of strategy would be quickly funded and implemented without the normal hassle.

Finally, establish a system of psychic and monetary rewards that pay off over the time frame needed to get strategic results, usually three to five years. Many companies are tying a significant portion of bonuses, stock options, and stock awards to strategic program accomplishments and long-term financial results.

▲ *Set a climate tolerant of mistakes.* Mitigate fear by being reasonably supportive of learning mistakes, miscues, and early-on failures. Change, by definition, involves learning and risk. Be tolerant and coach people through their failures. Obviously, you'll need to replace someone who continuously misses objectives and repeats mistakes. But you must expect a few mistakes on the part of talented hard chargers.

▲ *Quality assessment and control.* You need to assess and control the clarity, effectiveness, and quality of all organization processes, particularly when in the initial development and early implementation stages. Strategic planning is no exception.

When you are designing the process, developing procedures, and drafting manuals, solicit inputs from a broad spectrum of potential users. In addition, have one or two groups actually critique and road test the process before introducing it to the entire organization.

During your first year, your facilitator should actively solicit opinions on what's working and relevant and what's not, what needs changing in the process or content, and where the barriers to effective planning lie. You'll need this information to revise the manual and the process so that they work the second time around. It takes at least one and sometimes two revisions to make a manual and a process workable.

Finally, before you update your plan each year, you should step back and verify that your basic process still applies to your situation. Most good strategic planning processes work year in and year out with minor revisions. But if you have made substantial changes in your organization structure or in the number and nature of businesses within the company, you may need to redo your planning process substantially.

DO'S AND DON'TS

DO

- *Structure and document* the process. Don't leave it to chance or the whims of the organization.
- *Train* your people in planning.
- *Involve the organization* and encourage feedback during the development of the process.
- *Train people in process skills,* such as facilitation, team leadership, team building, and teamwork. These are more important than the plan itself because without them the plans won't be effective.
- *Perform quality assurance and control checks (QA/QC)* on the process to make sure that it is working and optimum.
- *Be patient.* Recognize that change takes time and that people often adapt slowly to a new order.

DON'T

- *Expect plans just to happen.* Simply sending out an outline doesn't ensure success. You have to provide structure and hand-holding.
- *Turn planning into a paperwork exercise.* Keep it sparse, documenting only the information and analysis needed to make correct key decisions.

Part Two

The Nuts and Bolts: Facilitating the Process Step by Step

Chapter 7

Situation Analysis: What It Is, How It's Done, Who Does It

Out of intense complexities intense simplicities emerge.

> —Winston Churchill, statesman and prime minister of
> Great Britain, 1940–1945, 1951–1955

Many a truth has been destroyed by an ugly scientific fact.

> —Erasmus Darwin, scientist and father of Charles Darwin

Assumption is the mother of screw-up.

> —Angelo Donghta, as quoted in
> *The New York Times*, January 20, 1983

The purpose of the situation analysis is to provide just enough information to make good decisions about your strategic priority issues, strategic thrusts, strategic fixes, and program ideas. Resist the temptation to let the analyses gobble up unwarranted time and become wasteful ends in and of themselves.

How much information and analysis is just enough? That depends largely on what level and type of planning your organization commits to. If yours is a small, entrepreneurial company or if this is your first planning effort regardless of company size, you'll probably be satisfied with a minimalist approach. Although such plans are substantially based on internal, gut knowledge and existing information, they can result in good strategic direction. Often, however, they define further work, such as external market research, that will be needed for later plans to refine or develop workable strategies in information-shy areas.

In contrast, the expanded, all-the-bells-and-whistles process incorporates the ideal combination of steps and analyses to produce a well-researched, fact-based plan. Only large, successful organizations with substantial resources are likely to take this approach to doing a first plan.

Most organizations view the expanded process as a menu of options and select the additional steps and analyses they need to make critical strategic decisions. They normally complete these additional steps over a period of several years.

This chapter presents the minimum process steps required. Chapter 8 covers the expanded analyses organizations can choose from to focus on their particular needs. Chapter 15 gives examples of two companies' situation analyses.

Prework I: Preparing for the Priority-Setting Meeting

The situation analysis is done in preparation for the priority-setting meeting (see Figure 7-1). Planning-team members need to arrive at the priorities meeting equipped with market, external environment, and financial information; analysis of this information in terms of strengths, weaknesses, opportunities, and threats; and preliminary recommendations for strategic thrusts and priority issues. This preparation, outlined under Prework I in Figure 7-1, includes the following tasks:

1. Evaluating the current and future external environment to define opportunities for profitable growth and threats beyond your control that could damage your business or thwart your ambitions.
2. Identifying the market segments available to you. For each important segment, determine customer needs, critical success factors, and your competitive positioning.
3. Defining internal capabilities and strengths that can be competitively leveraged for future growth.
4. Summarizing the assumptions about the external environment on which the plan's success rests.
5. Developing your strategic thrusts—areas in which you will gain a competitive advantage—and identifying internal strategies or thrusts needed to support these external thrusts.
6. Identifying internal barriers and weaknesses that need to be removed if the company is to have a successful future.
7. Defining a handful of priority strategic issues. These are those few basic and structural strengths, weaknesses, opportunities, and threats that the organization must address to ensure its future success.

Figure 7-1. Prework I.

A. Departmental/ Functional Area Input	B. Individual	C. Assigned and Circulated
▼ Lower-level input on SWOTs and priority issues	▼ Strengths ▼ Weaknesses ▼ Opportunities ▼ Threats ▼ Priority issues ▼ Programs	▼ Environmental analysis ▼ Financial: baseline history & forecast ▼ Market and competitive analysis; strategy ▼ Strategy statement ▼ Assumptions ▼ Organization audit

Given crisp, lean premeeting assignments, individuals and functional areas such as marketing, finance, and manufacturing evaluate the external opportunities and threats and internal strengths and weaknesses for the corporation, both overall and within their areas of expertise. Such careful prework ensures that the priority-setting and subsequent strategic planning meetings are used to make decisions, not to develop or convey large volumes of information.

Four types of prework are:

1. *Department input*—lower-level department views of corporate priority issues
2. *Individual prework*—assessments and recommendations privately prepared by each member of the planning team, often with the input of direct reports
3. *Assigned and circulated studies*—required staff studies assigned to one or more functions with resulting analyses circulated to the team
4. *Expanded analyses*—expanded special studies of key internal or external issues or functional areas assigned to internal and/or external personnel

Departmental Input

Preparation of the situation analysis provides a great opportunity for top-team members to involve their direct reports and other members of their functional departments by asking them to prepare for a departmental planning meeting by assessing individually both corporate and departmental SWOTs and priority issues and then presenting their program ideas for addressing those issues. At the meeting the lower-level workers arrive at a consensus on strategic and operating (short-term) priority issues at the corporate and the departmental levels. These are depicted graphically in Figure 7-2 and defined as follows:

Figure 7-2. Schematic of corporate and departmental priority issues.

	Strategic	**Operational**
Level I: Corporate	*Priority Issues for the Long Term* Structural issues that profoundly affect the corporation's long-term configuration, profitability, and ability to compete.	*Priority Issues for the Next Year* Issues requiring focused short-term action if the corporation is to meet its twelve-month numbers and operating objectives.
Level II: Departmental	*Priority Issues for the Long Term* Structural issues that profoundly affect the department's long-term contribution to profitability and the corporation's competitive advantage.	*Priority Issues for the Next Year* Operational issues requiring short-term action to meet departmental twelve-month numbers and operating objectives.

▲ *Strategic issues* are critical to the future of the organization and are structural in nature. They are likely to significantly influence the performance of the organization and its fundamental ability to compete in the coming three to ten years. Action on them needs to be started in the coming year. Examples of strategic issues are new technologies, new products and services, new distribution methods, entrance into new markets or exits from old ones, response to major government regulations, and acquisitions and divestitures.

▲ *Operational issues* are critical to achieving financial and operating results for the coming year. Examples include urgent customer service needs, cost reductions and staff reductions with a short-term payback, short-term capital expenditures, cash flow and financing, launching new products and extensions, pricing programs, and customer penetration targets.

▲ *Corporate issues* either require commitment of significant resources, or are so critical to the organization's future that management by the top team is required, or need the top team's involvement to coordinate actions between units and corporate or among several units.

▲ *Departmental issues* affect and are resolved by individual SBUs or staff support groups and are reflected in each unit's action plans and

Figure 7-3. Agenda for department priority-issues meeting.

3 hrs.	SWOT analysis — departmental and corporate
60 min.	Departmental strategic and operational priority issues
60 min.	Corporate strategic and operational priority issues
45 min.	Corporate program ideas
90 min.	Departmental program ideas/discussion/steps
15 min.	Meeting summary
7 1/2 hrs.	

budgets. Significant unit issues, of course, will be elevated to corporate issues if they have impact on the overall business.

Inputs can be gathered from a number of organization levels using this technique.

Although the subordinates' inputs will be heavily biased toward their own functional issues, their involvement increases their commitment to the process. In addition, there are often lower-level priority issues that are keys to corporate success and that are bounced up to the corporate list for consideration. If the cost and efficiency of an insurance company's claims processing are not competitive, for example, the operations vice president should bring this critical weakness to the attention of corporate executives.

All priority issues must eventually be dealt with, either at the corporate or at the departmental level, through well-defined programs with assigned accountabilities or through the delegation of objectives to designated individuals.

Figure 7-3 presents an agenda for a typical departmental meeting.

Individual Prework

Through individual prework, planning-team members define corporate strengths, weaknesses, opportunities, threats, and priority issues and

Figure 7-4. Minimum analyses.

FUNCTION	AREAS OF ANALYSIS
MARKETING	**EXTERNAL ENVIRONMENT**
	Markets/customers
	Competition
	Sociodemographics
	The economy
	Government/legislative
	Technology
	Factors of production
	MARKETS AND COMPETITION
	Segmentation
	Needs
	INTERNAL AND EXTERNAL STRATEGY
	ASSUMPTIONS
FINANCE	**BASELINE FINANCIAL FORECAST**
HUMAN RESOURCES	**ORGANIZATION AUDIT**

develop program ideas to address them. Each member of the planning team privately assesses the strengths, weaknesses, opportunities, threats, and priority issues for the overall business, identifying key strategic program ideas to address them. If a departmental meeting has been held as recommended, the planning-team member's assessment is based on that meeting's results.

The result of this work, summarized on simple worksheets, is brought to the priority-setting meeting.

Assigned and Circulated Studies

Assigned and circulated studies identify the key external trends that will affect the plan, describe viable internal and external strategies to capitalize on the trends, and evaluate the adequacy of financial and human resources to impel change. The minimum analyses shown in Figure 7-4 and detailed in this chapter must be performed for all first plans. They are usually assigned to individuals or teams in the marketing/ sales, finance, or human resources departments.

These analyses can take considerable time and effort, so it's essential to limit their scope and to provide plenty of time and support. The results are circulated to planning-team members well in advance of the priority-setting meeting. You will likely hold separate meetings to present and discuss the results of customer surveys or of other extensive analyses such as that on market segmentation and strategy.

Remember that, for the first plan, the objective is not in-depth research and elegance. It's simply to get existing internal knowledge into the open, make key strategic decisions on the basis of gut information, and identify information deficiencies that require subsequent detailed analyses.

Minimum Analyses

Marketing/Sales

Assignment 1: Environmental Analysis

▲ Define the top three opportunities in existing markets for long-term growth in or maintenance of profits, and propose programs for addressing them.

▲ Define the top three external threats in existing markets, and recommend ways to avoid them or to soften their impact.

▲ Define the top three opportunities to grow beyond existing markets, leveraging current or realistically acquirable capabilities and strengths.

▲ Identify the major external environmental assumptions on which the plan will be based and that must be continuously monitored for change.

▲ Complete an external environmental analysis, addressing the positive (helping) and negative (hurting) external trends, their impact on the company, and your potential responses. Examine each of the following areas:

— *Markets:* end markets/market segments, product/service, trends

— *Customers:* who they will be, their needs, how to reach them, customer profitability, and customer satisfaction, comparing your company to competitors

— *Sociodemographic:* trends in demographics, psychographics, and social behavior that will affect your customers and markets

—*Competition:* current and potential competitors, competitive strengths, weaknesses, structural competitive assets and capabilities, apparent competitor's strategy

—*Economic:* trends worldwide

—*Government:* legislative political action

—*Factors of production:* those key inputs used to produce your product or service, such as labor, management talent, professional personnel, raw materials, and utilities

—*Technology:* key product, manufacturing, or process technologies needed to compete effectively in the future

From this trend analysis, pick the top three opportunities and threats and no more than three critical assumptions about the external environment upon which the plan and its success will likely depend during the plan period.

A knowledgeable marketing person under the supervision of the sales/marketing vice-president usually conducts this marketing prework analysis. The marketing person summarizes and analyzes existing internal knowledge on the eight trend areas, first, by facilitating consensus by a team of internal marketing, sales, and service personnel on market, customer, sociodemographic, competitive, and economic trends, and second, by using input from the market segmentation analysis (described in this chapter) to bolster his or her thinking in the areas of markets, customers, and competition. Small companies in which personnel are focused on sales and not on marketing often use outside consultants to draw out this information and to challenge and crystallize thinking.

The analyst also gets input from or assigns the analysis to personnel in operations and R&D in the areas of factors of production and technology and draws on legal and trade association contacts for government and legislative information.

Assignment 2: Market and Competitive Analyses

▲ *Segment your current and potential markets* into groups with uniform needs.

▲ *Select those segments upon which to focus* and get and maintain a competitive advantage.

▲ *Define internal and external strategic thrusts for key segments.* Market segmentation and customer needs analyses underlie all internal and external strategy development. Although they appear complicated, they need not be. Using internal data or common knowledge, they can be accomplished by an individual or, preferably, by consensus of a group of key customer-interface and management personnel.

Ideally, such analyses are based on unbiased market research. If you find such research unavailable or unaffordable during your first year of planning, make every effort to obtain it for succeeding plans. Sources include commissioned custom market research on customer needs and competitive performance, multiclient surveys done by consultants, industry association studies and data, and custom analyses of market attractiveness, capability, and potential profitability.

Market segments are groups of customers within a broad market whose needs and wants are similar, who tend to purchase similar goods and services, and whose needs are different from those of other segments within the same market. Aerospace and consumer electronics manufacturers, for example, have separate and distinct product and service needs and are considered separate market segments by electronic component manufacturers.

After segmenting your current and potential markets, you can target each segment with tailored product, service, promotional, and other offerings. Such focused strategies not only win in the marketplace but result in more efficient, cost-effective, and profitable allocation of strategic resources. The steps in the process are:

1. Identify all of the markets that you do or could serve. Divide them into uniform segments.

2. Establish criteria for ranking the attractiveness of markets, such as their size, growth, potential profitability, competitive situation, and fit with your capabilities.

3. Characterize each market's fit with each of the criteria, using objective data if available or your best hunch if not. Use a tool such as the GE-McKinsey matrix to select those that are or will be attractive and those that should be deemphasized, and include the reason for your decision. This will let you rank your markets in order of priority or desirability for investment purposes and determine the growth posture that you will take toward the market: Grow share, hold position, milk for cash, divest share, exit, or ignore for now.

A supermarket chain defined the following postures for its categories (product markets):

> *Grow:* A market with a high fit on our attractiveness criteria that deserves a high level of attention and investment. "Grow" categories are usually managed to gain volume and market share.

They will show in excess of 10 percent per year market growth and have high profit potential in excess of three dollars direct profitability per week per foot squared. They are not price sensitive, have average to weak competition, and have a strong fit with our strategy, particularly the opportunity for strong differentiation on service and variety against an upscale market. They usually take priority for space, advertising- and promotion-dollar product variety, and higher investment in new-product, fixture, display, and communication methods than other markets.

Hold: Invest, spend sufficiently to maintain market position and share. A "hold" market has moderate ratings on many of our attractiveness dimensions and usually has 6- to 10- percent growth; medium profit potential; $2–$3 direct profit potential per week per foot squared; moderate market size ($10 million–$20 million); and moderate competition, price sensitivity, market maturity, and fit with our strategy.

Milk: Worth only minimum investment. This market is run for cash, and we will give up space and spending as they are needed for more productive categories and markets. A "milk" category has low ratings on many dimensions, such as growth, profit potential, and market size (usually small to moderate). There is relatively high price sensitivity, maturing or mature markets with lots of competition, and poor fit with our target market and strategy. "Milk" categories are usually strategically managed with the minimum of stock keeping units (SKUs) and space necessary to satisfy customers and are priced to make maximum profits. They must generate substantial positive cash flow.

A chemical company applied similar criteria to its end market segments such as automotive wholesale, automotive retail, utilities, aircraft maintenance, general manufacturing, automotive service, and electrical manufacturing.

4. Establish customer needs. For each important segment, identify the top five or six customer needs and how well you meet them in comparison to your competition. Present your results in importance/performance matrices identifying areas where you surpass your competition (potential strategic thrusts), areas where you are deficient (strategic fixes), and ideas for fixing problems or further developing areas of thrust. A key part of the segment needs assessment is the identification of customer product needs and the determination of your product priorities and posture, that is, which current and potential products will be placed in the grow, hold, and divest-share categories.

Figure 7-5 illustrates market segmentation for the Baptist Sunday School Board's religious conference centers. Figure 7-6 presents an im-

Figure 7-5. Market segments/penetration for religious conference centers.

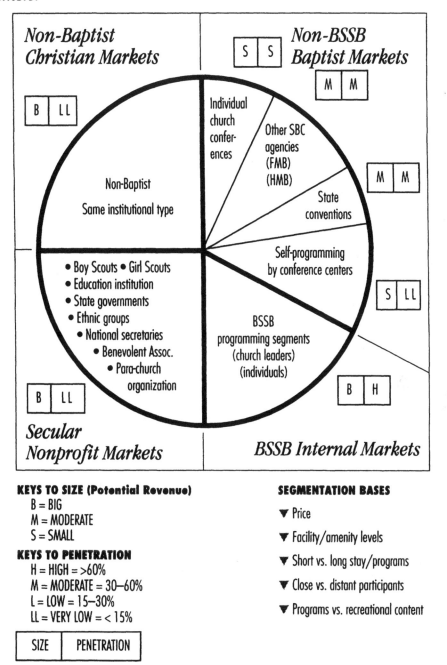

KEYS TO SIZE (Potential Revenue)
B = BIG
M = MODERATE
S = SMALL

KEYS TO PENETRATION
H = HIGH = >60%
M = MODERATE = 30–60%
L = LOW = 15–30%
LL = VERY LOW = < 15%

SIZE	PENETRATION

SEGMENTATION BASES

▼ Price

▼ Facility/amenity levels

▼ Short vs. long stay/programs

▼ Close vs. distant participants

▼ Programs vs. recreational content

portance/performance matrix for two poultry processors, with the lower-market-share company at an obvious disadvantage to a market leader.

It's not enough to identify needs in general terms such as service

Figure 7-6. Importance/performance matrix: major poultry processor selling to retail grocers.

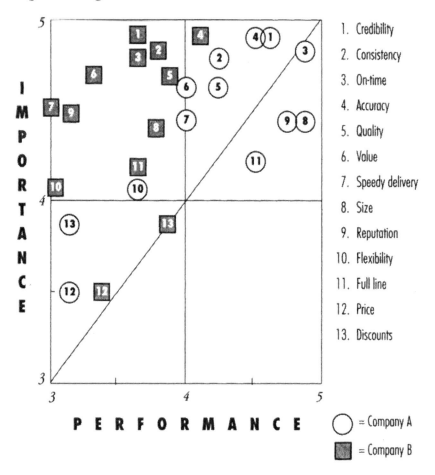

1. Credibility
2. Consistency
3. On-time
4. Accuracy
5. Quality
6. Value
7. Speedy delivery
8. Size
9. Reputation
10. Flexibility
11. Full line
12. Price
13. Discounts

○ = Company A
■ = Company B

or quality. You must define in detail what customers mean by each dimension and how they will judge success. According to a market survey, for example, wholesale purchasers of poultry products define service to include on-time delivery, quick delivery in case of emergencies, and flexibility in meeting special product, packaging, and service requests. Customers further narrow on-time delivery to mean delivery within two hours of estimated time, providing a clear-cut standard of performance for the vendor. This kind of specificity is critical to establishing programs to meet and exceed customer expectations. Of course, customer needs and their detailed requirements differ significantly by industry.

The chairman of Western Supermarkets describes market segmentation and customer need analysis as essential to the company's short- and long-term success. Instead of fragmenting its energy and frequently changing its focus in reaction to competitors' transient moves, Western has tailored its investments, new products, new stores, and merchandising efforts toward the specific needs of two top-priority customer segments: upscale, where service, quality, variety, and atmosphere are most important and price is relatively unimportant; and value, where quality and price are equally important and service somewhat less so. It also focuses on fulfilling three overriding customer needs: service, quality, and variety, detailing the meaning of each strategic thrust through customer focus groups and telephone surveys.

Western developed consensus on market segments and needs during one facilitated interactive session that included its entire thirty-person top-management team. The company later required the managers of more than thirty merchandise categories (business units) to align their objectives and product, pricing, promotional, and sourcing strategies to achieve high penetration of the selected market segments.

Assignment 3: Strategy Formulation

▲ Define the business's basic competitive advantage (cost, value, or differentiation).

▲ Specify the company's strategic thrusts, the top two to four specific external strategies that the company will use to gain and maintain an advantage over its competition. These thrusts must meet one or more high-priority customer needs better than the competition's efforts.

▲ Establish strategic fixes—ways of improving performance in areas where the customer considers you significantly inferior to the competition.

▲ Define internal strategic thrusts that must be implemented to support your competitive advantage strategic thrusts.

Summarize your strategies in a strategy statement that will explain and drive competitive strategy throughout the rest of the organization (see Figure 7-7). Note that the rarely achieved ideal competitive advantage fulfills three conditions:

1. It meets high-order customer needs better than the competition.
2. It plays to your key strengths.
3. It plays to your competitors' long-term weaknesses.

Choosing Your Strategies

1. Work with the high-priority segments within a business or business unit determined in Assignment 2.
2. Decide whether your overall competitive advantage will be cost,

Figure 7-7. Strategy statement for a packaging manufacturer.

Market Posture and Priorities

Grow: Regional and national pet food; milling; agricultural
Hold: Lawn and garden
Milk: Salt packaging
Explore: Snack food

Product Posture and Priorities

Grow: Multiwall, multiple-color paper
Hold: Multicolor plastic
Milk: High-density sheeting; other plastic packaging
Competitive Advantage: Differentiation

Strategic Thrusts

Superior Service:
   Being highly responsive to customer needs; being on time all the time; making complete shipments all the time; helping our customers solve their packaging problems
Quality:
   Putting out 100% defect-free packaging all the time; projecting and earning a total-quality image
Technical Support:
   Providing the market and our customers with alternatives to meet their emerging packaging needs and with solutions to their printing and packaging problems

Internal Strategies

To accomplish our external strategies we will have to build and maintain competencies superior to those of the competition in the following areas:
   Manufacturing systems: to schedule and quality-control production
   Service systems: to efficiently enter, expedite, ship, and keep customers informed of order status
   Technical staff: in manufacturing, customer engineering, and product and process development
   Printing technology: at the leading edge of multiple-color printing

Key Current Fixes

   New manufacturing MRP system
   Reconfigure, retrain current and new sales and service staff and systems
   Fix color quality with existing equipment and quality-control systems

Actual Example

value, or differentiation. Base this choice on your strengths, your competitors' capabilities and weaknesses, and customer needs.

3. Identify customer needs common to *all* high-priority segments. Select those that will become your overall strategic thrusts (need areas

where you will be at least on par with the competition or will maintain a distinct competitive advantage). Note that a significant competitive advantage usually requires meeting a bundle of needs better than the competition, not just one. For example, Henning Packaging, Inc. (a pseudonym), identified its umbrella strategic thrusts as a combination of (1) service, (2) quality of print and bags, and (3) technical assistance. These were needs common to all of its market segments. The company elaborated on each of its thrusts, deciding, for example, that service meant being superior to the competition according to the objective judgment of its target customers and that the key elements of customer service were delivering orders 100 percent complete and on time, responding instantly to inquiries, providing timely customer engineering services, ensuring high accuracy in shipments, and being flexible in meeting unusual requests.

Dell Computer, the creator of the low-price PC clone market, reacted to price cuts by Compaq and other computer makers by emphasizing a strategic thrust of customer service and security. In Dell's words, this meant providing services in the "three areas where you (the customer) want assurances—compatibility, quick answers, and fast service." To implement the thrust, Dell offered a "Guaranteed Response" program, promising toll-free telephone technical support within five minutes; a twenty-four-hour hot line to help Dell buyers get started setting up and operating their systems; next-day, on-the-spot technical service for difficult problems; a thirty-day, no-questions-asked return guarantee; and a three-year guarantee of upward compatibility between customers' existing Dell systems and new operating systems and applications software.

Dell accomplished all of this even as it maintained its price leadership by slightly undercutting the competition. It played to its major competitor's weaknesses: high cost structures, outdated distribution systems that used dealers instead of direct selling, a mediocre to poor reputation for service, and sluggish reaction to competitive moves. Thus, Dell, like Wal-Mart, sustained its position as a true value merchant, differentiating on service within the low cost-price market segment.

4. Isolate those needs areas in which your performance is subpar and in which you need to initiate strategic fixes before you can move forward. Identify the internal capabilities you must change to produce customer-specified performance. Henning, for example, focused on fixing its poor service by improving capacity forecasting and order entry and by introducing a manufacturing planning and control system.

5. Determine areas in which you should develop other unique subsidiary external strategies consistent with your umbrella strategies in order to meet the specific needs of individual segments. Pay particular

attention to fleshing out your detailed marketing strategies (the four P's: Product Services, Price, Place, and Promotion) for segments that you are either now in or about to enter. Henning, for example, focused on the pet food segment's unique needs for exceptionally high-quality four-color printing, quick turnaround of artwork changes, and delivery of large quantities on short notice.

6. Define your internal strategic thrusts, the key internal capabilities and linkages with functional areas needed to gain and sustain the overall and unique segment competitive advantages. Determine how these differ from your existing capabilities. Henning focused on redesigning its antiquated management information and control systems, ensuring that the new system would accommodate the advanced manufacturing planning, quality control, and sales service systems needed to support its strategic thrust. A strategic thrust for one health insurance underwriter was quick and accurate claims processing. To achieve its goal, the company realized it would have to install new, state-of-the-art data processing, claims handling, and customer service systems, as well as adding customer service personnel.

7. Identify any other subsidiary internal strategies that are key to your success, even if their value may not be directly recognized by your customers. While this step is not always important to the development of the top-level strategic plan, this is nonetheless a good time to flesh out these additional strategies for segments that you are now in or considering entering soon. For example, effective in-store and market communications are major success keys for supermarkets and many retailers. These stores therefore require superior internal marketing capabilities in advertising, display, in-store communications, and public relations.

8. Propose actions or detailed programs needed to implement your competitive advantage and most important internal and external strategic thrusts. These will be considered when strategic programs are selected.

9. Decide the growth or change routes that are appropriate for the business or to each segment (e.g., acquisition, joint venture, internal development).

10. Summarize your product and market postures and priorities, overall competitive strategy, strategic thrusts, strategic fixes, and internal strategic thrusts in a succinct strategy statement that can be communicated to the entire organization. Your strategies, once agreed upon, will drive and define all other external and internal support strategies (see Figure 7-7).

The market and competitive analyses and the strategy formulation process are usually facilitated during Prework I by the marketing/sales vice president and staff. They usually take about six to eight weeks and involve three intense periods of analysis, followed by well-facilitated meetings. The agenda for the first meeting is to reach agreement on market segmentation, the criteria for selecting markets, and market and product priorities and posture; the goal of the second is to examine customer needs and strategic thrusts and fixes, segment by segment; and the goals of the third are to decide on subsidiary external strategies and set marketing and financial objectives for each segment.

In addition, a meeting or series of meetings with the entire management team, including operations, finance, and human resources, is often held after the marketing work is complete to (1) present and agree on its findings, (2) determine the internal strategic fixes and linkages that must take place in nonmarketing functions if the external strategy is to be successful, and (3) set internal performance standards driven by external customer needs. If such a meeting takes place, the conclusions of the market analysis and the strategy formulation process are reviewed only at the subsequent priority-setting meeting, saving considerable time.

Finance

Assignment 1: Baseline Forecast

▲ Forecast company performance and results that can be expected if no changes are made in current strategy and internal structure.

▲ Identify what profitability and cash flow will be if the company meets industry leadership standards.

▲ Estimate future funds available for investment.

▲ Pinpoint problem or underperforming assets, businesses, markets, customers, or products.

▲ Define the top three financial issues/problems to be addressed and your recommended actions.

▲ Develop, from available records, a three- to five-year history and baseline forecast of revenue, profitability, cash flow, and balance sheet.

▲ Estimate how much future cash flow will be needed to sustain existing operations and how much will be available to fund growth and change.

▲ Include other key financial success measures, such as asset turns, return on equity and assets, SG&A (sales, general, and administrative) ratios, cash flow, and sales/productivity per employee. (Measures will, of course, vary by industry.)

A baseline forecast assumes that the company will make no investments in the business other than what is required under normal conditions in order to maintain operations and that it will make no structural
changes in its markets, distribution, technologies, and operations and
financing.

Human Resources

Assignment 1: Organization Audit

▲ Define organizational strengths and weaknesses.
▲ Identify the consequent top barriers to strategic progress and
  propose solutions to them.

At the minimum, the vice president of human resources should
identify the key personnel, skill, systems, cultural, and structural barriers to successful change, drawing on the vice president's own knowledge, informal employee and management interviews, succession
plans, and the collective opinions of key human resources personnel.
After the strategic plan is complete, an intensive organization analysis
will have to be completed to assess whether the current structure and
the key people who must manage change are adequate to deal with the
new strategies to be used.

Virtually all companies expecting and planning strategic change
have some significant organization barriers to success. Their organization structures and practices are the result of actions and activities
needed for success in the past and were developed in response to historical market and competitive conditions, not in anticipation of those
that will prevail in the future. New conditions and change usually mean
a different set of key tasks that must be performed at a higher level of
performance, often requiring new skills and organization forms and
practices.

Companies must therefore consciously configure their organizations for change prior to and during strategic change. Organization
change and structural changes precede or coincide with strategic progress. They do not result from it.

TARPON MANUFACTURING, INC. (pseudonym), a Small Business Administration national award winner, manufactures commodity plastic
parts for the automotive, consumer electronics, and appliance industries. It operates in a brutally price-competitive commodity environment. Before the company could identify and accomplish needed
continuous improvements in cost, efficiencies, and waste reduction, it
had to install work teams from the factory level on up.

Companies that don't remove or mitigate major organization barriers take 50–100 percent longer and spend significantly more money to accomplish their strategic goals—if, indeed, they succeed at all. Such companies resemble early gasoline engines. They are underpowered and unreliable, and they generate inordinate amounts of heat from organization friction. At best, this heat is harmlessly but wastefully dissipated.

Keys to Successful Facilitation of the Situation Analysis

Managing Behavioral Allergies and Other Glitches

There are parts of the early planning process that people like and are energized by and other parts they don't like and will need prodding to complete.

1. *Maximize likes.* Top-team members like to meet with their direct reports to prepare SWOTs and to identify priority issues prior to the top-team meeting. Their subordinates, in turn, are motivated and energized by the chance to participate and to vent problems, as well as by the opportunity to put their personal and functional priorities in perspective with the corporate picture. Similarly, the top team usually exhibits high energy, a sure sign of involvement and commitment, at the priority-setting meeting. Participants usually leave these meetings with a sense of real accomplishment, focus, and commitment to change.

You can make the most of this enthusiasm by carefully delineating what prework is to be completed and how staff is expected to complete it as specified in the planning manual. Keep meetings energized and productive by running them according to the formulas presented in Chapter 17.

2. *Manage dislikes.* People don't like assigned prework because it takes time away from their day-to-day schedules, adds to their workload, and is sometimes expensive. Furthermore, workers often get frustrated because good data are not available and because they don't know how to perform the prescribed analyses or present the data.

To facilitate these sometimes distasteful tasks, it is important to specify clearly in writing what is to be accomplished. Give the analysts plenty of time to accomplish their tasks. Bring in an outside or inside experienced professional who has a proven analytical framework to help gather and evaluate data so that you don't have to reinvent the wheel. This is particularly important for intricate market segmentation and operations analyses.

3. *Emphasize teams and deep organization involvement.* Involve people

in teams. It energizes, generates good ideas, coordinates diverse functions, and gains commitment to the process. Teams are used in the situation analysis to generate priority issues at levels below the top team, as well as in many of the market, manufacturing, and technology analyses.

Go wide and deep in asking for input. Tap at least the level beneath the top team in asking for priority issues. Go even lower if you have time. Seek input from people from many levels and functions within the organization for key analyses. Doing so motivates them, gets more and good information, and, again, gains their commitment.

DO'S AND DON'TS

DO

- *Conduct* a thorough, factual organization and strategic diagnostic, using an internal or external professional. The facts you uncover will drive action.
- *Use a professional* facilitator if you aren't one. It's better to let a skilled brain surgeon help you to operate on your nerve center than to tackle the job yourself.
- *Get consensus* on your target markets and on your competitive strategy. This will drive everything else you do. Incorrect strategy points the organization in a wrong direction that is difficult and expensive to change.
- *Fix problems* standing in the way of progress before you charge ahead with massive strides. You may have figured out where the business ought to go, but you won't get there if you trip over a land mine en route.
- *Pace the process* so that there is adequate time to accomplish good analyses for decision making while running the business. Defer to later years analyses that can't be mounted effectively now. Bad facts lead to bad decisions—garbage in, garbage out.
- *Give plenty of advance notice* on the year's planning schedule so that managers can plan their time. After all, you're adding a significant time drain and a new way of thinking to your organization without taking away any ongoing tasks. This should cause productive stress, but if people feel out of control, they'll make excuses that they lack adequate time and resources to do their jobs.
- *Heavily involve* key managers and change agents at all levels in identifying priority strategic issues and in deciding what to do about them. They have the data and the solutions. You need their commitment to resolve these issues.
- *Involve* each team member in on-their-feet facilitation during the early phases of planning so that they can teach team planning in their own parts of the organization.

DON'T

- *Get religion* and try to develop and set into motion a plan with all the bells and whistles in one year. It's important to select the elements of planning that need to be done in line with your culture, management style, business situation, and priority issues. Eventually you'll do it all—but initially craft, fit, and pace.

- *Get overly enamored* of fancy analyses. Most real issues exist at the gut level and are easily identified. The actions to resolve them are usually relatively simple and clear to define, if not to execute. Necessary facts, yes. Paralysis by analysis, no.
- *Wait* until the right team is in place to plan. Properly directed and stimulated, even nondoers and those who seem destined to fall to the axe of progress can usually think and contribute intellectually.

Chapter 8

Expanded Analysis

We are drowning in information but starved for knowledge
                                        —John Naisbitt, *Megatrends*

Never make troubles of trifles.

                                        —English proverb

Companies often need more information to make critical decisions than is provided by the minimum analyses presented in Chapter 7. You need pick from the expanded analyses only those parts that will help you to understand and address your highest problem and impact areas in the early months and years of planning.

For example, expanded analyses of future manufacturing, environmental control, and product technologies can be critical to technologically based aerospace and chemical companies, which usually have internal resources to evaluate them. Such analyses are probably irrelevant to fashion retail companies, which may focus expanded analyses heavily on customer, market, distribution, styling, and image assessments and trends. A turnaround company will focus heavily on guerrilla studies aimed at reducing personnel, losing operations, marginal products and customers, and overhead costs while seeking ways to increase profitable volume—all with the objective of quickly improving financial performance. Such a company will leave most "futures" thinking and analysis for a later, more stable time.

The most frequently used expanded analyses are presented in Figure 8-1.

The Top Planning Team: Strategic Alternatives

At some point in the strategic planning process, most businesses have to look at their strategic alternatives. All businesses can be strategically

Figure 8-1. Expanded analyses.

▼ **STRATEGIC ALTERNATIVES**

▼ **MARKETING/PRODUCT EFFICIENCY**

▼ **EXTENSIVE EXTERNAL BENCHMARKING**

▼ **IN-DEPTH ORGANIZATION ANALYSIS**

▼ **OPERATIONS ANALYSIS**

▼ **TECHNOLOGY ASSESSMENTS**

▼ **FUNCTIONAL PERFORMANCE**

structured and managed in different ways, each of which will result in different risk levels and outcomes. The outcomes are typically to grow, hold constant, milk, divest market share and revenue, or exit the business. Each outcome has implications for current profits and cash requirements. At the extremes, growth usually produces moderate profitability but consumes cash, whereas divesting share produces high cash flow accompanied by moderate to high profit levels.

There are a number of means or strategies by which these outcomes can be generated. Examples include new products, entry into new markets, acquisitions, mergers, joint ventures, licensing agreements, and divestitures of parts or all of the business.

The strategic alternatives open to a company are a function of its product/service and operations capabilities, its financial structure, and most important, the options available in the competitive marketplace. There is no canned way to develop your strategic options. They will be relatively obvious once the planning process is under way if you challenge conventional ways of thinking about your options.

One secret to pursuing the correct strategic alternatives is to devise, pick, and pursue the strategies before the market forces you to do so. Otherwise, you may find yourself at a competitive disadvantage. Such was the case with Compaq and IBM, which failed to reconfigure early to hop on the developing mail order and mass merchant markets for PCs—and paid the price in lost market share.

The process of developing strategic alternatives answers the questions:

▲ What are the market segment and product/service alternatives open to me? Are there segments I can open before the competition gets there? Can I be first in any segment?

▲ Which segments containing which competitors will my technical and financial capabilities let me successfully attack?

▲ What is the risk and the probable financial outcome of each product/market alternative?

Several examples illustrate the point.

A MANUFACTURER OF HIGH-TECH ELECTRONIC MATERIALS had limited capacity and found its markets maturing and its production technology expensive and of variable quality. Rather than continuing to pursue its earlier course of building additional inefficient capacity and trying to penetrate further a stagnating market under severe price pressure, it investigated six strategic options: (1) sell the business to a competitor; (2) sell the business to a large customer; (3) invest in a new, promising technology that might improve quality and cost; (4) stick with the existing business and process, fully intending to milk the business and close its doors when new investments were required and the business ceased to generate cash; (5) invest in process improvements that might make the operation adequately profitable; (6) seek a joint venture with someone with cash and/or the new production technology. Complicated.

These alternatives were the result of the management team's brainstorming after a situation and financial analysis revealed that the company would in all likelihood be out of business in five years if drastic action wasn't taken. After evaluating the risk and the probable financial outcome of the alternatives and given the company's limited technical and financial resources, management chose the options of vicious cost cutting, limited investment in improving existing processes, and limiting market share. These steps garnered modest profitability and a stable position in the market. Not great, but acceptable.

As the cigarette market approached commodity status, PHILIP MORRIS's premier, high-priced Marlboro brand suffered significant market share losses to low-priced generic cigarettes. Faced with increasing generic and private-label competition and with additional price increases forced by higher excise taxes, Philip Morris had many options, including: (1) maintain the high price of its Marlboro brand and lose share; (2) mount an assault on the generic market with generic brands and private-label smokes; (3) reduce its branded prices and go after the generic brands. Philip Morris chose the third option.

The COMPAQ COMPUTER CORPORATION had similar strategic options when market dynamics produced the low-price PC clone market, new and unconventional distribution channels such as mail order and mass merchants, and competitors who compete on service and by offering broad lines of software and equipment manufactured by other companies. Compaq chose to reconfigure its operation, drastically lowering costs and quickly bringing out price-competitive machines, rather than stay a manufacturer of high-performance, high-priced computers positioned in a declining product segment served by computer dealers of declining importance.

Strategic alternatives are usually developed in one of four ways: by the marketing team as it develops market strategy; interactively by the planning team during Prework I or, at the latest, during the priority-setting meeting; by the top-management team in conjunction with an outside strategy specialist; or, by a strategic simulation led by the facilitator and involving teams of key managers throughout the organization.

Strategic simulations are essentially role plays involving three or more multifunctional teams, one representing your company and the others of its key competitors. The teams are briefed together on the external environment, markets, and forecast trends and on the competitive and overall financial position of each competitor. Each team is privately briefed on the internal strengths and weaknesses and on the in-depth financial condition of its "company."

After the briefings, there are at least three rounds of "play." During each round, each competitor plots its strategy and presents it to the entire group and to a panel of expert judges. The panel consists of a few senior executives and inside experts who know the company and its industry well, often supplemented by objective outsiders, such as consultants or executives from other companies who are experienced in similar industries and competitive situations. The resulting market and financial position of each company is judged by the panel on the basis of the quality of the presented competitive strategies. The judges insert new, realistic changes in the environment before each round of play after the first.

At the end of the simulation, the alternatives open to your company are summarized by the facilitator and then discussed. The top-management team picks the most likely scenario on which to base its strategy, as well as any other scenarios for which contingency plans must be developed.

Regardless of the method used, the development of strategic alternatives requires good market and competitive analysis and data, crisp strategic thinking, and the eventual involvement of all of the top team.

Marketing: Marketing/Product Efficiency

Marketing/product efficiency analyses are usually used to analyze the marketing efforts for business-to-business selling. They evaluate three key areas:

1. *Product penetration and profitability*, both overall and by market segment and by key customer
2. *Sales force and selling activities*, taking into account productivity, cost, time utilization, and "loading"
3. *Customer service activities*, such as responsiveness and cost effectiveness of order entry

As a result of these evaluations, companies drop unprofitable products, customers, and internal activities and adopt new methods that lower costs, improve service, and increase market penetration. These actions often decrease costs and improve profitability, efficiency, and customer satisfaction.

Companies usually undertake such efficiency studies when poor marketing profits, deteriorating market share, and customer complaints about poor service signal inefficiencies and ineffectiveness. If a competitor adopts new methods, that too calls for an efficiency study.

HENNING PACKAGING, INC., is a major family-owned converter and printer of high-quality paper and plastic bags for the agricultural, industrial, food, and lawn and garden markets. When Henning did an intensive analysis of its sales force's call pattern, competence, and market penetration, it found that 30 percent of the sales staff's selling time was being used ineffectively. Most salespeople were not using effective personal account management and selling techniques, nor were they aggressively prospecting for new business. Henning reduced its sales force by 30 percent, trained the remainder in effective selling techniques, revamped its compensation system to provide generous incentives for making and exceeding both sales and profit budgets, and built in large upside potential. Significantly, with the participation of the sales force, management established new account targets in line with products and markets the company wished to emphasize strategically. It also installed a simple manual system for tracking salespeople through the lengthy qualification and sales process and made qualification of all new prospects a requirement of eligibility for sales bonuses.

The surprising result was, within four months, the qualification of forty-six out of ninety new target accounts, first orders from several, and identified potential equaling 5 percent of existing sales. In the second year of the program, potential demand exceeded capacity, partly because production did not have promised capacity in place and because new production and sales forecasting and scheduling systems did not work adequately. The company was in the uncomfortable position of having to allocate capacity and to choose between customers.

This was the unfortunate result of a situation often found during implementation of strategic plans: Significant changes in one part of the organization (sales) cause changes that are unanticipated or can't be handled in another (operations). Henning hired an experienced operations manager from another industry to straighten out its shop floor problems, bring new scheduling systems on-line, and bring manufacturing in synch with sales.

Finance: Extensive External Benchmarking

Benchmarking is an extremely valuable change tool that compares your company's performance against the performance and the anticipated performance of the best-of-class, often worldwide. Three types of benchmarking studies are common: competitive benchmarking, which compares financial performance, efficiency, and customer satisfaction to those of direct competitors; functional benchmarking, which compares the efficiency of an internal function such as customer service or warehousing to that of the same function in a best-of-class organization, inside or outside the industry; and internal benchmarking, which compares the performance of one function, such as data processing, at different locations within the same company.

You can benchmark your company's performance against industry norms and your top direct (current or potential) competitors; identify your company's financial strengths and deficiencies and compare them to those of the competition; and identify current strategic financial problems, their underlying causes, and recommendations for correction.

PHW, INC., for example, benchmarked the performance of its general insurance agency against financial performance statistics provided by a trade association for similar agencies. The company found that its agency was in the lowest quartile of industry performance and that it was exceptionally underproductive per salesperson. In addition, many spending and overhead items were grossly out of line with competitive, profitable agencies. This finding led to a line-item-by-line-item search for ways to improve, drastic overhead and personnel cuts, systems changes, and a management decision to either clean up or get rid of the profit-sapping unit.

Most companies can identify strategic financial deficiencies quickly and simply—at least at a gross level—by traditional financial ratio and trend analysis. This analysis, which is based on internal historical data compared to those of direct competitors and to industry average performance, can help a company pinpoint needed changes in standards and performance.

It is also useful to assess your competitors' existing and potential financial capabilities (e.g., assets, cash flow, debt/equity, financing capability) and to estimate their capacity to grow and to retaliate against your moves in the market.

Combining financial and market analysis can have profound effects on direction. A major but struggling worldwide manufacturer of electronic materials embarked on strategic planning with an eye to significant growth. Its off-the-cuff strategy assumed that, once high internal costs were cut and controlled, its supposed premium product could command a premium price in a performance-sensitive market segment. Reducing costs and concentrating on this segment, management thought, would return the company to profitability and growth within the market.

The company completed a market and financial analysis, evaluating several market penetration and financial scenarios. The reality was that its product "superiority" was not valued by the customer and would not command a premium price as the company had assumed. In addition, the company's admittedly inefficient process could be only marginally improved. The best financial forecast unfortunately envisioned few profits and modest cash flow. The situation analysis thus dictated that the company milk the business for cash, pay off its heavy debt burden, and exit this particular business in ten or fifteen years when its plant would need updating and replacing. Had it not done an extensive analysis, the company might have incrementally, year after year, rationalized throwing good money after bad.

In-Depth Human Resources Organization Audit

When there are symptoms of extreme dysfunction and when the barriers to success are dispersed widely or deeply within the organization, a more formal, in-depth organization diagnosis is needed. Relatively inexpensive to perform, such a study involves evaluating in detail five key areas of organization performance: culture, structure, management, systems, and people practices. Figure 8-2 shows the subdimensions of each of these areas that are frequently covered in such a thorough analysis.

The ideal diagnostic combines a limited number of qualitative interviews with a large-scale questionnaire survey to uncover the organization's perceptions of its own performance and effectiveness. The interviews should come first to help frame the questions to be asked by the survey questionnaire. Through interviews, your company can iden-

Figure 8-2. Five key areas of organizational performance.

Dimension	Sample Items
CULTURE	Openness to change, innovation, proactivity, collaboration, quality/customer orientation, time perspectives
STRUCTURE	Adequacy of structure, rules and procedures, job structure, decentralization, empowerment
MANAGEMENT	Goal setting/planning, delegating, feedback and communication, decision making, competence, succession
SYSTEMS	Goal setting/planning systems, performance appraisal, R&D, compensation, financial/budgeting, staffing, training
PEOPLE PRACTICES	Motivation, satisfaction, stress level, competence

tify a broad range of issues and gather rich data on the most important ones: What are the roots of these concerns? What are some potential solutions to existing problems?

Interviewees should represent management and employees across all levels and functions. In a small company, six to ten interviews will suffice. These interviews are confidential, of course, and can be conducted by a skilled, trusted internal human resources person or by an outside consultant.

To get the opinions of dozens or hundreds of people inexpensively, you can use questionnaires. Surveys are particularly valuable for identifying and quantifying the most significant problems. Most important, they determine where problems are most prevalent in the opinions of workers at all levels, in all business units, and in all functions.

The combination of qualitative interviews and quantitative questionnaires provides powerful data for the planning team to use in determining the top priority issues and what to do about them. Figure 8-3 presents common outcomes from a number of typical in-depth organization audits.

Operations

Operations means different things to different businesses. In manufacturing it is the facilities and organization that physically make the prod-

Figure 8-3. Actions resulting from organization audits.

Key Issues	Actions
Direction	
▼ Lack of direction, future vision, priorities, confused strategic thrust	▼ Strategic planning ▼ Market research
▼ Lack of priorities or resources, programs, activities	▼ Priority-focused short- and long-term planning at all levels
▼ Lack of market direction, strategy, few new opportunities identified	▼ Market segmentation, strategy development, new product program
Organization	
▼ Lack of accountability, poor delegation	▼ MBO, performance appraisal, program planning ▼ Plan and program review systems
▼ Poor teamwork, communication	▼ Team building, organization communication plan ▼ Introduction of teams
▼ Underperforming departments/managers	▼ Problem identification, counseling
▼ Operational problems, poor results	▼ Divestiture of losing products/businesses ▼ Restructuring of new key top and middle-level management ▼ Structural analysis of work flow to pinpoint cause of inefficiencies
▼ Short-term orientation, lack of proactivity, innovation	▼ Strategic planning and accountabilities ▼ Investment in product development, R&D

uct; in banking and insurance, it is the back-office organization that handles data and transaction processing; in a professional organization, it is the professionals who deliver the services and their backup staff.

In operations analysis, you identify weaknesses and opportunities in internal operations through extensive analysis. You also determine actions needed to get to par and to obtain competitive advantages in areas critical to future profitability, such as cost, and to customer satisfaction, such as quality and service.

Key Issues	Actions
Organization (continued)	
▼ Communication — lateral, up and down, involvement	▼ Build organization input into strategic, operation, and budget inputs; review results
▼ Lack of marketing thinking/orientation	▼ In-house key manager training in marketing, strategy ▼ New marketing executives reorganization
▼ Competency of people in selected functions and supervisory skills	▼ Training programs, personnel changes ▼ "ABC" personnel and leverage managers
▼ Overhead cost and effectiveness	▼ Structural evaluation of need, value added, and external options
Operational	
▼ Spotty customer service	▼ Research on needs/expectation ▼ Establishment of service standards and reporting system ▼ New service systems
▼ Poor marketplace performance — growth, share	▼ Market penetration, prospecting program ▼ Research to understand market needs, competitive positioning ▼ Sales force restructuring
Systems	
▼ Poor information systems, financial, cost and marketing	▼ Product/line cost/profitability systems, new MIS system

Although we look here at an example from manufacturing, in many professional and service-oriented organizations the key factors of production are people (e.g., lawyers in law firms, scientists and engineers in pharmaceutical firms, computer programmers in software companies) or technology (e.g., computer software for insurance companies). Whether the impact of such factors of production is assessed under the banner *operations* or included in other areas such as organization or technology is unimportant as long as it is assessed.

Many companies embarking on strategic planning for the first time do not have efficient operations for the simple reason that they have never looked at operations from a strategic, long-term point of view or compared it to competitive benchmarks. Rather, they have practiced incrementalism, making only modest improvements from quarter to quarter or from budget to budget. Almost any company can cut costs by 10 percent, often 20 percent, by reducing waste, staffing, and spending and by improving efficiencies. Meanwhile, customer satisfaction goes up!

The expanded evaluation we refer to requires extensive internal data collection and analysis. It uncovers trends in key strategic factors such as direct and indirect unit costs, labor, waste, efficiency, methods, overhead, manufacturing and information technologies, supervisory staffing, quality, service levels, asset utilization, and throughput. In manufacturing or information-based service companies, the analysis is often performed at each workstation or at every process step. The goal is not only to make existing methods more effective but to reconfigure or reinvent the production process to make it a competitive asset five to ten years out.

Where possible, companies should benchmark their performance on key dimensions against target competitors' performance, future customer expectations, and industry standards; if this is not possible, they should at least benchmark against targeted internal standards. Companies can often get help by exchanging information with comparable noncompetitors and with industry mutual help groups, as well as from suppliers/vendors, technical societies and conferences, and industry operations consultants.

Companies with sick and uncompetitive manufacturing or service delivery systems often use extensive operations analyses early in the planning process. These companies need to identify, understand, and fix detailed and complicated problems before they can make strategic improvements. Such "heavy" studies are usually championed by the CEO or COO and the vice-president of operations and often involve outside consultants.

HENNING PACKAGING, INC., for example, realized early on that its manufacturing costs were not competitive; in fact, costs, waste, and service inefficiencies were threatening to put the company out of business. With the help of a major operations consulting firm and through intense effort by managers and supervisors, Henning took 4 percent out of manufacturing costs within a year. This cost-cutting was a major contributor to the company's return to profitability.

The process was not without pain. It required excruciatingly long hours and weeks of effort. Some key managers and supervisors who could not handle the new professional work environment had to be replaced. In addition, once the consulting firm left, Henning found that many old-line managers were still poor at setting clear and achievable objectives, reluctant to hold people accountable for results, and reticent to reprimand for substandard work. Henning felt that it had little choice but to bring in a new manufacturing manager who would, among other tasks, instill a culture and management methods that emphasized measurable objectives and tough accountability for results.

R&D: Technology Assessments

Not every company needs to do a detailed analysis of core product, information, and basic scientific or manufacturing technologies. These assessments are important primarily in two situations: when the technology is key to strategic success in the marketplace (e.g., in insurance companies that rely on information systems and computers for both product development and efficient delivery of services) and in high-tech companies (e.g., Corning, whose future depends on basic research, product development, and engineering). Such companies need to stay on the leading edge of fundamental and applied technology in each technical discipline of every target market.

Technology assessments can be complicated, so we will only touch on expanded preparation here.

Your company should start by asking key internal technologists to compare current core technologies to the current and forecast state of the art and to assess the potential impact of new technologies on product, service, cost, and delivery.

If your company is in the midst of rapid and uncertain technical change, if you view technology as critical to your success, and if you have passed your first year of planning, you may want to consider several more-sophisticated analyses and information sources. You can get information on future technology development from external multi-client or proprietary consultant studies, predictions of experts and expert panels, and technological publications and societies, which often publish articles on or speculate on future technologies.

In the 1960s and 1970s, for example, CORNING ELECTRONICS, a division of Corning, Inc., used sophisticated technological forecasting techniques to predict future products and markets for passive electronic components such as resistors, capacitors, and inductors. This was during the heady, rapid-growth phase of the electronics industry after the commercialization of the integrated circuit. Corning's forecasts helped direct the company's initial strategic growth plan. To get the information it needed, Corning assembled a panel of market and technology futurists, applied the Delphi forecasting technique, purchased large multiclient studies from a consulting firm, conducted internal analysis, and used external experts.

As a result, Corning reduced its list of potential new-product categories from 485 to 13 that had high growth potential. By internal development or acquisition, it entered four of those markets. The business grew by 20 percent per year in a components market whose forecast growth was at best a few percentage points annually.

Planning technological development often leads to changes in core technologies. In the early 1960s Corning anticipated the growth of bioscience and recognized that its own glass and ceramics technologies would have potential applications in the new field. As a result, the company acquired bioscience capabilities through internal development, acquisition, and investment.

Functional Performance

Two circumstances call for analysis of the performance of an individual function, such as human resources or administrative services, whose "market" is principally internal: (1) the function is critical to effective implementation of strategy in the marketplace, and (2) the function needs significant improvement in performance, efficiency, or cost.

Analyses that are specific to individual functions will not be discussed in detail here. One that is universally helpful, however, is the internal customer survey, an analog of the external customer needs survey. Internal (and sometimes external) customers are asked to identify and rank the function's goods and services and to rate how well the function performs compared to expectations. With this information, planners can construct importance/performance charts, identify performance gaps, and seek solutions to significant deficiencies.

WALKER GROUP, a holding company for a number of market- and customer satisfaction-research companies, decided to reassess the question of whether a number of its central staff services belonged in corporate or in the operating companies, or whether they should be outsourced. Targeted services included accounting, human resources, advertising, public relations, facilities management, and finance.

Walker based its decisions partly on informally benchmarked standards of cost efficiency and partly on an internal customer satisfaction survey. The survey included a series of questions about where the services should be performed. Walker learned that, although satisfaction with corporate services was high, it could effectively delegate advertising to its business units and begin a transition to move some human resources and accounting activities to the operating units. It already used outsourced vendors for building maintenance and for tax and legal consulting services decided to keep the corporate staff very lean.

DO'S AND DON'TS

DO

- *Use expanded analyses sparingly* and only when key decisions can't be made without them. They take a lot of time and effort.
- *Use outside resources* to conduct the analyses unless you have insiders with plenty of experience, as well as the tools, such as software.
- *Look at your analytical needs each year* when you undertake planning. Over time, you'll probably end up doing many of the expanded analyses as you encounter new problems and opportunities.

DON'T

- *Overdo it.* Again, use only those analyses that you really need and then only to the extent necessary to make needed decisions.

Chapter 9

Facilitator's Guide I:
Priority-Setting Meeting—
Facilitating Agreement on
Strategy and Strategic
Priorities

It's hard to solve a problem when you don't even know it exists.
> —Fred Heiser, chairman, Heiser-Egan, Inc.

One must be aware of one's strengths; more important, one must know one's limitations. To be fully effective, one must know oneself.
> —Thomas R. Horton, former CEO, American Management Association

This chapter addresses the facilitator's tasks at the priority-setting meeting (summarized in Figure 9-1). It gives you, the facilitator, a guide on how to conduct the meeting, with step-by-step instructions for each section: environmental analysis and assumptions, market/strategy analysis, financial analysis, organization audit, strategic alternatives, priority issues, and programs. For each section, it includes information on what techniques to use, how much time to allot, and who is responsible for each area.

This structured framework is critical to the priority-setting meeting in order for information to be efficiently processed and decisions made in the limited time available. By working within it, planners can channel their creative energy into developing innovative ideas, achieving consensus on direction, and acting on assignments.

Figure 9-1. Priority-setting meeting.

A. Discussion	**B. Consensus**
▼ Environmental analysis	▼ Strengths, weaknesses, opportunities, threats
▼ Assumptions	▼ Strategic alternatives
▼ Market & competitive analysis; strategy	▼ Priority issues
▼ Strategy statement	▼ Strategic programs
▼ Financial history/forecast	▼ Key result areas
▼ Organization audit	▼ Summary
	▼ Assignments for planning meeting

Using the Facilitation Guidelines

The chapter covers all of the modular steps and procedures for a typical priority-setting meeting for the "typical" company. It presents alternative ways of processing many topics depending on the amount of expanded analysis accomplished and the decisions made about key issues, such as market strategy, before the meeting. You can select from these modules to design the exact process best suited to your company, given its problems, opportunities, business situation, and, particularly, the personality of the team.

A good process facilitator will be flexible as the meeting progresses. Expect to expand on or add topics where necessary, deviate from anticipated time allotments and techniques when needed, intervene when discussions get off the track, cut and fit prepared presentations that aren't on the mark, cause conflict where necessary, summarize frequently, tell planners what's practical and what isn't, and generally keep nudging the group until it reaches a consensus on important issues.

A typical meeting takes from two to two-and-one-half very intense days.

Objectives

The overriding purpose of the priority-setting meeting is to gain consensus on the company's strategic priority issues and on potential means and programs to address them. Achieving this purpose requires:

▲ Debating and understanding all the circulated environmental, marketing, financial, and other prework, with emphasis on understanding its implications for the future of the company and for each functional area

▲ Defining the strategic alternatives open to the company
▲ Establishing the strategic thrusts for the company and for each key business unit or market segment
▲ Beginning team building and decision making if these have been prior deficiencies

Prerequisites

It is critical that prework be thoroughly accomplished and circulated at least a week before the priority-setting meeting so that the meeting can be used to make decisions. Using it to develop and transfer a lot of information is a waste of everyone's time.

It is also key that the meeting site and setup be perfect so that, like a factory floor, the flow of materials and labor (facts and thinking) is efficient and results in a high-quality product. (See Chapter 17 for tips on meeting sites, setups, environment, and rules.)

Setting the Stage

How you physically set up and mentally position the priority-setting meeting is important. It sets expectations, establishes meeting discipline, and clarifies desired participant behaviors for the meeting.

Arrive early, if not the night before, to make sure that the room setup is perfect, all equipment and supplies are in place and functioning with adequate backup, and the facility staff understands break schedules and services required. Determine how the inevitable messages for participants will be handled.

Start each meeting precisely *on time*, and begin by covering:

▲ The agenda
▲ Decisions you expect to result from the meeting
▲ The meeting rules (Chapter 17)
▲ Helping and hindering behaviors (Chapter 16)

Philosophically, you need to condition the group for what's going to occur from an emotional, behavioral, and decision-making perspective.

First, this is the planning team's toughest and longest planning meeting. There will be a lot of debate, some conflict, and plenty of wrestling with unclear issues. Often, what's to be done will not be obvious. Participants will have to surface and understand facts, issues, and contrary or unclear points of view before they can reach conclusions.

Second, this is a complex process. The outcome is not mathematically decided by simply following the linear steps prescribed here. Rather, it is an interactive and building process, constantly referring back to prior steps to arrive at or modify conclusions. To identify priority issues and potential solutions, the group must process volumes of seemingly disjointed, incomplete, and unrelated information and personal experiences.

It ain't easy, and it ain't simplistic or formalistic. And it requires skilled, fleet-of-foot, flexible leadership and superior facilitation.

Finally, it's a chance for participants to both observe and practice facilitation techniques that they will use in the future to lead their own team meetings and teach their own people as team planning cascades downward over time.

Facilitation Tips

There is a tendency, especially among new planners, to spend too much time and energy on the first sections of the meeting: environmental analysis, market/strategy analysis, and organization audits. It is your responsibility to keep these sections on track and on schedule (Figure 9-2 gives the average time devoted to each step in the process), while ensuring that key trends are spotted and potential responses are workable. Intervene as necessary by summarizing trends and responses, and draw on your own content expertise when pertinent. In addition, start a hanging-issues list. Record the inevitable and important but peripheral issues that will be raised, and that will need to be discussed later in the meeting or in a separate meeting.

Section A
Environmental Analysis;
Assumptions

Objectives: Get consensus on the three to five key helping and hurting external environmental trends that may have a significant impact on the company's future performance.

Figure 9-2. Priority-setting meeting: typical agenda, sequence, and timing.

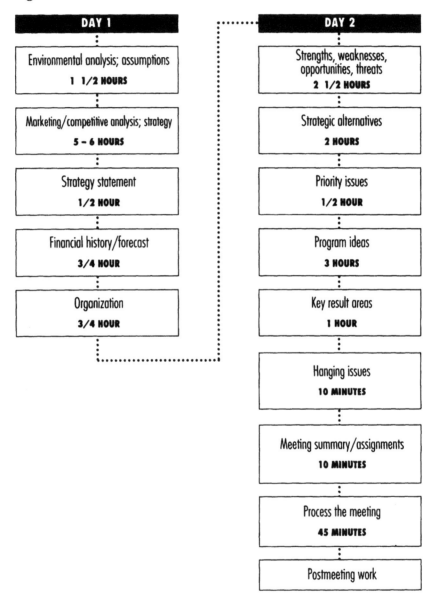

Agree on potential responses to them.

Agree on assumptions that underpin the plan's success and must be monitored as the plan is executed.

Techniques: Presentation, discussion, consensus building

Time: 1 hour, 25 minutes

Procedure

Each step includes the responsible person and the time allotted.

[30 min.]
Senior
marketing
executives

1. **Presentation of helping and hurting trends, with related opportunities and threats.**
   ▲ Ensure in advance that the content of this presentation has been previously circulated to the team.
   ▲ The presenter describes trends, opportunities and threats, and recommended responses for each relevant environmental area: markets, customers, competition, technology, economy, factors of production, sociodemographics, government/legislative.
   ▲ The presenter then summarizes the three or four most important trends and potential responses for each area. These responses will be considered later when choosing strategic thrusts, strategic fixes, internal strategies, and priority issues.
   ▲ Present the external assumptions on which the plan should be based, homing in on the three or four that will most influence performance over the plan period.
   ▲ The presentation may be supported by three to five charts on overheads or flipcharts. These should follow the formats in the planning manual.
   ▲ Allow no interruptions except for questions for clarification. Follow this procedure for all presentations.

[45 min.]
Facilitator

2. **Discussion.**
   ▲ Facilitate an open discussion on trends and responses. Are they right or wrong? Are there any additions? Go over one or two areas at a time, starting with markets and competition, and then move onto other areas that are most relevant to the company.
   ▲ Facilitate an open discussion of assumptions, particularly the three or four assumptions the presenter recommended for monitoring.

[10 min.]   **3. Consensus building.**
Facilitator   ▲ Summarize on a flipchart the three to five key
                trends, potential responses, and assumptions.
                ▲ Ask for agreement. Manage the group to a
                consensus on any differences over your
                summary.
                ▲ Record the final assumptions on a chart(s).
                Post them on the summary section of the wall.

Section B
Market and Competitive Analysis;
Strategy Statement

There are two methods for dealing with the market and competitive
analysis and subsequent strategy. Use the first if the group has thoroughly completed its marketing prework (Chapter 7, marketing assignments 2 and 3); choose the second if the group is starting from scratch
during the priority-setting meeting, which is often the case with organizations eager to get started in planning and unsophisticated in marketing. The first method is the most efficient and is preferred.

Option 1: Market Strategy Previously Determined

Objective: Review the previously defined market strategy and
                strategy statement for information only.
Technique: Presentation
Time: 10 minutes

Procedure

[5 min.]   **1. Present summary of market and competitive**
Senior   **strategy from prework.**
marketing   ▲ Criteria for selecting markets
executive   ▲ Current and potential market and product seg-
                ments and their posture (grow, hold, milk,
                divest)
                ▲ Your strategy statement (strategic thrusts, in-
                ternal strategies, and strategic fixes)

[5 min.]   **2. Answer any questions** but do not open the pre-
Senior   viously agreed-on strategies for reconsideration
marketing   and alteration at this point.
executive

Option 2: Develop Market Strategy From Scratch

Objectives: Agree on the strategic thrusts—the primary customer needs to be met—for the business overall and for high-priority market segments. To accomplish this, the group will first need to:

1. Agree on criteria for highly attractive market segments.
2. Identify major current and future segments.
3. Describe each segment's size, growth, and attractiveness.
4. Categorize market segments and product categories as suitable to grow, hold, milk, or divest.

For high-priority or problem segments, identify target customers or customer groups and their needs.

Designate strategic fixes, those areas where needs are not being met and where the business must be at least at par to survive.

Define internal strategic thrusts and linkage necessary to support external strategy.

Suggest ways to improve performance, get a competitive advantage, and correct deficiencies.

Define further marketing work needed now or in the future to better understand customer needs and the company's strategic position.

Techniques: Presentation, group discussion, small-group work sessions, summarizing, consensus building

Time: Approximately five to six hours (assuming two segments and two discussion teams)

Procedure

I. Determine Criteria for Attractive Markets/Segments

[15 min.]
Facilitator

1. **Elicit criteria** by asking group to define the characteristics of an attractive market and listing inputs on a flipchart.

[15 min.]
Facilitator

2. **Have open discussion and consolidate inputs.**

[10 min.]
Facilitator

3. **Get consensus.**
   ▲ Drawing from discussion, propose final criteria.
   ▲ Facilitate to consensus on criteria.

Figure 9-3. Examples of criteria for attractive markets.

Apparel Manufacturer and Wholesaler

Actual Example

Area	Weight
Potential Profitability	**(27%)**
Market	**(23%)**
Growth	
Stage of maturity	
Future size	
Fit With Competitive Advantages of Quality and Service	**(20%)**
Synergy with	**(15%)**
Manufacturing processes	
Existing distribution channels	
Competitive Situation	**(15%)**

Publisher of Religious Books and Materials

Fit with Religious and Business Vision

Market
>   Growth
>   Size

Profit Potential

Competitive Environment

Ease of Fix
>   (of problems preventing success in the market or extent to which have competencies to exploit)

Risk

Potential for Significant Revenue Growth
>   (through new products; share growth; per capita sales increases)

Figure 9-3 shows typical criteria for attractive markets or business opportunities for a manufacturing firm and a book publisher.

II. Develop Segments, Segment Data

[60 min. per market] **Facilitator**	**1. Give the definition of a market segment.** Ask the group to name the segments within each broad market open to it. List the segments on a flipchart and consolidate duplicates and subsegments into larger segments during the discussion. A good technique is to draw a circle and split the circle into wedges representing market segments and the subsegments within them.
[15 min.] **Facilitator**	**2. Characterize each segment's** size, growth, and current penetration. Ratings of high, moderate, or low are adequate as long as the ranges are defined.
[15–50 min.] **Facilitator**	**3. Rate each segment on its future attractiveness** and then decide on an appropriate strategic posture high (grow), moderate (hold), or low (divest share or get out). This may be done by asking for the group's gut reaction or by running through a formal exercise listing each segment and asking the group together to rate each segment on each criterion, calculating each segment's "score" and rank-ordering them.
	4. Agree on the segments requiring immediate attention—usually the most attractive segments and the problem segments, typically those with significant customer-perceived problems and eroding market share or intensifying competition.

III. Define Customer Needs, Strategic Thrust, Fixes, Means of Addressing

If there is more than one segment, each needs to be discussed using the following procedure. Divide the planning team into small groups of three to five members each, if the team is large enough, and assign each group a segment. The segments may then be parallel processed. The larger group will later review and gain consensus on the results of each team's analysis. If there are more teams than segments, you can have two teams work on the same segment and later consolidate their results.

[8 min.] Facilitator	**1. Configure the small groups.** Appoint a facilitator, and make sure that the group members have sufficient knowledge of the market and internal operations to analyze the segment. Establish the time allotment for the exercise, and specify that output will be presented on flipcharts. Suggest facilitation techniques for each step, and circulate among the groups during the exercise to keep them on track and to answer questions.
[3 hrs. per segment] Small-group facilitator	**2. Instruct small teams to follow this agenda and approximate timing:**
[30 min.]	a. Define and rank order needs of segment customers.
[20 min.]	b. Rate your company and your top target competitor on their performance in meeting the segment's top-ranked needs. c. Define and select the posture (grow, hold, milk, divest) best fitting the segment's current and potential products/services.
[10 min.]	d. Identify strategic thrusts and fixes.
[30 min.]	e. Identify and discuss any obvious strategic alternatives for the segment.
[30 min.]	f. Define what detailed actions must be taken to implement strategic thrusts.
[30 min.]	g. Define what detailed actions must be taken to implement strategic fixes.
[10 min.]	h. Identify what thrusts and fixes apply to all market segments and those that are particular to the one assigned.
[10 min.]	i. Identify information gaps—areas where further information is needed in order to make good strategic decisions for the segment.

j. Identify internal strategies and linkages needed to support external strategy.

[15 min.
per group]
Small-group
facilitator or
presenter

3. **Have presentations by small groups.** Each group presents its results to the entire planning team and allows brief discussion.

[15–30 min.]
Facilitator

4. **Achieve large-group consensus on each segment's strategies.**
   ▲ Sequentially, by segment, summarize what you think the conclusions should be, based on the presentations.
   ▲ Lead the entire planning team to consensus **segment by segment** on:
     —Definition of target customers and competitors
     —Market priorities and posture
     —Product/service priorities and posture
     —Strategic thrust and executional details
     —Internal strategic thrust and executional details
     —Strategic fixes and executional details
     —Strategic alternatives
     —If multiple groups discuss the same segment, point out any major differences among the groups' views. Then, following the sequence just given, present conclusions and facilitate the entire team to a consensus

[10 min.]
Facilitator

5. **Summarize and get consensus on strategic thrusts and fixes** that apply to all segments and will be considered for corporate strategies and programs.

[10 min.]
Facilitator

6. **Define further marketing work to be done** to understand customer needs and strategic thrust. This step is necessary if planners do not have adequate knowledge of customer needs and perceptions or competitive performance to select segments, thrusts, and fixes.

Section C
Strategy Statement

Objective:	Summarize and get agreement on the overall strategy statement.
Techniques:	Presentation, discussion
Time:	30–60 minutes

Procedure

1. **Based on the segment consensus achieved in the last section of the meeting, privately develop a succinct strategy statement for the entire business.**

   Summarize the strategy statement on a few flipcharts (see Chapter 7, Figure 7-7). Be sure to cover the following:
   ▲ Priorities and posture
     —Business unit
     —Market
     —Product
   ▲ Strategic thrusts
   ▲ Subsidiary external strategies
   ▲ Internal strategic thrust
   ▲ Subsidiary internal strategies
   ▲ Strategic fixes
   Note that this strategy statement assumes that you'll stay in the same business and won't pursue any radical alternatives such as sales of the business, divestiture, or significant reconfiguration. These strategic alternatives will be covered later.

Facilitator

2. **Present the strategy statement. Manage the group to consensus.**

Section D
Financial Analysis

Objectives:	Agree on the baseline forecast, i.e, the financial results expected in the future if no strategic or structural changes are made in the business.

Identify any critical financial issues that need to be addressed (e.g., cash flow, profitability, spending, equity funding).

Techniques: Presentation, discussion, consensus building

Time: 45 minutes

Procedure

[20 min.]
CFO

1. **Presentation.**
   - ▲ The presentation should be a crisp, bottom-line summary of circulated pre-work.
   - ▲ It should include:
     - —A financial history (usually the past three years' revenue, profitability, return on assets or investment, and any other key measures of the particular business)
     - —A three-year forecast
     - —Financial assumptions, such as projected interest rates and impact of expansions, reductions, and implementation of major programs
     - —The amount of cash beyond "running the existing configuration" available for investment in change
   - ▲ The presentation may also include analysis of financial contributions by product line, business unit, functional group, or cost center to pinpoint problems or opportunities.
   - ▲ It may also include benchmarking data (if prepared) comparing the company's financial performance to that of industry leaders and pinpointing areas for improvement if the company is underperforming.

[15 min.]
Facilitator

2. **Open discussion.**

[10 min.]
Facilitator

3. **Consensus building.**
   - ▲ Summarize forecasts, assumptions, and any critical financial issues to be addressed.
   - ▲ Ask for agreement. Facilitate the team to

a consensus around any major differences that surfaced during discussion.

Section E
Organization

Objective: Define organizational strengths and weaknesses. Identify the subsequent top 3 barriers to strategic progress and propose solutions to them.

Techniques: Presentation, discussion

Time: 40 minutes

Procedure

[15 min.]
Senior
executive,
human
resources

1. **Presentation.**
   ▲ The presentation should be a crisp, bottom-line summary of circulated prework
   ▲ It should include:
      —Organization barriers to strategic change
      —Leverage manager competence problems
      —Proposed solutions

[15 min.]
Facilitator

2. **Open discussion.**

[10 min.]
Facilitator

3. **Consensus building.**

Section F
Strengths, Weaknesses, Opportunities, Threats

Objective: Identify the top three strengths, weaknesses, opportunities, and threats to the organization.

Techniques: Round-robin activity, discussion, voting, optional small groups

Time: Approximately 2½ hours in total. Times vary by area, with weaknesses averaging 45 minutes and threats 30 minutes.

Procedure

Option 1: Small Teams

This procedure works best for a small planning team of four to six people. For teams of eight or more, use the procedure for a large team described under Option 2.

Although the following illustration describes the procedure for determining strengths, the process is *repeated sequentially four times*—once each for strengths, weaknesses, opportunities, and threats.

[5–10 min. per area] Facilitator

1. **Round-robin to collect individual prework ideas.**
   ▲ Go around the room to solicit ideas from participants (who should refer to their prework notes) one at a time, asking them not to repeat previously mentioned ideas. Stop when no additional ideas are forthcoming.
   ▲ Record and number inputs on flipcharts.
   ▲ Make it clear that some issues can appear on more than one list. For example, a threat can also be an opportunity; a company may have a strength in an area such as customer service but also have a weakness or deficiency in the same area. The important point is to get the key issues "on the board" somewhere so that they can be considered during selection of priority issues. It doesn't matter which list they appear on.
   This is the usual and preferred method. It results in long, rich lists of ideas to be discussed and consolidated. It has a number of advantages: Developing and discussing individuals' ideas in a group triggers additional ideas; misunderstandings are reduced as participants can illustrate and clarify their ideas with concise supporting comments; and the group has the opportunity to hear minority views, often from employees in functional areas, that may not make the final corporate list but are important in under-

standing key issues elsewhere in the company.

[10–40 min. per area]
Facilitator

2. **Invite consolidation/clarification/discussion.**
   ▲ Put all the flipchart pages on a wall. There will probably be a number of duplicate or near-duplicate entries. Consolidate duplicate points by asking the group which items are essentially the same or which can be combined under the same subject.
   ▲ Warn the group to resist overconsolidation. There is a temptation to lump lots of items under one heading so that nothing gets left out. This results in lack of focus. In general, keep items separate when their solution will require major resources, when the functions involved in resolution are different from those for related items, when an item's impact and resolution are so important that the item shouldn't be lumped with another item, and when consolidation would result in two "natural" programs sharing the same resources and leadership. For example, it might be tempting to relate all cost containment and cost reduction ideas under "cost." In reality, it would probably be better to leave manufacturing and sales, general, and administrative (SG&A) costs as separate items.
   ▲ Go down the consolidated list item by item, and briefly discuss or clarify any items that participants have questions about. It's helpful to reiterate the meaning of each item before discussing it. Stick to defining strengths, weaknesses, opportunities, and threats, and restrain the team from talking about solutions at this point in the process.

[5 min.]
Facilitator

3. **Vote for the top three strengths.**
   ▲ Sometimes the top three items are obvious and no vote is necessary. In that case, simply test for consensus. Otherwise:

▲ Give participants one to three minutes to pick their top issues individually.

▲ Allow each team member to cast three to five votes (three if the list of issues is ten items or fewer, five if it is long).

▲ Identify the three winning items. If there are ties or the first vote in inconclusive, discuss the highly rated items from the first vote and vote again.

[1 min.]
Facilitator

4. Summarize.
Once the top strengths are decided, neatly summarize them on a single flipchart to add to the summary section on the wall.

When the process is repeated four times, you will end up with four crisp charts, one each for strengths, weaknesses, opportunities, and threats.

Option 2: The Time Saver

Facilitator

1. Start with a predigested list.

▲ Ask team members to summarize their prework, combining items where appropriate, and to submit their individual top three SWOTs prior to the meeting.

▲ Summarize their inputs and bring the rank-ordered results to the meeting on flipcharts. These will provide you with a starting point from which to discuss each area.

[3 min.]
Facilitator

2. Presentation: Review the list.

[5–10 min.]
Facilitator

3. Round-robin.

▲ Solicit additional input. Ask the team for additional strengths, going around the room in a round-robin. Stop when few new ideas are forthcoming.

▲ List additional inputs on a flipchart. Ask the group if there are any further inputs before proceeding.

4. **Consolidate/vote/summarize,** following the process described earlier.
5. **Repeat the process for weaknesses, opportunities, and threats.**

Option 3: Small Groups for Large Teams

[30 min. per group per assignment] Small-group facilitators

1. **Initiate small-group activity to identify SWOTs;** time allotted varies depending on number of groups.
   ▲ Split larger planning teams into groups of four to six. Pick a facilitator for each small group.
   ▲ Assign one or more subjects to each small group. For example, if there are two groups, give one strengths and weaknesses, the other opportunities and threats. If there are four groups, give each one subject. Have each group use the round-robin process and record its conclusions on a flipchart.
   ▲ Ask each group, if there is time, to discuss and suggest what to *do* to resolve each issue. This is the right time to begin to discuss solutions, and the small-group setting is perfect for that.

[5 min. per subject] Small-group facilitator or presenter

2. **Have presentations of conclusions by small groups.** After each group presents its conclusions, allow a brief period for the entire planning team to ask questions for clarification or to discuss the conclusions and express agreement or disagreement.

[25 min.] Facilitator

3. **Build consensus,** area by area, ironing out any differences between the small group and the entire team.

Figure 9-4 shows SWOTs and the resulting strategic priority issues for a manufacturing company.

Figure 9-4. SWOTs and strategic priority issues for a manufacturing company.

Strengths
1. Customer service capabilities
2. Culture/work force
3. Service/quick turnaround
4. Market image/customer base
5. Diversified business

Weaknesses
1. Information systems
2. Manufacturing productivity/cost
3. Financial condition/undercapitalization
4. Profitability
5. Internal engineering
6. Responsibility/accounting for results
7. Inexperience/quality supervision staff/employees

Opportunities
1. Introduce new product "A"
2. Penetrate existing customers
3. Expand value added businesses
4. Improve manufacturing efficiencies/cost
5. Introduce new low-cost materials systems
6. Expand into new manufacturing technologies

Threats
1. Financial condition
2. Economic downturn/surge in interest rates
3. Decline in current cyclical markets
4. Concentration in a few large customers

Priority Issues
▼ Reduce costs and improve productivity
▼ Develop a total service capability package
▼ Provide investable funds
▼ Improve total engineering capability for customer engineering, product design, prototype production, and manufacturing engineering
▼ Increase penetration of existing markets "B" and "C"
▼ Develop cost, manufacturing, and financial reporting and control systems

Figure 9-5. Strategic alternatives for an electronic materials business.

> **1. Maintain**
> Maintain the business as is, not investing in new technology and cost reduction,
> eventually going out of business as become uncompetitive in 8 to 10 years.
>
> **2. Moderate Investment**
> Increase capacity through investment in process yield improvements; add no capital.
>
> **3. Internal Supplier**
> Cut sales to outside buyers; configure to supply parent company only.
>
> **4. Sell the Business**
>
> **5. Maintain and Reconfigure**
> Maintain existing business and add the next generation of production and materials
> technology through joint venture or licensing.

(Actual Example)

Section G
Strategic Alternatives

Objective:	Identify the three to five most probable strategic alternatives, their pluses and minuses given the company's strengths and weaknesses, probable financial and market outcomes, and the steps that must be taken to evaluate them and decide which to pursue.
Techniques:	Brainstorming, discussion, consensus
Time:	Varies from 10 minutes in option 2 to several hours in option 1.

Procedure

Option 1: Develop on the Spot

[15 min.] Facilitator	1. **Brainstorm all possible options.**
[20 min.] Facilitator	2. **Discuss,** add to the ideas, and consolidate to the three or four that are practical. Note that

this is where a facilitator's conceptual skill, practical business experience, and content skills shine and are most useful. Propose options or combinations of options, however unpopular or far out, that the group has not seen. Bring reality to the discussion by noting which options other companies have used successfully and unsuccessfully in similar circumstances. Businesspeople latch onto real companies and real examples better than onto abstract ideas.

[10 min.] Team members alone	3. **Ask team members to write down privately the pluses and minuses of each option,** along with the probable financial outcome and its risk.
[15 min. per option] Facilitator	4. **For each option, sequentially elicit its pluses, minuses, and probable financial outcome.** Do this rapidly with little discussion.
[20 min.] Facilitator	5. **During a break, consolidate and summarize the top three** pluses and minuses, probable outcomes, and risks of each option, and record each on a separate flipchart.
[30 min.] Facilitator	6. **Present the summary to the team.** Facilitate to a consensus on each option in turn.
[5 min.] Facilitator	7. **Suggest what needs to be done to evaluate the options further,** and ask the CEO to assign the work to an individual or to a team. The work typically involves both market and financial analysis and, often, includes assessing the technical feasibility of options involving unusual manufacturing or systems technology.

Figure 9-5 illustrates the strategic alternatives for an electronic materials business.

Option 2: Summarize Prework

[10 min.] CEO	1. **If the strategic alternatives were agreed on during prework, briefly present the conclusions on prepared flipcharts and for information only.**

Section H
Strategic Priority Issues

Objective:

Pick the three to five strategic priority issues that must be addressed by the planning team. Most priority issues result in programs and the allocation of resources to address them.

Techniques: Round-robin, discussion, voting

Time: 30 minutes

Procedure

Facilitator

1. **Review:** Put the summary charts for SWOTs, the strategy statement, and strategic alternatives up on the front wall.

[5 min.]
Facilitator

2. **Provide briefing.**
   ▲ Keep this step brief because the priorities are usually obvious at this point.
   ▲ Remind the team that priority issues usually come from strengths to be bolstered, weaknesses to be corrected, opportunities to be capitalized on, and threats to be avoided. They may also result from your strategic thrusts, strategic fixes, internal strategies, strategic alternatives, or market and product priorities if the issues raised by them were not included in the SWOTs.
   ▲ Convey that priority issues generally meet one or more of the following criteria:
     —Have long-term and major positive financial impact
     —Address a fleeting window of opportunity, for example, a developing new market, a temporarily weakened competitor, available acquisitions
     —Are critical to fix the ship, stop the bleeding, or correct any key structural weaknesses

[10 min.]
Facilitator

3. **Round-robin to compile issues.**
   ▲ Ask participants to select privately their top three issues from the list of SWOTs

and their pre-work. Give them sufficient time to scan the list and write down their top three. Remind them also to look back at the three they selected in their individual prework.

▲ Go around the room, asking each person to name his or her highest priority issue (from the top three) without repeating issues already mentioned. Keep soliciting issues until no more are forthcoming.

[10 min.]
Facilitator

4. **Elicit discussion/consolidation of issues.**
▲ Ensure that each issue is clear. Discuss the reason for proposing it, the positive impact of addressing it, and the negative impact of not addressing it.

▲ Priority issues are generally broad at this stage of planning. Typical examples are "cost," "profitability," "service levels and systems," and "organization effectiveness." Issues such as these are addressed by one or more programs that deal with specific subissues. For example, under the priority issue "organization," one company detailed programs in succession planning, critical management skills, and performance management systems.

▲ Be wary of issues that are too narrow. An item as narrow as "manufacturing reject rate and cost" is of minor strategic importance. The bigger issues might be overall manufacturing cost structure and manufacturing/sourcing configuration.

▲ Specific priority issues often stay on a company's list for a number of years until ongoing performance in the area is excellent. The specific programs addressing each issue, however, frequently change and become more sophisticated as progress is made.

5. **Ask the team to suggest any obvious omissions.** In addition, invoke the "rule of expertise." Sometimes a consensus is naïve, making sense to a team of generalists but not to a knowledgeable expert, who must raise

any omitted or overlooked issues at this point. For example, a team of retailers arrived at a list of five priority issues that did not address a problem obvious to their experienced facilitator: an uncompetitive cost structure throughout the organization, from purchasing through retail stores. Pointed out, this problem became their number one priority for a number of years.

[5 min.]
Facilitator

6. **Vote.**
   ▲ Ask team members to cast three votes as you sequentially go down the list of remaining priority-issue candidates. Identify the three to five issues that earn the most votes.
   ▲ Record *why* the team felt each issue deserved high priority.

Figure 9-6 shows priority issues for a variety of companies at the corporate and functional department levels.

Section I
Programs

Objectives:

For each priority issue:
▲ Sketch out one or more programs with measurable one- and three-year objectives and key action steps.
▲ Assign accountabilities for fleshing out program details before the next planning meeting (and, ultimately, for implementation).
It is important that *direction* be set for programs to guide the teams that have to flesh out the details.

Techniques: Small teams, discussion, consensus
Time: 1 hour, 10 minutes per priority issue per team

Procedure

Option 1: Small Planning Teams (Four to Six Members)

Note. By this point in the process planning-team members should be fully capable of facilitating parts of the meeting. Rotate the facilitation

Figure 9-6. Priority issues at the corporate and functional department levels.

CORPORATE/BUSINESS UNIT ISSUES
Common to Many Industries

▼ Need for mission/vision/strategic focus

▼ Organization: structure, skills, competence, motivation, succession

▼ Cost structure

▼ Product/technology innovation and development

▼ Top-team functioning

▼ Accountability/control

▼ Priorities on business units

▼ Marketing/selling methods

▼ Market penetration

▼ Profitability, capitalization

▼ New competition

INDUSTRY SPECIFIC
Corporate/Business Unit Issues

Retail Consumer Products

▼ Customer service

▼ Expansion

▼ Future store configuration

▼ Shrinkage/theft

Not-for-profit

▼ Funding sources

▼ Market-product-service definition

▼ Financial control and reporting

▼ Use of volunteer board

Manufacturing/Technology

▼ Process technology

▼ New product development system

▼ R&D innovation

▼ Cost/efficiency

Financial/Professional Services

▼ MIS systems

▼ Marketing/selling

▼ Service/product development

(continues)

Figure 9-6. (*continued*).

FUNCTIONAL DEPARTMENT PRIORITY ISSUES   *Actual Examples*

Human Resources
- ▼ Training
- ▼ Compensation systems
- ▼ Accountability systems
- ▼ Staffing levels
- ▼ Labor relations

Finance
- ▼ Cash flow
- ▼ Asset return/utilization
- ▼ Overhead cost
- ▼ Reporting/control/timelines
- ▼ Financial structure/capital
- ▼ Receivables management

Sales
- ▼ Penetration
- ▼ New customers
- ▼ Order entry/service
- ▼ Training/skills
- ▼ Sales-force efficiency
- ▼ Selling configuration

R&D
- ▼ New products
- ▼ Technical core competencies
- ▼ Technical career ladder

Operations
- ▼ Cost
- ▼ Quality
- ▼ Waste
- ▼ Maintenance
- ▼ Cost systems
- ▼ Standards, SOPs
- ▼ Capacity
- ▼ Raw materials supply

MIS
- ▼ Processing capacity
- ▼ New computer systems
- ▼ Response to internal customers
- ▼ Financial reporting
- ▼ Market reporting

Marketing
- ▼ New products
- ▼ Distribution systems
- ▼ Emerging segments
- ▼ Market penetration
- ▼ Pricing
- ▼ Customer satisfaction
- ▼ Marketing profit

---

of sections as noted and where there are capable facilitators. This gives team members needed experience, gains their commitment, and begins the process of disengaging the professional facilitator.

Facilitator	**1. Provide summary/direction.**
	▲ Put on the front wall and review the summary charts of priority issues, strategic thrusts, and ideas for programs to address priority issues made earlier in the session.
	▲ Remind the team members that they also recorded their personal program ideas in their individual prework.
	▲ Instruct them that they:
	—*Must* define programs to address the priority issues and development of competitive advantages in the strategic thrust areas.
	—Should avoid the tendency to select too many programs; three to five priority issues and five to ten programs are the most that can reasonably be executed and accorded senior-level monitoring. This doesn't mean that more programs aren't necessary to make the business succeed. Important programs that don't make the top-priority list are delegated to functions, SBUs, or individuals for incorporation into those units' or employees' own strategic and operating plans and budgets and accomplished as part of their ongoing jobs.
Facilitator or appointed facilitator	**2. Sketch out the programs.**
	▲ Assign a facilitator from the planning team to handle each program area separately. For *each* program area, the appointed facilitator should:
[5 min.]	—Frame the issue, describing it in a couple of sentences using inputs from the group. For example, if "uncompetitive costs" are the issue, they might be described as "total cost delivered to the customer is 15–25 percent higher than competition; key problem areas in man-

ufacturing efficiency, purchasing of raw materials, and administrative overhead."

[15 min.]

—Rough out one- and three-year objectives. Make the objectives as measurable as possible. Often, however, first-pass measures are subjective and directional (e.g., "improve quality significantly," "improve customer service"). Hard measures are added later when more data are available.

—Recognize when special approaches to objectives setting are needed. For example, it's sometimes difficult to come up with hard measures on some dimensions in the area of organization. Companies therefore sometimes use "word pictures" of people's vision of the organization in five to ten years. One company described its objectives for its future culture as "empower lower levels; reduce the number of layers; more teamwork; focus on key issues; less conservative management—be proactive; faster decision making; accountability at all levels; organization aligned with plan; better involvement and communication throughout." At other times, directional objectives may be undefined (e.g., "significant improvements in quality as measured by customer perception," even though it will take time to research what factors the customer measures and to develop means of measuring their perceptions objectively).

[15 min.]
Facilitator

▲ List subissues or underlying problems.
▲ Solicit as many as possible from the group in an open forum.
▲ For example, if manufacturing costs are a priority issue, subissues contributing to the problem may include overhead, staffing levels, waste, union work rules,

labor efficiencies, lack of standards, training, and supervisory competence.

[10 min.]
Facilitator

▲ Boil down the subissues to the few (80/20 rule*) that drive the area and require action. Ask for a consensus:

[12 min.]
Facilitator

—Develop a list of potential solutions to the key issue areas.
—Brainstorm actions that might be taken.
—Give the list to the program leader to sort out later.
—Examples: The company that created the word picture of its future culture developed a number of programs aimed at reaching its desired state. These included formal team building, lower-level involvement in planning, new accountability and reward systems, zero-base restructuring of the organization after strategy was agreed on, and modeling of desired behaviors at the top.

[5 min.]
Team
facilitator

▲ Set key "what, when, who's."
—List the two to four key steps that the program leader or team is expected to accomplish in the next year.
—Determine tentative timing.
—Identify any groups and/or individuals with whom the program leader must coordinate to ensure that the program can be accomplished.

Facilitator

▲ Summarize these key points on two or three flipcharts.

[2 min.]
CEO

3. **Assignments/clarification.**
▲ After all the programs are completed, select a team leader and members for each program.
▲ Clarify assignments. Each program leader must meet with the program team to prepare and circulate a formal action plan prior to the next planning meeting. The action plan should conform to the stan-

---

*That means that 20 percent of all causes account for 80 percent of the problem.

dard format in the planning manual. To develop the plan, the program team should get input from knowledgeable and potentially involved people throughout the organization. Doing so helps ensure that programs are well designed to produce the desired results and that time requirements and resource estimates are reasonable.

Option 2: Large Planning Teams

1. **Break the team into small work groups** of three to five members.
2. **Appoint a facilitator** for each group.
3. **Assign each group one or more priority issues** to work on. Make sure that the functions and individuals represented in the groups are suitable for the assignment. Each group should include the likely program leader and representatives of functional areas that will participate heavily in implementation.
4. **Have each work group use the procedure** outlined under "Small Planning Teams" for *each* issue assigned. The issues should be processed one at a time to completion.
5. **After all groups have processed one issue, convene the entire planning team** and ask the facilitator of each group to lead a three to five minute presentation of results and discussion, isolating and resolving any differences. Repeat this sequence of work teams/group presentations until all of the issues/thrusts have been presented.
6. **Assign more than one team or all of the teams to work on the same issue when the issue is of overriding importance to the company,** affects many functions, is highly complicated, or has high emotional content. A typical example is organization—e.g., skills, structure, competence of groups/individuals, reward system, and accountabilities.
7. **When multiple groups work on a single issue, have one group present** its results without comment from the rest of the team. The

facilitator of that group then takes additional inputs from the remaining groups, integrates them, *and gets a consensus on the consolidated work.*

Section J
Key Result Areas

Objective:

Define the key result areas (KRAs) and measures that the organization will use to establish objectives and to measure strategic and financial success. Objectives will be determined during the next phase of planning.

Definitions:

A key result area is an area of business activity in which the business must excel to meet customer needs, beat competition, and meet stake/shareholder expectations. Organizations must gain consensus on:

1. **Their key result areas,** for example, financial performance, customer service, organization health.
2. **How they will measure success in each KRA.** For example, success measures in the customer service KRA might be performance on a customer satisfaction index based on customer surveys, the number of complaints, and returns per million cases shipped.
3. **Specific long-term objectives,** for example, a composite customer satisfaction index of 98 (nearly perfect) with a five-point margin over the nearest competitor.

KRAs are generally derived from several sources: (1) common financial measures driven by stakeholder demands and industry standards; (2) the strategic thrust and key internal strategies; (3) critical success factors; (4) key elements of the mission, vision, and value statements (such as quality, service, profitable growth, organization/culture) and new products/services/innovations (assuming that work has started on the mission statement—if not, KRAs may be modified to include these elements during the subsequent strategic planning meeting); (5) measures of performance in priority-issue areas.

Most organizations have four to six KRAs. Each KRA usually has only one or two strategic objectives.

It's important to limit KRA measures and objectives to the critical few in order to focus on the really important areas and to avoid the tendency of most organizations to micromanage many detailed objectives that are best delegated.

Background: Key result areas are a difficult concept to grasp. They are therefore best introduced during the priority-setting meeting by the facilitator, using Method 1, described in this section. Method 2, requiring prework by the CEO or CFO, is occasionally useful, particularly when the organization is experienced in planning and the facilitator and CEO have time to work on KRAs and measures in advance of the priority-setting meeting.

Techniques: Presentation, discussion, consensus

Time: 55 minutes

Procedures

Option 1: Team New to Strategic Accountability

This method is generally recommended for organizations in which team members have not been accountable, will struggle with being held accountable, and need to work through the logic behind KRAs and measures.

Facilitator

1. **Reiterate what KRAs are** and how they will be used in setting objectives.
   Solicit KRA ideas and associated measures from the group, allowing comments only to seek clarification. Use the solicitation as both a teaching tool and a method for developing ideas. List ideas, stopping when no new ones are offered.

[40 min.]
Facilitator

2. **Consolidate.** Combine similar ideas for both KRAs and measures.

[10 min.]
Facilitator

3. **Open up discussion of potential KRAs and measures of strategic success.**
   ▲ How well do the measures evaluate the extent to which the company is fulfilling its vision and meeting the needs of the outside world, including customers?
   ▲ How do team members feel they should be held accountable by management?
   ▲ To what extent are the data available to measure strategic success? Recognize that measurement data may not be quickly and readily available. Some companies have established the need to measure customer service, for example, but realize that it may take several years to create the systems to do it.
   ▲ Be sure that lead measures of strategic success (e.g., share of market, service, quality, innovation, organization competence) are strongly addressed and separated from traditional financial measures (e.g., return on investment, revenue growth, asset turns, cash flow) that result from successes in the strategic areas.

[5 min.]
CEO

4. **Select KRAs.**
   ▲ Propose appropriate KRAs and measures to the team, and test for consensus.
   ▲ Help the team resist the temptation to throw in lots of KRAs and measures. Many teams try to include all the measures that they can think of—most of which are appropriate for evaluating operations or lower-level functions and jobs but not the strategic plan.
   ▲ Note that there may be some—probably slight—additions or changes after the next planning meeting, during which the team will formulate the mission of the organization.
   ▲ Assign development of objectives to the CEO and CFO in preparation for the next meeting.

Option 2: Team Used to Strategic Accountability

This method is appropriate when the organization is used to being objectively measured and the concept of key result areas has been previously taught.

[10 min.] CEO or CFO	1. **Present tentative key result areas and measures** based on prework. As usual during presentations, allow questions for clarification only.
[15 min.] CEO	2. **Solicit additions** and brief reasons for them from the entire team. 3. **Open discussion** (as for Method 1). 4. **Select KRAs** (as for Method 1).

Figure 9-7 presents KRAs for a variety of companies at both the corporate and the departmental levels. Figure 9-8 shows the KRAs, measures, and first-year objectives set by Burlington (Vermont) Electric, a public utility.

Section K
Hanging Issues

Objective:	Ensure that any major hanging issues are resolved, assigned to individuals for resolution, or carried over to the next meeting.
Technique:	Discussion
Time:	10 minutes

Procedure

Facilitator	1. **Review the hanging-issues list,** and discuss those that haven't been dealt with. You will find that most important hanging issues have already been dealt with or no longer seem important in light of the meeting's conclusions. 2. **Assign action steps** if necessary, but resist assigning too many tasks to team members. First-time planners have a tendency to try to

Figure 9-7. Typical key result areas at the corporate and some functional levels.

Examples

CORPORATE
- ▼ Strategic plan/strategy
- ▼ Innovation
- ▼ Financial performance/numbers
- ▼ Organization/cultural health
- ▼ Financial health
- ▼ Corporate image
- ▼ Strategic market position
- ▼ Service
- ▼ Quality

MARKETING/SALES
- ▼ Sales
- ▼ Long-term marketing strategy
- ▼ Long-term marketing performance
- ▼ Market penetration
- ▼ New products
- ▼ Sales MIS
- ▼ Pricing
- ▼ Contribution margin
- ▼ Distribution
- ▼ Customer satisfaction
- ▼ New-product launches

FINANCE
- ▼ Cost of capital
- ▼ Receivables level
- ▼ Reporting — timeliness/quality
- ▼ Capital availability
- ▼ Bad-debt level invested
- ▼ Debt-equity ratio

MANUFACTURING
- ▼ Unit volume
- ▼ Service level
- ▼ Raw material supply
- ▼ Cost
- ▼ Efficiency
- ▼ Safety
- ▼ Quality
- ▼ Capacity

HUMAN RESOURCES
- ▼ Management proficiency/training
- ▼ Attitude/morale
- ▼ Labor relations
- ▼ Adequacy of staffing
- ▼ Compensation/wages
- ▼ Succession planning
- ▼ Training
- ▼ Recruitment
- ▼ Safety
- ▼ Compliance

Figure 9-8. Key result areas, measures, and objectives for a public utility.

KRA	MEASURES	OBJECTIVES
Cost	Cost per KWH (total revenue requirement divided by total retail kilowatt hour sales)	In years 1 and 2 there will be no increase in rates beyond the January 1986 rate filing. In year 3, rates will increase no more than an average of 7% due primarily to an increase in generation from small power producers.
	Rates vs. Green Mountain Power (GMP)	To be lower than GMP
Reliability	Reportable customer hours out of service divided by total possible customer hours of service	99.9% reliability or better
Safety	Average days charged (severity rate divided by frequency rate)	Exceed National Safety Council standards
Customer Satisfaction	To be determined upon completion of the benchmark survey	A benchmark survey will be performed to determine what is important to our customers, how we rate now, and how we could improve. Measures and objectives will be completed by December 1987.
Financial Health	Meet revenue and debt-service requirements in each year.	1988 — $8.9 million 1989 — $9.4 million 1990 — $9.9 million
Employee Morale	To be determined upon completion of attitude survey	By spring 1988 a benchmark survey will be done to establish attitude and morale measures.
Supply of Electricity	Ability to supply: Capacity (MW) and Energy (MWH)	1988 —79.1 MW 353,000 MWH 1989 —80.4 MW 358,000 MWH 1990 —81.5 MW 365,000 MWH

Actual Examples

fix everything. Organizations are better off trying to evoke change a few pieces at a time, particularly if they are doing it with the same resources they had before planning.

Section L
Meeting Summary

Objectives: Summarize the entire meeting to reinforce conclusions, make sure that your perceptions of conclusions are accurate, and reconfirm assignments.

Wrap up the meeting, give the group a strong sense of accomplishment, and motivate them to continue the process with a high level of energy and ownership.

Techniques: Flipchart preparation, presentation
Time: 5 minutes

Procedure

Facilitator   1. **This is one of the most important parts of the meeting, so prepare in advance by summarizing all of the conclusions (usually about ten) on flipcharts.** You may use the summary flipcharts already produced or new, cleaned-up ones. Prepare the summary the evening before the final day and during breaks so that only last-minute additions need to be made. This summary will be used to produce the written meeting summary and list of action steps. It should contain the following sections:
   ▲ Summaries of sections: summary charts with conclusions from each section of the meeting (environmental analysis, marketing analysis, strategy, SWOTs, priority issues, etc.)
   ▲ Summary of programs to be fleshed out after the meeting with assignments
   ▲ Summary of other action steps: who is to do what and when

2. Presentation.
▲ Present the summary concisely. You do not need to hit all points.
▲ Do not allow discussion or the reopening of issues.
▲ Clarify any inaccuracies in the summary, and make sure that assignments are clear.
▲ Remind the group of all of the prework assignments for the next meeting, the due and circulation dates, and the date and place of the next meeting.
▲ Close by complimenting the group members on their progress, noting honestly how far they've moved in their thinking and team development since planning started. Also note tasks that still need to be done on the plan and on team developments. Leave the team on a high note, motivated to complete the job well and get on with implementation.

Section M
Process the Meeting

Objective:	Get participants' perceptions of the meeting's accomplishments.
Techniques:	Round-robin, questionnaire
Time:	1–2 minutes per participant at the meeting, 15 minutes after the meeting

Procedure

Facilitator

1. In a round-robin, leaving the CEO until last, ask each person to address:
▲ What the meeting accomplished
▲ What it should have accomplished but didn't
▲ How the meeting could have been improved
2. Immediately following the meeting, send a brief questionnaire to all participants to get

direct and confidential feedback on the quality of the meeting itself, what they personally thought it achieved or didn't, its potential impact, the quality of prework processes and materials, facilitation quality, and potential improvements.

Section N
Postmeeting Work

Procedure

Facilitator

1. **Immediately after the meeting, read over the meeting summary.** Make sure that it is clear and captures all of the key points and conclusions from the meeting. Make pencil notes on the summary and on important detailed charts produced by the meeting. Your recall will be best right after the meeting, and this is your only record of the many working hours spent.

2. **Clean up the summaries** of each segment of the meeting and any other material that needs to be captured. Be particularly careful to reproduce the results of work teams and program discussion teams, because they capture participants' interest and will be used by participants to flesh out their own postmeeting assignments.

3. **Circulate,** within a couple of days of the meeting, a summary in this order:
   ▲ Action steps and assignments resulting from the meeting
   ▲ The meeting summary
   ▲ Appendices (keep them to a minimum, capturing only the important records, such as summaries of each meeting segment and details from work groups)

DO'S AND DON'TS

DO

- *Custom-structure each meeting*, picking the agenda and the techniques from the menu in this chapter. Create a mental picture of the way the meeting will unfold as you create the agenda.
- *Be incredibly prepared*. Review all prework thoroughly, have all agendas and presentation charts prepared, and make sure that participants do likewise. Ensure that the meeting setup is sent to the facility in writing and adhered to. Terrorize the facility manager so that the ambiance is perfect.
- *Make sure participants understand* when and how they are to participate and the format and media to be used for their personal presentations.
- *Keep the pressure on* to move through the agenda smartly. Quickly curtail divergences from the agenda and topic. Demonstrate what a quality meeting is really like.
- *Be flexible* and ready to dance a different dance to a different tune on the spot. Some techniques won't work, and others will have to be substituted. You'll have to deal with a new topic or slant that you didn't anticipate. You'll think of a better way. The order of the meeting may have to be changed to go with the natural flow.
- *Get into group work fast*. It produces involvement, communication, interplay, commitment, and results.
- *Liven up the meeting*. Applaud after presentations. Tell jokes. Keep a chart of funny sayings from participants. Insert your personal humor. Stick appropriate pins in people's balloons. Some of the techniques sound hokey, but they work to lighten, personalize, and motivate serious grind-it-out work.
- *Review results* and what's to be covered next at the end of each agenda topic.
- *Summarize and clarify* issues frequently throughout the meeting.
- *Model, demonstrate*, and let the participants know what facilitation techniques you are using and why.
- *Carefully configure groups* with the right mix of personalities, functional areas, and natural facilitators.
- *Draw out everyone*, particularly quiet people who have an opinion but won't voice it.
- *Confront issues* positively, and make the group resolve them.

DON'T

- *Allow too much discussion*. Move on when the main points are out, discussion is getting peripheral, or people are bringing in other or personal agendas or are talking just to hear themselves talk.
- *Let the meeting burn out* on early topics, leaving insufficient time and energy for the remainder of the meeting.
- *Allow political infighting* or let personal agendas intervene.
- *Be negative*, hypercritical, or annoyed, even if you think that the group is not doing a good job. Remember, your job is to get the absolute best that is possible from this group, not to achieve nirvanalike perfection. The definition of *best*, of course, varies from group to group and from business situation to business situation.

Chapter 10

Strategy Meeting Prework

The best way to predict the future is to invent it.
> —Alan Kay, director of research, Apple Computer Company

The very essence of leadership is [that] you have to have a vision. It's got to be a vision you articulate clearly and forcefully on every occasion. You can't blow an uncertain trumpet.
> —Theodore Hesburgh, former president,
> University of Notre Dame

Most of the tough thinking and analysis needed to accomplish Prework II (Figure 10-1), the preparatory work for the strategy meeting, has been done. This step requires expanding on the direction the top team has already agreed to, looking at ways to pursue that direction, and putting all these ideas into writing so that they can be communicated, debated, and ultimately chiseled in stone—well, maybe putty!

Prework II should yield the following outputs:

▲ Drafts of a mission statement and a statement of long-term strategic and financial objectives
▲ Details for programs identified during the priority-setting meeting
▲ Drafted statement of strategic alternatives and related competitive strategies
▲ Identified internal strategies, specific to individual functions, that are critical to the success of corporate strategy

The Mission Statement

Minimum Assignment

The CEO drafts and circulates a mission statement to all planning team members for them to critique. (The statement will be finalized at the

Figure 10-1. Prework II.

A. Individual	B. Assigned/Circulated
▼ Programs to address priority issues	▼ Draft mission/statement ▼ Draft objectives ▼ Final strategy statement ▼ Resource balance

final strategy meeting.) The statement should include the overall vision, business definition, and external and internal values, all derived from what's emerged from the process to date.

Many CEOs consult key planning-team members and other thoughtful and influential people in the organization as they put the draft statement together. It's also helpful to refer to the mission statements of other companies for ideas on format and content.

Expanded Assignment

Instead of depending on informal input, the CEO may choose a more structured way of involving the planning team before actually writing the draft. This expanded process starts with a team "storyboarding" session to choose and define the key words to go into the statement. The CEO drafts the statement on the basis of the output of this session, then delivers it to the team for finalizing at the strategy meeting. (Storyboarding is explained in detail in Chapter 17.)

To run a storyboarding session on the mission statement, the facilitator begins by listing the concepts to be addressed and the questions to be answered for each concept. Typical concepts and questions are:

▲ *Numbers.* How big should the company be? How profitable? By when?

▲ *Five words.* What five words will best describe the company overall five to ten years from now?

▲ *Business definition.* In one column list your current market segments, target customers, products and services, geography, channels of distribution, and critical technology(ies). In a parallel column list what you think they should be in the future.

▲ *Strategic thrusts.* In which areas of customer need will you be superior to your competitors?

▲ *Internal values.* What do you want your people to say about the company?

▲ *External values.* What do you want the community to say about the company?

▲ *Financial values.* What do you want the financial community to say about the company?
▲ *Shareholder values.* What do you want your shareholders to say about the company?
▲ *Vendor/supplier relationships.* What do you want your vendors to say about the company?

Using the structured storyboarding process, the team members progress from responding to these questions to agreeing on the key words for the mission statement. Using this input, the CEO drafts the mission statement prior to the strategy meeting.

This technique can be used in a variety of ways. First, the exercise can be run much earlier in the planning cycle. It is a stimulating technique that requires no preparation and works whenever time is available or the planning process needs to be energized. A "missionizing" or "visioning" session can be made part of any retreat when the timing seems right.

It's also helpful to use the technique to get input from lower-level employees in the organization. Lower-level groups can address only those areas that are within their experience and job scope, such as selection of vendors or employee values, and feed their results to the top team. Your company will benefit from their ideas, participation, and buy-in. Examples of mission statements are contained in the Appendix.

Strategy Statement and Strategic and Financial Objectives

The CEO circulates the final version of the strategy statement that was agreed on during the priority-setting meeting and drafts the objectives that the top team will review and finalize at the strategy meeting. Assisted by the CFO, the CEO sets measurable objectives for each key result area designated at the priority-setting meeting.

The draft statement needs to encompass both financial and strategic objectives. *Financial* objectives define the revenue, cost, and profit performance you want to result from the actions you will take. *Strategic* objectives define qualitative and quantitative outcomes in areas such as product innovation, customer satisfaction, service, market share, and organization succession. These are the outcomes that underlie, precede, and predict the future financial results you want.

Pay particular attention to first-year objectives, which will become your next year's budget, and to your objectives for year three or the final year of your plan. The latter are the stars by which you'll set your course and steer (although you should expect deviations from the direct route as you proceed).

Objectives need to be doable within the resources of the organization and the realities of the marketplace. Unrealistic objectives frustrate and alienate the organization, which finds itself underperforming through no fault of its own. It's a good idea to point out in the draft where objectives fall short of or exceed industry norms and where you anticipate the greatest difficulty in achieving the objectives and why.

The CEO should draft just a handful of corporate objectives and circulate these to the planning team. Ultimately the team will break these down and delegate pieces to lower-level businesses and functions, which will in turn translate them into subobjectives and actions. There may also be some important key result areas that are normally the domain of lower levels, e.g., facility safety, but where performance is unacceptable and objectives and programs to meet them are initially set and monitored by the top team level. Once continuing satisfactory results are achieved, these objectives are delegated intact to a lower-level function and monitored under its strategic plan.

Recognize that this is just the beginning of the objective-setting process. For some KRAs, it may take considerable time to obtain the information necessary to complete objectives and develop mechanisms for measuring performance. Setting objectives for customer satisfaction, the United States Tobacco Company (USTC) surveyed wholesale and retail customers to determine their definitions of service and quality and measured the company's baseline performance on those attributes. Only then could it establish objectives and set up a process to measure its performance against customer expectations. Establishing measures and getting data took USTC two years.

Resource Balance

The CFO prepares the following information covering the upcoming three to five years:

▲ *Discretionary cash flow available*—cash throw-off from operations, after taxes and interest and loan payments, that will result from the existing businesses. This money, combined with funds available from loans, capital markets, and lines of credit, can be used for funding capital spending and strategic programs and for financing growth in the baseline business.

▲ *Incremental spending to maintain the business*—expense items and program spending that have been requested to maintain and expand the existing base business. Examples include staff increases, raises, and product improvement expenses.

▲ *Capital* needed to keep the baseline business healthy.

▲ *Key infrastructure capital and expense requests*—items such as MIS, building maintenance, training and development, and electronic systems needed to keep the baseline business healthy.

▲ *Incremental strategic program requests* for capital, expense money, and people, the latter in conjunction with the vice president of human resources.

Program Development

At the priority-setting meeting, the planning team identified potential programs to address the priority issues facing the company and designated a program leader for each. Now each program leader adds flesh to the output from that meeting and puts together a preliminary program to address the issue for which he or she is responsible; this program will be finalized at the strategy meeting.

Each program should include:

▲ Measurable one-year and long-term objectives
▲ Three to five key action step—including who, what, and when—that must be accomplished in the next year
▲ Coordination requirements—functional and financial assistance needed from areas outside the program leader's control
▲ An impact statement assessing the program's projected financial and strategic gain, capital and expense costs, payback and rate of return, and people requirements—number and skills required and where the people will come from

Programs should be recorded in a standard format similar to the one shown in Figure 10-2.

Hints for Good Programs

▲ Don't go into infinite detail in program action plans. Include only a few benchmark steps for the top team to monitor. Detailed plans will come later, developed by those who must implement them.
▲ Don't waste time on detailed financial estimates. Ballpark figures will do. Leave the number crunching for budgeting time.
▲ Pay a lot of attention to coordination requirements. Many action

Figure 10-2. Program action plan formats.

PROGRAM ACTION PLAN

Program # _____ Program Manager _____

Program Name _____

Priority Issue _____

Objective: 1-year _____

_____

3-year _____

_____

	What	**Who**	**When**
Step			

IMPACT ESTIMATE

Record incremental impact only — resources beyond those currently available to the program.

	YR 1	**YR 2**	**YR 3**
Revenue			
Sales:			
Gain			
Profit:			
Cost savings:			
Total:			
Cost			
Expense:			
Capital addition:			
Working capital changes:			
Net results			
Net cash flow:			
Net present value:			
Profitability index:			
People			
# of people:			
Time required:			
Special skills:			

COORDINATION REQUIREMENTS

Group/Division/Person	*What's Required*	*When*

plans fail because a critical function or department didn't sign off on the program and didn't have resources available when required. One company's direct marketing program stalled because of the program leader's failure to get commitment from MIS.

▲ Recognize that it takes time to bring new people on board and up to speed and that using existing people for new programs diverts them from their ongoing jobs. Inadequate people planning can foul up both your existing business and your strategic change plans.

▲ Involve the organization. Get input from a multilevel team of knowledgeable and potentially involved people how much time the program will take, what resources you'll need, and the best ways to implement steps and reach objectives.

Strategic Alternatives

Executional details for each strategic alternative identified during the priority-setting meeting need to be developed sufficiently to allow evaluation of risk and financial return.

Financial, marketing, and technical staff teams from the electronic materials company cited in Figure 9-5, for example, spent about twenty-five worker-days of managerial time and sixty worker-days of analytical support time evaluating the technical feasibility, cost, profitability, and competitive risks of many equipment, process, joint venture, and licensing approaches to their five alternatives. They, by the way, selected a middle-of-the-road option that required relatively safe incremental investment, yielded modest gains, and left the door open for riskier, higher-payback alternatives at a later date—if the currently active competition doesn't coopt their future markets first.

Facilitation Tips

Strategic meeting prework requires very little input from facilitators. The planning team is usually well grounded in planning principles, is committed to the process, and has clear direction and a good manual to follow.

Facilitators do need to be available to answer questions, serve as sounding boards, or facilitate lower-level meetings; they should also touch base periodically with those carrying out assignments to make sure they are on track.

DO'S AND DON'TS

DO

- *Stick close to the CEO and the CFO.* They are often the ones with the least time and the most thought-provoking assignments—mission statement and objectives.
- *Support the functional heads.* Make sure they understand the role of their functions in implementing corporate strategy.
- *Train lower-level teams and individuals* in what the company's planning principles are and how to set objectives, write action plans, operate as a team, and facilitate meetings.

DON'T

- *Confuse issues* by adding assignments or involving people in additional data collection or analysis. Now is the time for employees to assimilate what they've done and narrow its focus.

Chapter 11

Facilitator's Guide II: Strategy Meeting—Guiding the Team to Consensus on Each Part of the Plan

Tell me and I'll forget; show me and I may remember; involve me and I'll understand.

—Chinese proverb

People don't resist their own ideas.

—William Werther, professor, University of Miami

This chapter, like Chapter 9, is addressed to the facilitator. It presents a step-by-step process, summarized in Figure 11-1, that includes techniques and tips for conducting the strategic planning meeting, which is responsible for creating the final plan document. It also offers examples you can use as models to guide the work of the planning team.

By this point in the planning process, the corporate direction and priorities will be apparent. The planning team should have jelled and become skilled and relatively efficient in process techniques, and it should now be ready to complete the plan. The strategy meeting serves, therefore, to summarize the plan, get buy-in, and decide how to get the plan implemented.

Objectives: The final outcome of the meeting is a planning document that is ready to be implemented. To achieve that end, the team will need to:
▲ Finalize the company's mission and strategic thrusts.

Figure 11-1. Strategic planning meeting: typical sequence and timing.

Consensus on:	▼ Strategy	▼ Resource allocation
▼ Mission	▼ Key programs	▼ Communications
▼ Objectives	▼ Action plans	▼ Review structure

▲ Select programs to address the priority issues and strategic thrusts.

▲ Allocate strategic resources.

▲ Do a reality check in terms of financial impact, resources, and strategy.

▲ Establish a review process to track progress and imbed accountability.

▲ Develop a communications plan.

▲ Establish postmeeting actions and responsibilities.

Preparation: Review the recommendations in the Prerequisites, Setting the Stage, and Facilitation Tips sections at the beginning of Chapter 9. The same advice is applicable here. Figure 11-2 presents an agenda and the typical sequence of steps and time allocations for this meeting.

=====

Section A
Mission, Strategic Thrust, and Values

Objectives: Agree on the organization's mission (including the vision), strategic thrust, business definition, and value statements.

Techniques: Presentation, work groups, discussion, consensus building

Time: 3 hours, 20 minutes

Procedure

Each step shows the time allotted and the responsible person in the left-hand column.

[10 min.]   **1. Presentation of mission statement.**
CEO   ▲ CEO presents entire mission statement.

Figure 11-2. Strategic planning meeting: typical agenda, sequence, and time allocations.

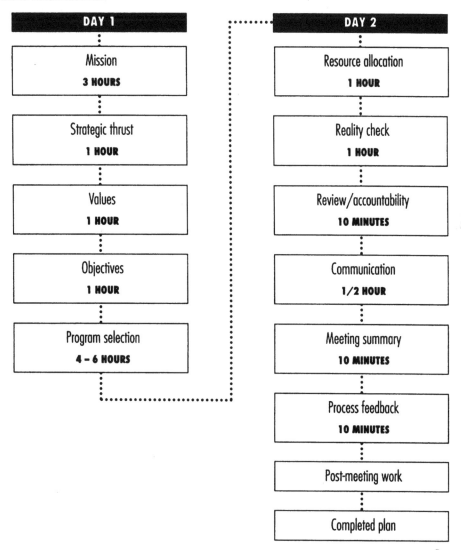

DAY 1	DAY 2
Mission — 3 HOURS	Resource allocation — 1 HOUR
Strategic thrust — 1 HOUR	Reality check — 1 HOUR
Values — 1 HOUR	Review/accountability — 10 MINUTES
Objectives — 1 HOUR	Communication — 1/2 HOUR
Program selection — 4 – 6 HOURS	Meeting summary — 10 MINUTES
	Process feedback — 10 MINUTES
	Post-meeting work
	Completed plan

[30 min.] **2. Critique of the mission statement.**
Facilitator

▲ Facilitate an open discussion of the mission statement—including desired financial performance, market position, core products and services, pivotal internal and external values, and—important—the strategic thrusts.

▲ Ensure that the team answers the following question: "Does the statement clearly and concisely capture the essence of the company and clearly communicate (1) our purpose (why we exist), (2) what we want to become in the future, (3) our core values, and (4) how we're going to get there—our strategic thrust?

[1 hr., 15 min.] 3. Strategic thrusts (optional).

Small groups
▲ Your strategic thrusts are included in and discussed with your mission statement. They are one of the most important topics in planning. Considerable time and thought should have been spent in defining your strategic thrust prior to this meeting. It is critical that there be agreement on it and that each thrust area be turned into operational programs and actions to allow the company to gain or maintain its desired competitive advantage. *Make sure that needed actions are incorporated into your priority programs or explicitly delegate to functions or individuals.*

▲ *If the strategic thrust was not agreed on prior to this meeting, e.g., during development of marketing strategy or in the priority-setting meeting, follow the optional procedure below.*

▲ Divide the team, if there are six or more members, into two groups. Have each group appoint a leader. (If there are fewer than six members, stay in one group.)

▲ Ask both groups to critique the strategic thrust. Each group should take one to one and one-quarter hours to:
—List and agree on any additions to the statement.
—List any areas with which it disagrees and recommend changes.
—Define, in detail, what is meant by each thrust and how the organization will turn it into action, measure success in each area, and get results (if this was not accomplished as part of the prework exercises).
—Grade the company's performance A, B, or C in each area, and recommend corrective action in the C (need significant improvement) areas and positive actions in B and A areas that it thinks the company must put more effort into.

▲ Instruct groups not to get hung up on details

and numbers. Only general agreement is needed on the numbers, which are merely directional and need pass only the test of reasonableness. Nor should groups spend time searching for the precisely apt words to express their ideas. The groups' job is to modify concepts and bullet-point descriptive words and ideas, not to write precise language. The exact wording will be completed by the CEO or a team member after the planning meeting.

▲ Instruct work groups to record their recommendations on flipcharts for presentation to the entire group.

▲ An example:

—One manufacturing company in a highly interactive planning meeting decided that its thrust of "superior customer service" meant (1) being judged objectively superior to the competition by its target customers, and (2) that the key elements of customer service were delivering orders 100 percent complete and on-time, responding instantly to inquiries, rendering customer engineering services in a timely fashion, ensuring high accuracy of shipments, and being flexible in meeting unusual requests.

—Operationally, the thrust meant significant increases and changes in staffing, processes, and methods for order entry, manufacturing planning, and customer service; improvements in computer systems servicing those areas; and creation of a customer engineering function.

▲ Agreement on strategic thrust:

—Have each group leader make a five-to-seven-minute presentation, giving recommended changes and the reasons for them. Allow questions for clarification only.

—Lead the entire group to consensus on the summary strategic thrust.

[30 min.]
Facilitator

4. **Critique of business definition.**

▲ Facilitate an open discussion of the business definition—the company's target markets, target customers, and geographic scope; the role of technology; and products and services offered. The business definition should be well honed at this point if, during the situation analysis, careful work has been accomplished in identifying the current and potential target market segments served and the range of products and services that might be offered to them.

▲ Ensure that the team answers these bottom-line questions:
—Are we going after the right markets and customers?
—Are we offering the right products and services?
—Have we clarified the types and character of businesses that we want to pursue in the future?
—Are our product and market priorities clear?

▲ Remember that the business definition must be wide enough to give people plenty of opportunities to achieve your mission and objectives but narrow enough so that they are clearly focused and do not try to be all things to all people.

▲ Some examples from a footwear company:
—*Too limited:* penny loafers for the upscale market via wholesale distribution channels
—*Too wide:* accessing the multibillion-pair male footwear market
—*Appropriate:* addressing the upscale, professional men's footwear market for dress and casual, high- to mid-price, traditional fashion shoes and accessories, sold through high-grade clothing and footwear retail stores and direct mail within North America

[55 min.]   5. **Critique of internal and external values.**
Small groups   ▲ Break the planning team into two or more groups to put flesh and meaning on each word or statement.

▲ Divide the work between the groups by assigning customer values and shareholder values to one group, for example, and employee and community values to the other. For each value, the groups should address these questions:

—What do we mean by this word?

—Operationally, how will we turn the value or direction into action and get results?

▲ The groups should also add values that they deem missing and challenge values that they think are inappropriate.

▲ The groups should also grade the company's performance A, B, or C in each area and give recommendations for corrective action in the C (need significant improvement) areas.

▲ An example: One company decided that community service meant "being viewed by the community as highly involved and interested in the progress of the community socially and economically; moreso than any direct competitors." Operationally, this meant encouraging employee involvement in service activities of their choice, requiring such involvement by key officers and putting it into their MBOs, and giving money to employee/managerial-directed community causes.

[20 min.]
Facilitator

6. **Reconvene the entire team, and have each work group report its results.**

▲ Allow three to five minutes per group for presentation of conclusions. Then spend five to ten minutes getting consensus on both the values/directions to be put in the mission statement and the operational steps to be taken in areas where performance is inadequate. Revisit the mission statement to confirm that the most important values have been included in that succinct summary of direction. Record any changes on the flipcharts.

▲ Assign the final rewriting and wordcrafting of the mission statement to the CEO or to another team member, who will present the finished document for the CEO's blessing.

Section B
Objectives

Objective: Agree on the long-term objectives by which the success of the business will be measured.

| **Techniques:** | Presentation, discussion, consensus |
| **Time:** | 1 hour |

Procedure

**[10 min.]
CEO or CFO**

1. Presentation of key result areas, measures, and objectives.
▲ Summarize the precirculated key result areas, measures, and objectives (in that order and preferably with industry norms for comparison). Be sure to focus on terminal objectives for what's expected in the next year and for three years out. Be realistic. Pie-in-the-sky objectives rarely get accomplished and may, in fact, be demotivating rather than motivating.

**[50 min.]
Facilitator or CEO**

2. Discussion and closure.
▲ Lead a discussion, key result area by key result area, noting any changes or disagreements with the presented objectives as you go along.
▲ Summarize changes and get consensus from the group on them, one at a time. Vote if the consensus is not obvious. If there are disagreements over objectives, the CEO decides.

Section C
Program Selection

Objectives:	1. Select and rank high-priority programs.
	2. Gain consensus on the programs' objectives and on the key steps to be monitored during the plan period.
	3. Coordinate tasks to be accomplished by different functions within the organization. Agree on follow-up steps for each program.
Techniques:	Presentation, discussion, consensus
Time:	Probably 4–6 hours, varying with the number and the complexity of programs and the quality of homework done in advance. In general, allow 30 minutes per program.

Programs are the major means that you will use to implement your strategies and to achieve your objectives. As we discussed in Chapter

1, the sources of programs are your priority issues, strategic thrust, and mission statement. Your programs:

▲ Must address your priority issues
▲ Must address your strategic thrusts
▲ Should address areas where you are underperforming and areas where you have both secondary opportunities with high potential impact and resources to address them (or can get them)

The programs to be presented were assigned at the priority-setting meeting and their action plans circulated to the planning team. Since then, team members may have identified additional programs as they thought further about the earlier meeting's results, completed their homework assignments, and did the prework for this meeting.

Additional program needs may also have been identified during *this* meeting. Although complete program action plans cannot be presented for these on-the-spot programs, their general outlines, resource requirements, and priority can be addressed.

Procedure

Facilitator

1. **Introduction and scheduling of program presentations.**
   ▲ Post list of programs to be reviewed, in sequence and with allotted time. Note any programs that were added during this meeting or between the priority-setting meeting and this meeting

[30 min. each]
Program
leaders

2. **Program presentations, discussions.**
   ▲ Each program leader should briefly (seven minutes maximum per program) present each of the following elements of the program:
      —Objectives—one-year and three-year
      —Key action steps—who, what, when—no more than three or four
      —Coordination requirements—major responsibilities of units not under the control of program leader
      —Resources—major financial return, expenses, and capital; people requirements
   ▲ Use overhead transparencies of the precirculated program plans or prepared flipcharts to present each program.

▲ Allow interruptions for questions for clarification only.

[60 min. maximum] Facilitator

3. **Program discussion.**

▲ With a list of the proposed programs or flipcharts summarizing all the programs on the walls, guide a free and open discussion of the programs, focusing on the issues: Have they been well thought out? Are the objectives clear and measurable? Do they address the priority issues, strategic thrusts, and vision? Can they be realistically accomplished and coordinated internally? Are there deficiencies in the common problem areas of time, money, or skills needed to accomplish them?

▲ The facilitator should note any potential changes on a flipchart page.

▲ If some programs require more discussion than time will allow, set them aside until all the other programs are discussed. That way, they won't eat up all of the group's time and energy, and the team will have an overall perspective when it finally picks programs. Discuss these difficult programs later in the meeting, or, if they require significant time and additional inputs, address them after the meeting.

[10 min.] Facilitator

4. **Consensus.**

▲ Get the team's agreement on each program and on the members' roles in implementing it.

[20 min.] Facilitator

5. **Program ranking.**

▲ Before team members rank the programs, review the five factors that govern program selection and priorities:

—Financial impact. The higher the long-term impact, the better.

—Alignment with the mission.

—Window of time. How important is it to do this now? Is there a fleeting opportunity resulting, for example, from a new market opening up or from the failure or short-term weakness of a competitor?

—Resource availability. Do you have the skills and dollars to implement the program?

Some programs, however desirable, may have to be deferred.

—Infrastructure necessity. Some programs, while difficult to evaluate in terms of strategic impact, are nonetheless necessary (e.g., MBO systems, some computer systems, additional physical space).

▲ Remind the group also that there are many options when selecting programs and allocating resources. They can:

—Shift program timing—either in or out—depending on its urgency and availability of resources.

—Shift responsibility for execution outside, for example, to an external vendor. This is particularly useful when critical skills are short or lacking.

—Cut the program.

—Defer the program.

—Use creative options such as implementing only a key part of the plan.

—Execute the plan in a modified form—improve service systems for a few key customers and with limited services; accomplish a venture or new product as a joint venture to bring in additional resources; use guerilla or skunkworks techniques, instead of doing it by the book.

▲ Manage the group to consensus on the three to six high-priority programs and their ranking. If the ranking isn't obvious, vote. Resist the temptation to have too many programs. If you are in doubt, it is better to err on the side of having too few programs, all of which are critical and well resourced.

Section D
Resource Allocation

Objectives:

1. Allocate strategic resources—people, time, and money—to those programs and activities that will have the highest positive long-term impact.

2. Select the strategic projects that will be funded.

Techniques: Presentation, discussion, "mental Monopoly money"
Time: 1 hour

Procedure

[15 min.]   **1. Definition of available strategic resources and de-**
CFO   **mands for them.**
                 ▲ Preferably in advance of the meeting or, alter-
                   natively, on the fly during the meeting, the
                   CFO prepares and presents the following in-
                   formation covering the upcoming three to five
                   years:
                   —Capital needed to keep the baseline busi-
                     ness healthy
                   —Incremental strategic program requests for
                     capital, expense money, and people
                 See Chapter 10 for a more detailed explanation of
                 information required to complete this step.

[10 min.]   **2. Agreement on baseline spending.**
Facilitator   ▲ Facilitate an agreement on the minimum per-
                   centage of the discretionary cash flow that will
                   be needed to take care of the baseline business
                   and infrastructure spending and the percent-
                   age that will remain for strategic and change
                   programs.

[20–30 min.] **3. Consensus on spending.**
Facilitator   ▲ Give each team member "mental Monopoly
                   money" equal to the amount of discretionary
                   cash flow available for strategic and change
                   programs.
                 ▲ Tell team members that they can vote for a
                   project only by completely funding it from
                   their pile of money. Partial funding is not al-
                   lowed. In addition, they must vote all of their
                   funds. Once their funds are depleted, they
                   have no further votes, even though there may
                   be additional projects that they feel are of
                   merit.
                     Sequentially, ask each team member how
                   he voted his funds, and record the results.
                   Where there are wide discrepancies in how
                   funds were voted, ask why.
                 ▲ Make sure team members are considering "hu-

man" capital. In implementing change, allocating people skills is often a greater problem than apportioning money.

▲ Confirm consensus. When every project has been vetted, there should be a clear consensus on where money should be spent. If not, it is up to the CEO to make the final allocation on the spot.

[5 min.]
Facilitator

4. Closure.

▲ Summarize on a flipchart any changes and further action steps required of team leaders.

[5 min.]
CEO

5. Follow-up assignments.

▲ Assign team members to take the raw programs back to the organization that must implement them, and:

—Fine-tune or change them, given the meeting output, to ensure that the program can be accomplished.

—Delegate action steps to those individuals who must execute them, ensuring that the programs are included in individual MBOs for the coming year and that required financial and people resources are budgeted.

—Write a final program summary for inclusion in the program summary book to be produced after the meeting.

Section E
Reality Check: Financial Impact/ Resources/Strategy

Objectives:

1. Test the reality of the plan.
2. Verify that the plan will yield the desired results.
3. Confirm that the company has the necessary financial and people resources to carry out the plan.
4. Verify that the plan addresses the strategies that will win.
5. Summarize the approximate incremental financial impact of chosen programs and the incremental resources—money, people, time, and skills—required.

It's easy to pick lots of desirable programs. It's even easier to fail in their accomplishment because the resources and time aren't available to implement them properly. This is particularly true for groups new to planning, who have not learned to balance the time necessary to meet ongoing business demands and the time devoted to strategic change.

It's extremely important to pick only those programs that can realistically be resourced and well executed. To ensure that this happens requires a final reality check.

CFO, CEO; senior management, human resources; senior management, marketing

1. **In-meeting preparation.**

   Ideally, the CFO, CEO, senior management for human resources, and senior management for marketing should come prepared with preliminary summaries based on assignments taken from precirculated program descriptions and adjusted on the spot for any last-minute changes. Alternatively, they can develop the summaries during breaks or evenings at the meeting.

   In preparation for their presentations, they should outline their conclusions on no more than two flipcharts. The summaries should include the following:

   ▲ Financial items (CFO)
   —Baseline revenue, profits, and profitability
   —Incremental costs—expense and capital— showing the buildup from each program and in total
   —Incremental gain from each program and in total
   —Gap analysis, comparing the baseline figures plus the incremental gain from the programs to the financial objectives agreed upon earlier
   —Answers to these questions: Will the plan and programs produce the financial results that we want? Are the financial resources available to accomplish the plan?
   —(If there are gaps between your anticipated results and the objectives) recommendations to reevaluate the objectives, do more to meet them, and/or add additional programs in the future in order to meet them
   —(If there are insufficient resources) recommendations to get additional funding or to cut back programs and ambitions

▲ Human resources issues (senior management–HR)

—Additional human resources requirements (numbers of people and particular skills and additional time load on existing personnel)

—Answers to these questions: Do we have enough people and the right skills? If not, can we get them? Do existing personnel have time to both execute the plan and do their ongoing jobs?

▲ Strategy issues (CEO or senior management–marketing)

—How well the programs address the strategic thrust and nonfinancial objectives for the key result areas

—Answers to these questions: Are we doing enough to close any strategic performance gaps? Are we doing enough to get needed competitive advantage?

Techniques:	Presentation, discussion, consensus
Time:	1 hour maximum, probably less

Procedure

[20 min.]
CFO

1. **Financial reality check.**

   ▲ Make a ten-minute presentation, summarizing the financial impact and resource gap. Focus on:

   —What are the problems?

   —How realistic is the plan?

   ▲ Allow ten minutes for questions.

   ▲ List any major concerns or deficiencies on the hanging-issues list for resolution after the planning meeting.

   ▲ This financial summary plus the baseline forecast and objectives become the basis for the financial section of the plan.

[20 min.]
senior
managment,
human
resources

2. **Human resources reality check.**

   ▲ Make a ten-minute presentation on skill and people resources requirements. Focus on:

   —What are the problems?

   —How realistic is the plan?

   ▲ Allow ten minutes for questions.

   ▲ List any major concerns or deficiencies on the

hanging-issues list for resolution after the planning meeting.
▲ This human resources summary is reflected in the plan's financial projections and becomes the basis for the staffing section of the plan if significant new resources and skills are required.

[20 min.]
CEO

3. **Strategy reality check.**
   ▲ Make a ten-minute presentation on the extent to which the strategic programs and other actions delegated to team members will:
   —Fix strategic weaknesses.
   —Move the organization significantly toward meeting its strategic objectives and fulfilling its mission.
   —Gain a significant competitive advantage.
   ▲ Allow ten minutes for questions.
   ▲ List any major concerns on the hanging-issues list for later resolution.

[20 min.]
Facilitator

4. **Overall reality check (optional).** Use if you think there are significant unsurfaced barriers to the plan's success.
   ▲ Discussion: Ask the group to list the key barriers to getting the plan implemented.
   ▲ Get overall consensus on whether the plan, particularly the first-year tasks, can be accomplished.
   ▲ If there are significant barriers, allow time later in the meeting or at a later date to address and resolve them. Alternatively, decide what part of the plan or ongoing activities should be cut to permit the proper balance between implementing strategic change and running the business.

Section F
Review/Accountability

Objectives:

Clarify:
▲ The plan and program review process
▲ How plan objectives and programs will be incorporated into individual MBOs

▲ How plan results and costs will be incorporated into the budgeting process

Technique: Presentation

Time: 10 minutes

Procedure

CEO

1. **Presentation.** Include:
   ▲ How accountabilities will be established and how the plan is to be reviewed. (For details on making the plan operational and reviewing and keeping the plan on track, see Chapters 12, 13, and 18.)
   ▲ The timetable for implementation. Record projected timing on a flipchart.

Section G
Communications Plan

Objectives: Agree on:
▲ What results from the planning process as a whole are to be communicated
▲ To whom they should be communicated
▲ When the communication should take place

Techniques: Presentation, discussion, consensus

Time: 30 minutes

Procedure

Facilitator

1. **Presentation of recommendations for communications plan.**
   Recommendations should include:
   ▲ Audiences that need to be addressed:
     —Senior management/boards
     —Their subordinates
     —Other exempt and nonexempt employees
   ▲ How to determine what to tell each audience:
     —Tailor information to the jobs and positions of the audience.
     —Take into account the information that it needs to carry out its part in the plan.

—Be sensitive to the group's need to know proprietary information and/or the strategies agreed upon.

—As a general rule, the more people know about the vision and strategic plan, their role in it, and its effect on their job, the better. This helps direct spontaneous action, plans, and programs at lower levels in the organization. It also reduces working at cross purposes and misunderstandings about what is strategically important (e.g., quality versus cost reductions).

▲ The best method of communicating the plan:

—Develop scripts and good visual aids for each major target audience so that a uniform message is conveyed.

—Have a senior manager, preferably a member of the planning team, present the plan to each target group.

—Leave time for employees to ask questions and get answers, preferably in small groups with managers facilitating them and recording issues.

▲ Typical methods for communicating the mission statement for the first time include:

—Sending it out, complete, in writing.

—Making it "plaquable" (summarized in a few key words or sentences for desk or wall plaques).

—Putting it on wallet-size cards—a popular and much used method.

—Producing a video featuring the CEO and top team explaining the mission. The video is useful for new employee indoctrination, for workers in remote locations, and for initial presentation of the mission.

2. **Note that plan and mission communication is not a one-time event.** It requires consistent effort and attention on the part of the CEO and top-team members to effectively communicate the mission, particularly the vision, values, and strategic thrust, to everyone in the company. They must use every opportunity to reemphasize the company's direction.

3. **Lead a discussion and manage the group to consensus on the elements of plan communications.**
4. **To gain closure, record the results on a flipchart.**

Section H
Meeting Summary

Objectives:

1. Summarize the entire meeting to reinforce conclusions and put all the detailed work in perspective.
2. Leave the group feeling good about its progress. (A sterling, punchy summary can put thick and tasty icing on the cake and make both the facilitator and the team look good.)
3. Review and get final agreement on the action steps.

Prework:

This is one of the most important parts of the meeting. The summary presentation will be used to produce the written meeting summary and action steps and the written plan itself. Therefore:

1. As the meeting progresses, prepare and keep a neat, serial flipchart summary of each section of the meeting (mission, strategic thrust, objectives, programs, etc.) for review at this time. These summaries will be added to the summary charts of SWOTs and priority issues from the priority-setting meeting. If logistically possible, keep the summary charts visible and in sequence on one wall of the meeting room so that participants can watch their progress over the course of the meeting.
2. Prepare a list of all major action steps resulting from the meeting to help people reaffirm or modify their commitments.
3. Pay particular attention to the summaries of programs and to the list of other follow-up assignments. They are the most important output of the meeting.
4. Finish your summary the evening before the final sessions so that only last-minute additions need to be made.

Technique: Presentation
Timing: 8 minutes

Procedure

Facilitator

1. **Presentation of summary.**
   ▲ Make the summary quick, punchy, motivational, and to the point. You do not need to hit all details.
   ▲ Include:
   —Summary of each topic. Talk from the summary charts, presenting conclusions from each section of both the priority-setting meeting and this meeting (major external trends, SWOTs, priority issues, mission, objectives, strategic thrusts and other strategies, program priorities, resources, and communications). This is the summary of the entire plan.
   —Summary of action steps: who is to do what and when.
   —Postmeeting follow-up: how you will track progress in completing action steps and other assignments made as a result of this meeting.
2. **Do not allow discussion or the reopening of issues.** Allow questions only to clarify inaccuracies in the summary or action steps and to ensure that assignments are clear.

Section I
Process Feedback

Objective: Improve the process and future meetings.
Technique: Round-robin
Time: 10 minutes

Procedure

Facilitator

1. **Round-robin.**
   ▲ Ask each person (with the CEO speaking last):
   —How useful was the prework, and how could it be improved?
   —What did the meeting accomplish?

Figure 11-3. Post-meeting work.

▼ Completion of action plans	▼ Delegation of objectives/action steps
▼ Coordination of programs	▼ Final strategic plan

—What should it have accomplished that it didn't?

—How could the meeting have been improved?

2. **Send a confidential quality control survey form to all participants** within twenty-four hours of the meeting to get detailed ratings and feedback while the meeting is fresh in their minds.

Section J
Postmeeting Essentials: Capturing and Circulating Results and Assigning Accountabilities

Figure 11-3 summarizes poststrategic planning meeting work to be accomplished.

There are two steps: production of a meeting summary and a final meeting to confirm the plan.

Procedure

1. Meeting Summary

1. **Read over the meeting summary** to make sure that it is clear and that it captures all the key points and conclusions from the meeting. Make any pencil notes on it immediately after the meeting. Your recall will be best then, and this summary will be your only record of many working hours spent.

2. **Clean up the summaries** of each segment of the meeting and any other material that needs to be captured.

3. **Circulate,** within a couple of days of the meeting, the action steps and the meeting summary (in that order). The revised program summaries will prob-

ably not be complete immediately after the meeting. The meeting summary and action steps
should be circulated without them.

2. Final Meeting

[*Many companies have a brief meeting to do a final review of the program
priorities, coordination issues, and resource allocations before delegating action
plans throughout the organization. This meeting should take no more than half
a day and can be done as soon as the program leaders have filled in some of the
details on their programs.*]

Section K
Completed Written Plan

Write a concise summary plan (Figure 11-4 gives an outline for this),
omitting any unnecessary detail and including no background material.
Circulate this plan in two documents:

    1. *The Strategic Plan Summary.* This summary includes these sec-
tions: assumptions, priority issues, mission, KRAs and objectives, strategic thrust and other strategies, and a list of the programs. An
appendix should contain relevant and concise financial summaries, a
summary of SWOTs, and any parts of the environmental and marketing
analyses that are relevant to the long term. (Appendix II of this book
contains examples of two strategic plan summaries and a mission statement.) *This three- or four-page summary is the most important planning document you will produce.* It will be used to communicate the plan and
referenced frequently. It is the starting point for your annual plan
update.
    2. *Programs:* A compendium of the final approved program sum-
maries. This section will be used during quarterly review meetings to
evaluate progress on the programs.

Follow-Up Tips

The postmeeting facilitation tips presented at the conclusion of Chapter
9 apply for this meeting also.

Figure 11-4. A typical outline of a written strategic plan.

I. Priority Issues (1)*
- ▼ Priority issues and rationale for each

II. Mission (1-3)
- ▼ Vision, business definition, and values

III. Objectives (1/2-1)
- ▼ KRAs, measures, 3- to 5-year objectives

IV. Strategy Statement (1-2)
- ▼ Routes of change
- ▼ Market and product priorities; postures
- ▼ Competitive advantage
- ▼ Strategic thrust, subsidiary external strategies
- ▼ Internal strategic thrust; subsidiary internal strategies
- ▼ Strategic fixes

V. Program Summary (1-2)
- ▼ Brief summary of rationale, objectives, and key action steps for all priority-issue programs

Appendices

A. Numbers
- ▼ Detailed financial tables needed to support the plan, including P&L, balance sheet, and cash flow statement (2-4)

B. Background Information
- ▼ Environmental analysis (1-2)
- ▼ Assumptions (1/2)
- ▼ Market segments and segment strategies (1-2)
- ▼ SWOTs (1)
- ▼ Strategic alternatives (1/2)

C. Programs
- ▼ Full program action plans for quarterly reviews (15-25)

*approximate number of pages

DO'S AND DON'TS

DO

- *Follow up* after the meeting to make sure that the written plan and programs are completed and circulated quickly.
- *Quickly obtain needed input* from lower-level employees so that the plan can be tied off at some point and folded into the budgeting or upper-level approval cycle.
- *Communicate* to the troops fast.

DON'T

- *Put out a thick plan.* Include only the minimum essentials—probably a dozen pages, excluding program plans.

Part Three

Implementing the Plan

Chapter 12

Making the Plan Operational

Remember, nothing that's good works by itself, just to please you. You've got to *make* the damn thing work.

—Thomas A. Edison, inventor

Good thoughts are no better than good dreams, unless they be executed.

—Ralph Waldo Emerson, author, philosopher

Remember, gentlemen, an order that can be misunderstood will be misunderstood.

—Helmuth von Moltke, chief of the German General Staff under Bismarck

Now comes the tough part—making it happen. The first step in this arduous process is to break down the strategic objectives, programs, and tasks and assign them to teams and individuals who have the resources and the motivation to execute them.

If you've followed our advice, your organization has participated heavily in the development of the plan. If so, by now the people who will carry out the plan should be strongly committed to the priorities that will be delegated to them and should have identified ways of overcoming the tangible and organization barriers to accomplishment. In other words, before the organization commits itself to the tasks of change, people throughout the company should agonize over how to accomplish them. This follows the model of the Japanese (taught to them by a few Americans who were not yet prophets in their own land).

Relevance, Resources, Alignment, Accountability

The four critical concepts that together make up the secret to strategic implementation are:

▲ *Relevance*—making the mission, priority issues, and actions that need to be taken relevant to and understood by those who must execute. This is as important for a junior production superintendent charged with shortening setup times as for a senior officer asked to embark on an acquisition program. How their actions directly affect strategic success must be explained and understood.

▲ *Resources*—ensuring that you have the right skills, backed by adequate time and money, available in the right place and at the right time.

▲ *Alignment*—making sure that throughout the organization all actions, including ongoing tasks, support the mission and the strategic priorities. It makes sense for a company that identifies customer service as a competitive advantage to set up an elaborate customer service and order entry organization. But it makes no sense for the same company to allow the people in manufacturing to go on thinking their job is to achieve the lowest possible cost, and the customer be damned.

▲ *Accountability*—giving everyone who has a strategic task to perform at any level the ability to win or lose on the basis of how they carry out their charge.

Making the plan operational also involves:

▲ *Communicating the mission, strategic thrust, and priority issues,* putting into place the communication plan you developed at the strategy meeting
▲ *Identifying the leverage individuals, teams, and functions*—those who will be on program teams and those who manage and deliver in areas that support your critical success factors
▲ *Having the right people with the right skills in the right leverage slots,* and dealing quickly and effectively with those who don't have the skills or who resist change
▲ *Driving the plan down through the organization,* making assignments, providing resources, and holding people accountable

This chapter looks more closely at each of those steps.

Communicate the Mission, Strategic Thrust, and Priority Issues

The mission sets the overall philosophy, direction, and framework for strategic action. The principal parts of the plan that people actually turn into action are the priority issues and the programs to address them. Do not underestimate the importance of communicating these issues and programs fully throughout the organization.

The first step in making the plan operational is to ensure that the mission, strategic thrust, and priority issues are driven home and understood at all levels. Provide complete copies of the plan to all people who have key roles in implementation, or at least give them copies of the mission and strategy and details of the programs that affect their areas.

Execute the communication plan developed at the strategy meeting (see Chapter 11). Prepare the scripts and the visual aids for addressing your target audiences, and use them to hold communication meetings at which planning team members describe the plan and managers facilitate small question-and-answer groups.

Hand out wallet-size cards entitled [*Year*] *Strategic Focus* to the entire organization. The cards should explain in a few phrases the company's mission, strategic thrust, key values, and four to six strategic priority issues that must be addressed during the coming year. This message will help focus the organization at all levels. When instructions for developing operating plans and budgets are distributed, preface them with this same succinct message.

Each year when you update the plan, update the focus card also. If you have done your planning job well, the strategic thrust will change rarely and the priorities only moderately from year to year.

The cards have as much public relations as information value. The PR works when actions and deeds are aligned with the message.

Identify Your Leverage People

For the most part, you will have decided what senior leadership will be responsible for each strategic program during your planning meetings. All that remains is to elaborate on the implementation organization.

First, you need to identify the leverage positions, individuals, and functions that will have the most impact on plan implementation. Typically, they are those who will head up or participate in teams assigned to implement priority-issue action plans and those who manage and deliver in areas that support your critical success factors and competitive strategy. For example, if your competitive strategy focuses on customer service, your leverage functions are your service organization and support systems, such as order entry, production planning, and materials management. If a major thrust is to acquire companies with products to sell through existing distribution channels, your acquisition specialist, chief financial officer, and marketing functions are likely to be key.

It is my experience that only 5–10 percent of the organization needs to be the movers, shakers, rattlers and rollers, and tough change agents. The remaining 90–95 percent are worker bees who, if reasonably skilled and well managed, will produce.

Make Sure You Have the Right People With the Right Skills

If the strategic organization isn't structured properly or your high-leverage people aren't superior, the plan won't work. To execute your plan, you need people with the highest level of leadership, technical, managerial, and teamwork skills. You cannot afford to settle for whoever is available.

When You Don't Have the Talent

Most strategic programs involve significant change in the way a company does business. Effective program implementation requires people who are not only technically competent but willing to change and to lead change. That is a rare combination. Moving into the future may require advanced skills your company doesn't have. Get people with the skills you need, from inside your organization if you can or from outside if you must. If you neglect this, you doom your programs to failure or, at best, mediocrity.

One chemical company struggled for three years, waiting in vain for its tired and disinterested R&D management and staff to implement pivotal plans to increase new product output. Setting and reviewing stringent objectives failed to bring around the moribund function. Only when the company finally replaced its R&D director and key staff did it begin to make progress.

If time is on your side, you are in a good position to develop the new skills you need inside in your organization. Although cash-rich and highly profitable, the United States Tobacco Company recognized that, in the future, being the leader in the smokeless tobacco industry would not be enough. To position itself strategically, the company needed world-class organization and methods of production. Although not pressured from the marketplace or by bankers, USTC took on the toughest challenge of all: self-motivated change. Led by its manufacturing, R&D, human resources, and marketing functions, it accomplished a more studied, slower change that involved fewer people changes and disruptions and more retraining. Emphasizing improved productivity with existing people, the company's progress was nonetheless striking over a six-year period.

Build Program Teams

When your programs are for multifunction, multilevel projects, your implementation organization is going to look somewhat different from the functional structure you may be used to. To tackle programs such as cost reduction, new product development, and customer service improvements, you'll need to form formal program teams with members drawn from a variety of functions and levels. During the life of the program, these members will devote the majority of their time and substantial resources to its implementation.

If just one or two functions dominate the implementation of a program but there is a need to seek advice from other functions from time to time, the more likely organizational approach is the informal program team. These are short-lived and task-oriented, and, except for the leaders, members are not dedicated full-time to the program. A typical example is the development and launch of a marketing program to promote and expand the market for an existing product. Marketing and marketing communications carry the brunt of the assignment, but some advice is needed from manufacturing, engineering, and information systems in order to pull the program off.

Chapter 16 focuses in detail on the characteristics, impact, and requirements of teams, team leadership, and team members.

Use Individuals Effectively

It is practical and efficient to delegate a program to an individual or to a single function when little coordination between functions is required and the resources reside within one functional area.

For example, one company designated the installation of MBO and new compensation systems to its human resources department. While the project required interaction with a number of functions and frequent solicitation of approvals as various options were proposed, the inputs and approvals were concise and could be handled in the course of ongoing day-to-day business.

When You Get Resistance

Early in the process, deal appropriately with those who can't or won't work on strategic programs or who can't adapt to the team environment. You have only three options in dealing with people who can't cope: Move them to jobs where they can productively contribute with necessary retraining, retire them early, or separate them. You need to move quickly, for you can't afford to hold back strategy with inadequate change agents. Business is not a social movement. Its job is to get results. Be kind but forceful in quickly removing human progress barriers.

A mid-size, family-owned manufacturing company found itself in a back-to-the-wall turnaround situation that was at least partly attributable to decades of sloppy standards in hiring and developing people and holding them accountable. For a company that was kindhearted to a fault, taking the necessary action meant biting a very big bullet. But in the course of nine months, the firm retired, separated, or moved to other positions approximately one-third of its top managerial force. In addition, it substantially redefined the content of nearly all of the top fifteen managerial positions, adding several that didn't exist and eliminating others. The result? Far fewer people and almost immediate and measurable increases in productivity, both internally and in the marketplace.

Ontario Chemicals, Inc. (OCI), a pseudonym, is highly profitable, but with many of the same organization problems, it could afford to take a more leisurely pace. Faced with a market that was rapidly becoming more competitive and undergoing significant structural change, OCI developed a plan that called for aggressive cost reduction, more competitive pricing, higher service standards, and major improvements in technical innovation. Over three years, the company retired or replaced five of its nine top managers because they couldn't perform at required higher skill levels or couldn't function in the new team-oriented culture.

Drive the Plan Down Into the Organization

If you have done your homework and involved the organization in the development of the plan, there will be few surprises when the plan is finally handed down.

Pass the Torch to Program Team Leaders

Have a top-team member meet with every designated program team leader to:

▲ Explain the final program, clarify the objectives, and outline key action steps.
▲ Emphasize the need to check with teams and subordinates to:
1. Ensure that they can buy in to the tasks, resources, and, especially, due dates.
2. Work out any detailed subaction plans to ensure that the master plan can be implemented.
3. Identify the top three to five barriers to success. Most teams have one or more meetings at this point to flesh out the plan and get organized. You should allow for these in your planning cycle.
▲ Schedule a second meeting about two weeks later, at which time the program team leader should come back with a written list or recommended changes and modifications to the action plans. The top-team member is responsible for approving or disallowing these changes.

Generally, changes in objectives and programs are few, and little time is spent here. Most teams (and individuals) know what's coming down and are anxious to get started.

Ensure Alignment: Hold an Alignment Meeting

An alignment meeting is a creative technique for ensuring that lower-level strategic objectives and programs support the corporate plan. After circulating a book containing all program action plans, the CEO convenes the management team to review detailed lower-level program action plans developed after the strategic planning meeting. During the meeting:

▲ The CEO lists the top five strategic objectives that everyone must support if the plan is to succeed.
▲ Each top team member:
—Traces objectives and program action plans supporting each corporate objective down three levels within his or her own organization
—Describes in detail the steps to be taken and the processes to be used to accomplish one objective, for example, price increases, to ensure that his or her implementation thinking is effective
—Presents the top two strategic priorities for his or her own group that are not on the corporate list so that the top team sees the principal functional jobs to be done

After each team member presents, the team discusses what it does and doesn't agree on and coordination requirements.

The first time that the Resins Group of HERCULES, INC., a complicated multiproduct, multinational business, followed this procedure with its top fifteen managers worldwide, it found many gaps in its implementation programs, including:

▲ Lots of missing lower-level "ties" to corporate objectives. For example, some numbers, such as sales revenue, didn't add up to the corporate totals.
▲ Lack of key actions needed to support top-level objectives.
▲ Lack of mutually agreed upon coordination steps ("joints," in Resins Group's terminology) with departments outside their control whose contributions were needed to implement the plan.
▲ Lack of a precise understanding of what was meant by and what was expected from a number of program action plans.

After the meeting, the team members said that the process had clarified their task. It heightened their awareness of the need to drive action and accountabilities doggedly down into the organization, making sure that they were understood. It also highlighted the complexity of the process, the many factors behind future success, and the need to have excellent people who could execute complex tasks without close scrutiny.

Build Strategic Change Into Operating Plan Objectives

In some areas of strategic change, new programs are not required; all that is necessary to achieve the new objectives is for lower-level functions to improve performance within ongoing jobs and systems. In these cases, when the new objectives are passed down, they are incorporated into the annual operating plan. For example, if a company already has a responsive service system, its performance objectives may simply be modified to reflect a higher level of desired performance and ability to deliver. It's up to the lower levels to figure out how to meet the new standards.

Get the Plan Budgeted

Instruct your organization to incorporate the strategic programs and resource requests into the budgeting cycle. This is normally a mechanical step. Some companies separate strategic spending from operational in their budget reporting in order to simplify tracking.

Put Program Objectives Into MBOs

It is the joint responsibility of top-team members, program team leaders, and the functional managers of team members to see that program objectives and action steps are appropriately incorporated into personal MBOs.

If you don't have a management-by-objectives or a personal performance management system, you must get one. Without personal accountability for plan components, employees will not produce the desired results.

But don't do it all at once. MBO systems aren't, as some think, simply a matter of paperwork, sending out objective-setting and performance appraisal forms and follow-up reminders. That belief is what gave MBO a tainted reputation in the late 1960s and early 1970s. Properly designed and implemented and tied to compensation, MBO does work to empower people and to hold them accountable.

To do MBO right, start with those individuals who are key to implementing your strategic programs and those operating personnel whose contributions are critical to short-term and strategic success. Installing an MBO or performance management system is a major task that requires an immense amount of preparation, training, counseling, and auditing of effectiveness. Done best, such systems tap various layers and parts of the organization at different times and generally take two to three years to become effective in moderate-size to large organizations.

Make Sure Programs Are Happening

There are three ways for a chief executive to ensure that the key plan elements are being acted on at lower levels.

First, verify that the top-line strategic program objectives are included in the MBOs of your direct reports during MBO reviews, year in and year out.

Second, the first time you delegate the plan, ask to see the MBOs of those reporting to your direct reports and of each key team leader. At a minimum, have your facilitator, an organization behavior consultant, or a staff member audit the process by looking at one or two major programs. The auditor should trace the tasks as they are broken down and delegated to ensure that the objectives and actions required are imbedded in MBOs at all levels.

While this may seem excessive, it's not. More than one company has been unpleasantly surprised to discover that lower-level people did not understand the true thrust of the company mission, the strategic programs, and their own part in them. This lack of awareness, combined with normal confusion about how to set meaningful objectives, led to some muddled and poorly executed tasks.

The third, and most comprehensive, step to ensure the enactment of programs is to install and implement the formal process of progress detailed in the next chapter.

DO'S AND DON'TS

DO

- *Focus on the few leverage managers,* programs, functions, and teams who will execute the plan. Make sure you use the right people; motivate and reward them.
- *Overcommunicate* the mission, priority issues, and objectives to key people on every possible occasion to reinforce alignment.
- *Check* to make sure that programs and objectives have been delegated and accepted.
- *Install accountability systems* early in the process if they're not already in place. If they're in place, enforce them.

DON'T

- *Hesitate to remove the losers* who can't implement your plan.

Chapter 13

Keeping the Plan on Track

People accomplish what you inspect, not what you expect.
—Business folklore

The purpose of this chapter is to help you keep the plan on track once implementation is under way, reallocate resources as you accomplish goals or your strategic situation changes, imbed accountability for program accomplishment with every implementer, and reward results to ensure commitment and continued top level performance.

The keys to keeping the plan on track are:

> *Review, review, review.*
> *Revise, revise, revise.*
> *Reward, reward, reward.*

The Review Process

There are five reasons for reviewing the plan:

1. To become aware of when you need to allocate and reallocate valuable strategic resources to the programs that require them. New allocations have to be made swiftly and decisively in response to changes in the outside markets and in your competitive situation, in the rate of accomplishment of various programs, and in the resources available internally. Although the strategic priority issues rarely change, their relative importance and what you do to address them do change during implementation. Your success depends on flexibility and on the dynamic reallocation of resources as your strategic situation changes— which it will, frequently.

2. To assess the performance of individuals and teams.

3. To suggest solutions to problems and to remove internal

blockages to progress, particularly those that can be addressed only by the top team and that require top-level interfunctional coordination.

4. To motivate strategic teams and individuals through visibility, recognition, and praise.

5. To ensure that action is in alignment with the vision and the plan and that plan priorities are being enforced.

Reviews are more complicated than simply establishing where you stand. They are the primary mechanism for reinforcing strategic priorities. By conducting them, you demonstrate your commitment, and this behavior helps reinforce or change the culture of the organization.

How to Review

There are three review mechanisms: the quarterly plan review, individual performance reviews, and informal contact with plan implementers.

The Quarterly Plan Review

For keeping the plan on track, the most important review is the quarterly plan review, in which the top team assesses:

▲ Program performance as it compares to the written plan
▲ Progress in meeting strategic numbers, such as service levels, quality levels, market share, and profitability

Before starting the quarterly plan review, establish the ground rule that the review meetings are for making decisions and allocating resources, not for transmitting information. To prevent reviews from turning into lengthy, uninformative dog-and-pony shows in which people exaggerate their accomplishments and bury their deficiencies, follow this procedure:

1. *Prework.* One week before the review, have each team or individual responsible for a strategic project circulate a short (at most two pages) summary that states:

▲ What has been accomplished
▲ What hasn't been accomplished that was promised
▲ What major issues or problems need to be discussed and resolved
▲ Recommendations for actions to be taken, including changes in timing, program steps, and resources required

▲ A self-assessment of performance on both accomplishment and
timing of accomplishment: excellent, good, fair, or poor

In addition, the summary should indicate how the team is performing against program budget, including revenue, profit, spending,
capital expense (where relevant), and any changes in forecast results.
(See Figure 13-1 for a typical review form.)

The detailed review of the program takes place before the meeting
with the top team and is the responsibility of the program team. Obviously, functional bosses of program team members, often members of
the top team, should be kept well informed about performance in their
functional areas.

It's also the responsibility of program teams to work out solutions
to their own problems before the top-team review. For example, one
company's new product development team faced a threat to its critical
product launch date when a major packaging equipment problem surfaced. Rather than wait to present the problem at the quarterly review,
engineering held extensive meetings with the vendor and developed
solutions that, while neither ideal nor inexpensive, kept program delays
at a minimum.

2. *Review meeting.* During the meeting, allocate only twenty-five
minutes or less to each strategic program. This includes ten minutes for
the team to summarize the five points summarized during the prework
and fifteen minutes for discussion and decisions on the team's recommendations. If decisions can't be made in the allotted time, place the
program and its weighty issues on a hanging-issues list. You'll need
to set aside time later in the day or at a later date to go back to the
hanging issues.

This procedure allows equal time to everyone, preventing the quarterly plan review from bogging down in detailed discussions of only
one or two issues. When you know in advance that a program requires
extensive discussion, it's a good idea to schedule that discussion before
or after the quick quarterly reviews. Sometimes, particularly with scientific and engineering projects, some members of the top team want extensive briefings on some programs. These can be scheduled as
interactive sessions for those who wish to attend prior to the formal reviews.

It is critical that each program team be "graded" excellent, good,
fair, or poor during the meeting and in front of other teams. If the
project team and the top team disagree on the appropriate grade, the
reason for the differences must be identified and discussed.

Quarterly plan reviews need to be scheduled a year in advance,
in a quiet location, often off-site. They are unchangeable, must-attend

Figure 13-1. Quarterly program review form.

___ Quarter, 19 ___   Program Manager: _____

Program Name: _____

Program Description: _____

Long-term Objectives: _____

Short-term Objectives: _____

_____

Program Ratings (E, G, S, or P): ____

▼ **Key results:**

▼ **Problems/issues to be addressed:**

▼ **Steps/objectives due but not accomplished:**

▼ **Changes in timing, objectives, resources requested:**

The Numbers:	**Budget**	**Project to Date**	**Forecast**
Incremental			
Sales ($)			
Gross margin (%)			
Net profit			
Cash flow			
ROA			

resulting from this program since your plan was approved and you began to make changes.

If hard data are not available, state what incremental returns you think are resulting from this program. On what evidence?

What have you spent so far versus what you planned to spend?

Actual Expenditures ($)_____   Planned Expenditures ($)_____

meetings for all involved. When a meeting is in progress, no interruptions can be allowed.

3. *Postreview.* After the review, send out a summary of program changes and key issues and items to be addressed during the next review. This provides continuity from meeting to meeting and ensures that program teams are not allowed off the hook on items they promised to accomplish.

When program objectives, action steps, and timing of actions change during implementation, it's important to retain traceability and a record of the changes in original programs. Note changes and add new elements on the original program plan so that original objectives, steps, and timing are always visible. That way, people can't simply revise their programs and put out new action plans every time they get off track, creating the false appearance of perfect performance.

Who attends?

Obviously, because coordination is a major reason for using teams, the whole top team must attend. Each program team needs to be represented by people who can quickly review the program, make decisions, and, later, motivate the entire execution team. It is often sufficient to have the program team leader present the review, supported, perhaps, by one or two key program team members. At least once a year, however, it is helpful to have the entire program team present to give members visibility, motivate them, imbed accountability, and allow the top team to ask questions directly of those usually not present.

Individual Reviews/Performance Appraisal

Even though teams may be responsible and rewarded for team accomplishments, people on each team must be held individually accountable for both their team's accomplishments and their functional contributions to the team's efforts. If you have an MBO or performance management system as noted in Chapter 12, you will have incorporated team objectives and individual contributions to the team effort into each team member's personal objectives.

A marketing manager, for example, may have ongoing responsibility for the sales, marketing, development, pricing, and profitability of an existing product line. In addition, that person may be part of a team charged with developing a major new product. In that case, the marketing manager's annual objectives would include objectives related to ongoing responsibilities, objectives set for the team, and any specific functional objectives that the manager is to accomplish for the team, such as designing and testing the product packaging or overseeing market research or consumer testing.

The factors going into the manager's year-end appraisal would therefore be weighted for ongoing job performance, the overall performance of the program team of which the manager is a member, and the manager's specific functional contribution to the team.

Informal Review

The ancient and effective practice of wandering around, touching base with key plan executioners, and sniffing for the perfume of potential success or the smoke of a future conflagration is the best way to detect the need for early corrective action or praise. Such interventions, and that's what they are, should be informal, unobtrusive, and not meddlesome, but frequent enough to put a different spin on events, if needed, early in the process and, if significant changes are needed, to allow top-level action to be initiated quickly.

Intervening to Keep Programs on Track

Your top team or the individuals on it may need to make one or more of four interventions to keep strategic programs on track.

1. *Counseling* a program team or individuals on it. Program team members often need advice, particularly if this is their first project. They may need functional advice for solving specific problems, and they may need behavioral advice on how to get recalcitrant members on board and performing or on how to run meetings.
2. *Influence.* Sometimes a senior manager simply has to use muscle to get a team the resources it needs. It may take high-level persuasion to convince a function, such as data processing, to provide a team with needed support.
3. *Skill development.* Individuals and teams may need training in team management or in functional expertise. In one instance, a newly appointed sales manager had to learn sales management skills in order to launch effectively a new selling and distribution system. In another situation, an entire project team had to be trained in team and project management principles. Up to that point, the company culture had never encouraged collaborative efforts, and team members simply didn't have the experience and skills to manage as a team.
4. *Direction.* There are times when teams simply get off track and don't know how to get back on. It may be necessary to tell them what to do.

Rewarding the Winners and Withholding From the Losers

Reward is an all-important motivator, particularly for strategic tasks that take a long time to play out to the bottom line.

Rewarding Individual Performance

Obviously, money does and should play a big role in rewarding good work. Many organizations have compensation schemes that reward long-term performance and the accomplishment of strategic programs and tasks. One company's system of annual individual bonuses provides a good model. Each bonus is contingent upon the extent to which:

▲ The individual accomplishes strategic program objectives (or his or her part in them) on time and within the budgeted cost. Note that this rewards people for accomplishing one-year strategic objectives and tasks that may not pay off at the bottom line for several years.
▲ The individual meets or exceeds the objective of his or her ongoing job.
▲ The entire corporation meets its financial objectives.
▲ The individual exhibits positive behaviors and cultural values cited in the value statement.

The level of bonus award is tied to the company's performance and to the importance of the individual's job. The weight given to each factor depends on the time allocated to it, the importance of the tasks, and the individual's impact on the eventual results.

Rewarding Team Performance

Team members should be rewarded for the results that the team gets, not for each individual's perceived contribution to the team. In other words, if the team gets an excellent rating, every team member gets the same rating; if the rating is poor, everyone suffers. Obviously, within a team, the time given and the relative importance of each function's contribution will vary.

One way of rewarding team performance is to rate team performance during periodic reviews. Each individual has three potential levels of involvement:

▲ *Facilitator*, with significant functional responsibility for execution.

▲ *Key member*, with significant functional responsibilities to accomplish.

▲ *Ordinary member*, with lower-level team effort required. Their roles are principally to give opinions and to coordinate the contributions of their functions.

Part of each individual's MBO, annual time distribution, and potential bonus is allocated to team efforts, with facilitators having the highest allocation and ordinary members the lowest.

Rewarding individuals for team performance pushes the team to be self-policing on performance and personnel competence. The team can't afford to have a laggard, because everyone's performance rating and bonus will suffer. Teams have rejected and asked for replacement of underperforming team members for this reason.

Some adventurous compensation advisers suggest awarding a bonus pot to the team and delegating to team members the task of splitting it up on the basis of their own perception of each member's contribution. For the most advanced teams, this might be the ultimate empowerment; for others, it could precipitate a feeding frenzy.

Nonfinancial Rewards

Don't overlook psychological rewards, which can outpace money for motivating performance. Herald and publicize the winning programs, and formally recognize the winners.

One company holds an annual conference for its product managers, in part to reward successful strategic planning. The meeting format includes substantial travel awards for the plans that have resulted in the best bottom-line results, as well as for the most innovative and most promising plans; show-and-tell presentations for the winning plans plus one or two others that were particularly well done or creative; education in one or more planning or strategic subjects that will lead to better long-term results; and a showcasing of internal and external resources, for example, market research, that can improve effectiveness.

Time Saved, Effectiveness Gained: A Case Study

A major Fortune 500 company mired its research, development, manufacturing, and engineering managers in endless quarterly reviews of dozens of strategic technical projects with the senior vice presidents of research and manufacturing. These two-day reviews were virtuoso performances of data transmission, technical theatrics, and program hype.

It took a Sherlock Holmes to detect reality. The meeting's purpose and agenda were further confused and presentations subsequently made guarded by the self-invited attendance of senior corporate officers "for their information."

Installation of the review process we have described in this chapter, combined with a new plan focus on a few high-priority programs, cut review time to two hours each for manufacturing and engineering. Outside personnel were not permitted to attend. Over a year's time, reviews became crisp, direct, issue- and decision-oriented, and honest. Complicated discussions and detailed technical reviews were held outside the review meetings when necessary. Focus, execution rate, and satisfaction with the process rose substantially.

DO'S AND DON'TS

DO

- *Establish and publicize a review mechanism,* stick to it, and make it one of your immutable management mechanisms and calendar fixtures.
- *Keep informally in touch* with key plan executioners between reviews to anticipate problems and to help forward movement.
- *Reward strategic success* psychologically and with money.

DON'T

- *Assume that plans and programs will happen* simply because people have committed to them and they're in writing; they won't. Implementation requires careful nurturing, review, and in-transit changes and reresourcing.
- *Hesitate to change the plan or resources* as soon as it's evident that it's needed. Don't wait for reviews and for events to run their course.

Chapter 14

After the First Plan: Updating and Improving With Much Less Pain

Any plan is bad which is not susceptible to change.
—Bartolommeo de San Concordio
Florentine painter and writer

The second year of planning, when the focus is on revising the priority issues and turning them into action, is a lot easier than the first. The plan does not need to be redone from scratch. You can revisit the situation analysis and assumptions, see what, if anything, has changed, and jump right to defining priority issues and determining action plans to address them. The second and subsequent years of strategic planning usually take less than one quarter the effort of the first.

The purpose of this chapter is to guide you as you:

▲ Update the situation analysis and determine if there have been or will be significant changes in the inside or the outside environment and in your assumptions.
▲ Involve many levels of the organization in updating the strategic and operational priority issues.
▲ Revise existing priority issue programs or develop new ones.
▲ Extend the strategic objectives, and link the objectives and strategic programs into the operating plan and budget.

The Continuing Process

In Figure 1-4 we present the continuing strategic planning process used after year one. Its steps are:

Corporate Prework

1. Update the situation analysis and financial forecast.
2. Update the internal analysis.

Lower-Level Meetings

3. Dip down into the organization to define strategic and operating priority issues at select lower levels.
4. Bubble up the strategic priority issues to be addressed at the top.

Corporate Priority Setting

5. Determine the new or revised priority issues, program suggestions, and objectives.

Program Development

6. Develop programs to address them.

Annual Planning Meeting

7. Extend and revise strategic and next year's objectives.
8. Agree on final programs, and allocate resources.

Implementation

9. Delegate the programs and objectives for accomplishment and fold them into the annual operating plans, budgets, and accountabilities.

Updating the Situation Analysis

Three parts of the situation analysis must be surgically updated: the external environmental analysis, the internal analysis, and the financial forecast.

External Analysis

To reaffirm or redefine external opportunities and threats, ask the individual or department that did the original external analysis to update it for changes and to circulate the revision to the top team. Pay particular attention to signaled structural changes in markets, customers, technological trends, and competitive activities that you must address.

Unless you developed your market strategies thoroughly the first year, consider a customer survey and market research to determine customer needs and market trends and how well you and your competition are responding to them. Then segment your markets and develop your marketing strategy.

Internal Analysis

You may want to circulate an organization diagnostic questionnaire probing the strengths and weaknesses of the organization in terms of culture, structure, managerial practices, systems, and personnel. Whether or not you did such a questionnaire the first year, do one now if the organization is not functioning well or is resisting change or if significant changes are under way and it is necessary to measure the extent of those changes (see Chapter 8). If a recent review of strategic programs has not been done, you should circulate a summary of the company's progress in adhering to last year's strategic objectives and programs.

Finally, review the results of any special studies, such as market research or organization diagnostics, prior to your priority-setting meeting.

Financial Forecast

Update the baseline forecast produced in the original plan, accounting for first-year plan results and experience.

The Priority-Issue Dip-Down

You can elicit lower-level involvement through the annual dip-down, which defines for most levels and functions:

▲ *Priority strategic issues*—issues that each department feels need to be addressed at its level and at the corporate level, along with ideas for new programs or modifications of current programs to address them
▲ *Priority operating issues*—issues that must be addressed to get operating results in the coming year at both the departmental level and the corporate level

The issues pertinent to the organization as a whole are passed up the managerial ranks for consideration at the top-level priority-setting meeting; those issues that are pertinent to action at lower levels stay there and are considered when putting together lower-level operating plans and budgets.

This annual lower-level involvement serves three purposes. First, it forces people to step back and think and surface critical issues. Second, it sends the most important issues to the top team. Third, and most important, it stimulates people at lower levels to think strategically about their jobs and departments and brings their activities into alignment with the corporate mission and priorities. This not only motivates people throughout the organization but also helps the subsequent implementation by getting lower-level employees to think about solutions to problems and issues before they are asked to act. After all, they are the implementers. With their extensive and early involvement, the solutions to problems will be more creative, employee commitment will be greater, and the results will be more impressive.

Top-Team Prework

Ask top-team members, as they do their personal prework, to answer this question: Has anything changed from the prior year, and, if so, what should we do about it? Top-team members should come to the priority-setting meeting prepared to present their personal perceptions of (1) changes in critical external factors, such as market conditions, competition, and technology, and in the company's strengths, weaknesses, opportunities, and threats; (2) where the company is and is not making progress in achieving the written vision directions; and (3) corporate priority issues and ideas on how to address them. Their preparation should include the dip-down for information described earlier in this chapter.

The Annual Priority-Setting Meeting

The annual corporate priority-setting meeting is the pivotal event in the planning calendar. All key strategic and operating actions throughout the organization in the next year will be based on its results. The meeting and the process leading to it are scaled-down versions of those described in Chapters 7 and 9. With adequate prework, the meeting itself is usually completed in one to one-and-a-half days.

A typical agenda is shown in Figure 14-1.

In reality, priority issues for most organizations don't change much from year to year. What you do about them as you make progress does

Figure 14-1. Annual priority-setting meeting agenda.*

90 min.	1. Review of current plan—SWOTs, assumptions, markets, competition, and trouble spots; continued validity of strategies. Are there changes? If so, what are their implications?
120 min.	2. Review of mission statement. Are any changes needed? How is the organization moving toward achieving the vision and the strategic objectives? Are there gaps? How will they be addressed?
15 min.	3. Summarize accomplishments in addressing last year's priority issues.
70 min.	4. Presentations from staff and line managers on their divisions' strategic and operating priority issues and the programs they will develop to address them (maximum of ten minutes per manager).
60 min.	5. Consensus on top five strategic priority issues for the next year.
60 min.	6. Consensus on top five operating priority issues for the next year.
15 min.	7. Identification of issues for program development.
90 min.	8. Tentative programs to address priority issues. Assignment of responsibility for program development.
8 3/4 hrs.	•••

*The timing suggested is approximate.

change, however. For example, Western Supermarkets has for years had five to six priority strategic issues, three of which were on the list for at least five years. These three were customer service and friendliness, cost structure, and "out-of-stocks" (defined as percentage of frequently purchased merchandise on the shelf at all times in all stores).

Western began specific programs to address customer service and friendliness, providing simple "smile" training and basic motivational programs to create a positive associate-customer interface—in other words, to stop clerks from snarling at customers! The company progressed through the years to more sophisticated and less obvious programs, most successful but some not, that included providing video carts to help shoppers locate items and identify special promotions; introducing scanning systems that record specific customer purchase patterns and offer customers discounts on frequently purchased items;

initiating frequent-shopper reward programs; and offering training in product use and preparation in departments such as meat, seafood, and wines.

Similarly, cost containment and reduction programs progressed from simple actions to reduce staffing and overhead to far more complicated and long-lasting structural changes. For example, the company installed sophisticated computer-driven systems for ordering, inventorying, and tracking store deliveries and for monitoring the cost and profitability of merchandise.

The Annual Planning Meeting: Fleshing Out and Approving the Programs

After the priority-setting meeting, the top team delegates the priority issues, objectives, and program suggestions to individuals and teams whose task is to design programs to address them. These plans are presented for top-team approval at the subsequent annual planning meeting. (See Chapter 10 for program development procedures.)

The top team then holds its strategic planning meeting for approximately one-and-one-half to two days to fine-tune the new high-priority programs, allocate resources, and establish revised strategic objectives and those for next year's operating plan and budget.

Linkages Between Plans and Budget

If you have designed and sequenced your planning process well, you should have a smooth fit among your strategic plans, your operating plan, your functional plans, and your budget. The keys to a smooth process, as laid out in the flowchart in Figure 1-4, Chapter 1, are to:

▲ Allow plenty of time to complete each step.
▲ Train key managers in what's required.
▲ Document the process in a simple, paint-by-the-numbers annual planning manual.
▲ Use strategic and operating priority issues as the thread from which you weave the whole cloth of budget and action plans for achieving long- and short-term results.
▲ Base individual accountabilities at all levels on these priorities, as well as on the numbers.

It takes several years to develop a smooth planning process. Once developed, however, the process will operate almost seamlessly, allowing people to concentrate on the few priorities that will result in meaningful change and operating results.

When to Start Over From Scratch

You should redo your strategic plan from scratch under two circumstances: first, when the outside world changes significantly and existing actions are not adequate to respond to them, and second, when you're getting stale and plans start to rehash old ideas and simply dust off previous years' thinking. In practice, this usually means starting over every four to five years.

When the World Changes

All bets are off when the outside world changes. For example, a significant new competitor may enter the market, as happened to IBM and Compaq when Dell Computer strode into the market in the mid-1980s, threatening their markets with PC clones and eroding their profitability. IBM and Compaq did not adequately respond. Pushed in 1992 by a forceful new chairman who was unhappy with profitability, market share, and stock price declines, Compaq radically reconfigured its strategies in just 120 days. Its new but belated strategy included direct marketing and the mass merchandising of inexpensive PCs. This new approach allowed Compaq to successfully enter new product and market segments, gaining major market share. Or the market may undergo a pivotal structural change. For example, uncertain oil supplies, shortages, and stringent environmental regulations caused successful chemical companies to alter drastically their external and internal strategies in the 1970s and 1980s. When you encounter circumstances like these, you should assiduously go through the entire planning process, paying particular attention to the external analysis and the extent to which you are internally configured (i.e., have the appropriate resources) to respond.

When You Get Stale

It's all too easy to get complacent and assume that the world is not going to change and that you're doing just fine. To counteract this kind of thinking, it is a good idea to redo your plan from the ground up, beginning with a good organization diagnostic, every four to five years. An objective outside facilitator and consultant can help you avoid ingrown thinking and warmed-over plans.

A major publisher of religious books and curriculum materials had been going through the motions of strategic planning for years with little structural change in its businesses and was facing a significant loss of market share. The company's fatal flaw was that each operating unit used the strategic plan to justify budget expenditures rather than objectively looking at its marketplace, responding appropriately and innovatively to changes, and bubbling key issues to the top for decision and allocation of resources.

The Bumpy Road to a Smooth Process

It takes time to merge the strategic planning process with the annual operating planning and budgeting processes that exist in most companies. The focus is usually on the budget, just the opposite of where it should be. The budget should be based on programs developed during the strategic and operating planning process.

The evolution of the process at ONTARIO CHEMICALS, INC., is enlightening. OCI was producing something it called a strategic plan every three years, along with its annual operating plan and budget. Unfortunately, the strategic plan was based on numbers and not on incisive analysis, and the annual operating plans mixed strategic and operating thinking, containing a situation analysis and other features that were also part of the strategic plan. OCI failed to assign crisp accountabilities and programs for either strategic or operating priorities. In short, the planning process produced tons of paper and incremental year-to-year profit improvements, but little measurable structural strategic progress.

In response to a radically changing marketplace and dissatisfaction with internal performance, OCI's new president attempted to make strategic planning a tool for change. In the first year, the company's top team identified the key issues to be addressed: organization competence, product innovation, marketing effectiveness, manufacturing cost, and top-team teamwork. It made little headway in addressing these issues, however; it tried to do too much too soon. The strategic plan was developed painfully and was out of synch with the operating plan and budget. There was confusion about what belonged in which document. A cumbersome, detailed market segmentation and strategy exercise sapped energy from overstressed sales executives, some of whose ability to handle additional work and to think in marketing terms was questionable. Action plans were still not crisply defined, and the tendency was to do more of the same: Stay very operational and make next year happen. The planners jumped right to the budget and of course requested more people to accomplish strategic change rather than think about ways to reconfigure or reinvigorate the organization to invoke strategic change without inordinate increases in cost.

In the second year, OCI streamlined the process. Work that was repeated for writing both the strategic plan and the operating plan was eliminated. The process began on time, allowing plenty of time to complete the tasks. The focus was on developing the priority issues and the programs to address them and on placing accountability on the shoulders of those responsible for executing the programs. However, the president of the company was distracted by his search for acquisitions and new personnel. In addition, a number of poor-performing top-team members were replaced. The result was good focus on priorities but less-than-stellar execution.

By the end of the third year, virtually all the top-team members whom the president had inherited had been replaced and members were beginning to function as a true team. Most key employees were familiar and relatively comfortable with the planning process. The president simplified the process further by focusing the top team on developing its priority issues early on in the annual planning process. Team members dipped down into the organization for a view of departmental and corporate priorities, subsequently agreeing (in a top-team retreat) on the priorities that would be funded and acted upon. Action on the priorities was then driven down into the organization through objectives and program action plans.

The president refocused his energies internally. He became more of a hands-on manager to ensure that plan execution was good. He commented, "How nice it is that at last my people hold meetings and make decisions without me and just get on with the job." That was a direct reflection of having highly competent people with a strong direction and a strong plan—one that they helped formulate and buy in to and one that *they* will execute.

DO'S AND DON'TS

DO

- *Revise* your plan annually, focusing on changes in the market and on competitive activity.
- *Look at the outside world* and redo your plan from scratch when there are significant structural changes.
- *Get all levels to focus* on priority strategic and operating issues. This is your most important recurring planning task.

- *Have a simple annual process* that addresses priority issues through concise, focused operating plans, budgets, and individual accountabilities.

DON'T

- Make your annual process *paper-heavy and cumbersome.*
- *Focus on the planning process* itself instead of on the issues and actions that need to be taken.

Chapter 15

Five Years of Planning: Benchmarks of Accomplishment

Draw from others the lesson that may profit yourself.

—Terence, Roman poet

Whether you install a companywide planning process or put out fires in your first year of planning, it will be years before your process is fine-tuned and you reap major strategic results. What follows is a realistic five-year planning schedule, based on more than twenty case histories. It describes our typical moderate to large organization as it goes through the strategic change process introduced in Chapter 3, identifying anticipated planning accomplishments and tangible business outcomes. (Figure 15-1 presents highlights of the five years.) The chapter concludes with two case histories.

Year One: Recognition/Elation: Identify the Issues

The job of first-year planners is to design the process as the company enters the "recognition/elation" stage and decides to do something about its strategic situation. Planners facilitate development of the first plan, focusing on developing a mission, strategic thrusts, and solutions to the most pressing strategic and fix-the-ship priority issues.

The Planning Job

▲ Conduct a brief strategic and organization audit.
▲ Design a process.

Figure 15-1. Benchmarks of accomplishment.

	1. Elation/Recognition YEAR 1	2. Unfreezing/Muddling YEARS 2–3	3. Strategic Change YEARS 3–5	4. Constant strategic renewal YEAR 4 PLUS
PLANNING	▶ Design a process ▶ Set corporate strategy ▶ Define priority issues and programs	▶ Install accountability systems ▶ Install planning at lower levels ▶ Continue priority-issue focus	▶ Place facilitation in company's hands ▶ Integrate strategic operating, budget planning	▶ Begin ground-up situation analysis ▶ Perform informal internal and external audits ▶ Maintain strategic performance indicators
BUSINESS	▶ Costs cut ▶ Key people and organization structure decisions identified ▶ Modest priority program results obtained	▶ Removal/replacement/restructuring unproductive people, businesses, organization units ▶ Higher profitability and market performance decisions ▶ High rate of priority program accomplishment ▶ Systems infrastructure barriers fixed	▶ Strong strategic results in new products, acquisitions, internal structural change ▶ Top quartile industry/market niche performance new products, acquisitions, internal structural change ▶ Top quartile industry/market niche performance	▶ Continued operation at higher performance levels ▶ Strategic thinking and change process imbedded throughout organization

TIME →

KEY ACCOMPLISHMENTS

▲ Through formal and OJT methods, train top officers and key managers in strategic planning and implementation.

▲ Understand critical success factors and the internal competencies needed to support them for chosen target markets.

▲ Agree on the corporate strategy, particularly on the mission, target markets, products and services, objectives, and strategic thrust.

▲ Identify information gaps, particularly regarding external markets, competitive information, and culture/climate and when and how you're going to do something about them.

▲ Agree on the priority issues that affect the company's ability to move forward strategically or constitute barriers to progress.

▲ Develop programs to address the priority issues.

▲ Delegate these programs to leverage managers and the organization pressure points that must implement them.

▲ Install accountability systems if none exist.

▲ Monitor and review to make sure that objectives and actions support priority-issue programs throughout the company as planning progresses.

▲ Enforce accountability of pressure points and others responsible for programs and tasks.

Tangibles

▲ First evidence that company is beginning to solve problems and remove barriers to future success.

▲ Obvious cuts in overhead and operating costs.

▲ Enforced accountabilities and a lot of hands-on help and monitoring by top management in an effort to get immediate results with existing products, customers, and people.

▲ Frustration with poor key managers and functional areas unable to cope with change.

▲ Elimination of some, but not enough, unproductive people, unprofitable products and customers, and wasteful internal programs.

▲ Addition of or search for a few key people needed to cause change.

▲ Painfully drawn decisions to replace most underskilled, underperforming leverage people; restructuring of the organization to meet future needs; beginning of actions to implement these decisions.

▲ At best, moderate success in executing strategic programs and achieving strategic objectives. The organization is struggling to reallocate resources from the short to the long term, find a planning pace it can handle, learn to set realistic objectives, deal with changes in people and culture, and face up to its problems.

Years Two and Three: Unfreezing/Muddling: Remove Barriers

In their second and third years of planning, most businesses delegate the process, install accountabilities throughout the company, refine their priorities, see some significant results, and make needed organization changes.

The Planning Job

▲ Audit the process and the organization: what's working and what's not.

▲ Refine the process, which should be seated and understood at the top level.

▲ Get lower-level inputs into corporate priority issues, and then delegate strategic objectives and programs back down for implementation.

▲ Evolve the programs to address priority issues. The issues will be largely unchanged, but the programs should be more concise and implementable and at a higher level of sophistication and expansion. One or two issues may be added and one or two dropped or delegated to day-to-day operations as they are resolved.

▲ Install planning in lower-level departments and business units not initially covered so that they plan and develop priority issues and executional programs for their own functions.

▲ Conduct training in facilitation for key team members and leaders at all levels.

▲ Install adequate systems for monitoring and measuring short-term and strategic results.

▲ Determine how you stack up against the competition in terms of product line success, customer and market segment profitability, customer service levels and customer satisfaction, and market penetration by benchmarking profitability, innovation, cost, and efficiency.

▲ Install performance management (MBO) and compensation systems that reward strategic performance and enforce accountabilities.

▲ Fine-tune the strategy based on first-year feedback and more formal and extensive market research and input from customers and from within the organization.

▲ Use internal cofacilitators at top levels, begin to involve other levels in facilitation, and begin phaseout of intensive external facilitation.

▲ Do team building if needed.

▲ Undertake key market and customer surveys to increase your understanding of the marketplace.

▲ Continue planning education, and communicate its importance to strengthen it and to convince skeptics.

▲ Integrate the strategic planning process into the annual operating plan and budget.

Tangibles

▲ Beginning of resolution of major barriers to strategic progress

▲ Removal of unprofitable businesses or those with poor prospects, marginal people, and marginal products

▲ Replacement of deadwood with new, key change agent personnel, particularly at senior management levels

▲ Completion of organization restructuring

▲ Increase in new competencies and higher productivity among old personnel as a result of training, planning, coaching and counseling, and new methods and systems

▲ Strategic change in organization structure, such as new customer service structure, with appropriate new personnel and systems, new manufacturing control systems, and so on

▲ Increased market penetration and improved profitability of existing product and markets

▲ New products introduced and accelerated

▲ Work begun on identifying new markets, customer groups, and products/services for future entry

Years Three to Four: Structural Strategic Change

Overlapping the period of removing barriers, years three to four should see strategic planning become relatively well accepted as a way of life at many levels. By now, its importance to long-term results and personal rewards should be recognized throughout the company. The process should be pared to a bare minimum and smoothly integrated into the operating plan and budget. Facilitation should be fully in the organization's hands as top management focuses on ensuring that the process continues to work and devotes a higher than historical percentage of its time to setting future strategy, while lower-level management thinks about strategy and continuous improvement of productivity for its own function.

This is a period of structural strategic change as the organization imbeds the process, gets meaningful results, and focuses on strategic priorities as a way of life.

The Planning Job

▲ Update key parts of plan only on the basis of changes in inside and outside worlds.
▲ Review and refresh priority issues, and address those that retain their urgency with greater sophistication. As success in handling issues becomes a way of life, put the old problems to bed and confront new ones.
▲ Use advanced market research and competitive analysis techniques, as well as new management methods, to address barriers and move ahead of the competition.
▲ Turn most facilitation over to company employees.

Tangibles

▲ Elimination of short-term strategic barriers, such as debilitating cost structures, poor personnel, and lack of teamwork
▲ First results from earlier strategic programs, particularly lasting structural changes, including productive new organization forms, new products, acquisitions, entry into new markets, and improved customer service position and perceptions
▲ High rate of strategic program implementation throughout the company
▲ Noticeable cultural changes, including higher organization energy, better focus, improved teamwork and coordination, higher standards, and better innovation and creativity
▲ Noticeably improved bottom line. The company approaches or reaches top quartile performance for its industry or market niches

Years Four and Five: Constant Strategic Renewal

By now, the process is fully installed at the corporate level, in the business units, and throughout all departments. The company is getting significant strategic and operating results at all levels and in most functions. Benchmarked against the competition, it is in a strong position in targeted markets. Strategic thinking, action planning, and accountability and continuous productivity improvement are a way of life for key leverage managers and pressure points throughout the organization. The culture dotes on positive change and teamwork and naturally selects people who impel it.

As the process becomes standard operating procedure, however, there's a danger that it may get stale. Organizations need to refocus on priorities and changes in both the outside and the inside world to prevent insularity. Some companies may need to redo the plan completely.

The Planning Job

▲ Keep doing formal and informal internal and external audits to ensure that the organization is on track, is not getting complacent, and is in touch with changes in the outside world.
▲ Through market research, monitor key strategic performance indicators (e.g., market share, quality, service, image, new products, customer needs).
▲ Do another thorough situation analysis from the ground up, and reexamine the organization's mission, objectives, and strategies.

Tangibles

▲ Eighty-five percent success in meeting strategic objectives and accomplishing strategic projects on time
▲ Approaching industry/market segment leadership in profitability, creating increased shareholder value
▲ Recognition as an industry or market sector leader in critical success factors
▲ High achievement on priority-issue programs
▲ Organization pride in its strategic results and its continuing planning process

Evolving and Imbedding the Process Over the Years: Holistic Planning in a Large, Complex Company

In the early 1980s WESTERN SUPERMARKETS, a billion-dollar-plus regional chain, dominated metropolitan markets in three states and extended into several neighboring states. Its 180 stores served a broad population with a wide selection of merchandise in five groups: grocery, dairy, frozen, general merchandise, and perishables, including in-store restaurants and take-out food services. Within these five business groups were more than sixty important categories ranging from fresh fish to photo processing. Western's complex operations also included massive warehouses, a transportation and real estate company, and manufacturing operations producing milk and dairy products, eggs, take-out foods, and bakery items.

Although it was a public company, Western was controlled and managed by members of its founding family. It needed to make the managerial and generational transition from father to two sons and from its old-line, top-down, paternalistic style to that of a professionally managed corporation. At the same time, it faced a mature, relatively stagnant market, new competition from food discounters and a local upscale supermarket chain, and a dearth of desirable new locations for expansion within its existing market area.

Management started formal planning with three aims. One was to instill financial and strategic focus, first at the top and then throughout the organization. Another was to protect the company against erosion from increasing competition. The final aim was to grow beyond the chain's stagnant geographical area into underserved adjacent markets.

First there were significant cultural, personnel, management-systems, and cost issues to be addressed. Most personnel had grown up with the business. Managers of departments and categories proudly stated that they had started at low-level positions such as bagger and had risen through the ranks. While they were good at buying, advertising, displaying, and selling merchandise on a day-to-day basis, they weren't used to thinking in terms of target markets, competitive strategies, or category innovation or even efficiently managing internal costs, inventory, and communications.

Year One

Western started its change process with team building, led by a professional psychologist, who worked first with top management and subsequently with lower levels. It was the first step toward changing Western's top-down organizational character into a culture emphasizing teamwork, delegation, and accountability. With one of his sons in the position of president, the chairman removed himself from day-to-day operations so that the son's authority would not be undermined.

During the team-building sessions, top management developed a mission statement. Before moving on to objectives, competitive strategies, and action programs, however, the team engaged a strategic planning consultant to conduct a brief audit.

Taking an issue-oriented approach, Western identified the priority strategic issues, using inputs from three levels of managers and staff. A thirteen-person top-management group distilled inputs and identified the final five corporate priorities. Key meetings were facilitated by the consultant. The resulting priority issues were: (1) customer service and focus; (2) geographic expansion; (3) efficiency of operations; (4) quality of the perishable foods department; and (5) store standards: stock, service, and conditions.

The planning consultant and the psychologist structured a two-and-one-half day retreat for the top thirty-five managers in the corporation. After the president presented the company's financial and growth goals, cross-functional teams developed fifteen programs to address the five priority issues. Appointed team leaders were to be held accountable for implementing their action plans.

Execution rate during the first year was mediocre, with about 60 percent of the action plan objectives and tasks completed. Hindsight showed the reason for the delays: There were too many programs, objectives, and action plans, some of which were not very measurable. Significant problems arose in coordinating joint actions among the numerous departments. Strategic programs ran into time conflicts with the day-to-day activities needed to keep the business running, and the president observed that there was inadequate change in the cultural pattern of reacting to short-term pressures and avoiding responsibility and accountability for strategic programs and long-term results.

Although the first-year programs resulted in significant improvements in teamwork and customer orientation within the stores, strategic thinking and accountability were largely absent.

Year Two

Management completed the organization and strategic audit and took additional steps toward better strategic thinking and management.

First, all senior managers attended a week-long in-house seminar in strategic marketing. They learned the strategic planning process and the principles of competitive market strategy. They also drew up a profile of Western's target customer: simply stated, the nonprice buyer, primarily in the middle- to upper-income range, who shopped for service and quality. They agreed on their strategic thrust: service; variety; and new, innovative, and advanced products, services, and concepts. And they determined which key departments, products, and services would be used to implement that thrust and the executional details of how they would do it. They also embarked on a program to build or acquire stores outside their existing markets.

Agreeing to focus on service and variety of product targeted toward an upscale market eliminated an historic strategic seesaw. No longer would the company switch its competitive strategy back and forth between price and service according to transient changes in the competition and market share.

Second, the company took steps to improve implementation of operating and strategic objectives and accountability of those responsible for executing company plans and programs. It installed management by objectives and performance appraisal systems at senior management levels and called in a compensation expert to help design a compensation and bonus system that rewarded performance. While the reward system improved strategic focus and results, it had the unwanted side effects of narrowly focusing people on their proprietary projects, inhibiting their cooperation with others who needed their help, and causing grumbling about provincialism. In subsequent years the reward system was changed to include assessments of teamwork. Meanwhile, the planning system was modified to emphasize up-front, prebudget commitment of the interdepartmental resources needed to accomplish each strategic project. These moves drastically improved needed cooperation and coordination.

Western refined its annual process to identify and refresh corporate strategic and priority issues, determine the year's strategic programs, and conduct the annual retreat. The results were codified in a manual that could be used, with minor modification, from year to year. Key changes from the first year included: encouraging team development of programs and action plans before the annual retreat; using the retreat to critique, modify, and coordinate program action plans instead of developing them on the spot; and taking steps to ensure agreement on interdepartmental actions and sharing of resources where mandated.

Finally, after the second-year retreat, top management shared the plans with lower levels and implementors who were not present at the meeting. Only after their input was received were plans "chiseled in stone" and parts incorporated in individuals' personal objectives.

Management turned the documented annual planning process over to human resources to manage but continued to use organization behavior and planning consultants to facilitate key meetings and processes. A complete strategy document summarizing the company's mission, target markets, products and services, financial objectives, and competitive strategies was written and communicated to key managers.

The execution rate for programs and objectives rose to 80–85 percent that year, thanks to clearer and more doable objectives, better coordination, and improved accountability. Nonetheless, problems still impeded efforts to coordinate interdepartmental actions and to push strategic thinking, action, and accountabilities down to the managers of the fifty to sixty key merchandise categories.

In addition, the performance of new stores within Western's current market and in some new markets was not up to expectation. Management determined that its store format and market-entry strategies were in some ways flawed, and steps were taken to help ensure better site selection, management, and profitability of future expansions. To allow management to work on improving profitability and moving the existing business forward strategically, further expansion was put on hold.

Year Three

Western made staff changes in operations, marketing, and some merchandise categories to put more aggressive, action-oriented people in key slots, and the MBO system went into effect throughout the company. The firm pushed planning down to the category-manager level, where twenty-two category managers and assistants oversaw sixty categories. The category managers were to become business managers for their categories, taking on responsibility not only for merchandising and buying and for month-to-month and annual financial results but also for innovation and long-term direction.

The company developed a planning manual for category managers, trained them in the planning process, and provided outside assistance to help them through their first set of plans. Significantly, priorities were put on merchandise categories, and category managers were charged with developing strategic plans for identified high-potential or problem categories. To ensure that the proposed plans would use wide functional inputs to make key strategic decisions, allocate strategic resources well, and assign accountabilities, the plans went through a review system that required the approval of the company president. To review category-plan progress, the company established a quarterly review system. To motivate managers to plan thoroughly, immediate decisions were made to allocate resources to projects of merit and to withhold resources from inadequately planned projects.

Several high-quality plans with significant and measurable financial impact resulted, including the introduction of one-hour, in-store photo processing and display, product, and merchandising improvements in the candy and greeting card departments. That year, Western instituted a category managers' conference to train category managers in new planning or category management skills, showcase potentially useful internal functions such as market research and information systems, and highlight and reward with foreign trips the plans that had the highest impact or that demonstrated the greatest creativity.

Despite all this, the first year of category planning was rough. Plans were sometimes poorly done, and there was cynicism about management's commitment to the process and about the ultimate impact of the plans. In addition, because an in-house staff coordinator was running the process, the merchandise vice presidents didn't truly own and embrace it.

After a year of category planning, Western recognized that overall plans for the five major merchandising departments—grocery, dairy, frozen, perishables, and general merchandise—should have been completed first. This would have put the responsibility for success firmly on the shoulders of the merchandising vice presidents and given their subordinate category managers the overall framework within which to develop their plans. The company created a new position, senior vice president of merchandising, and appointed a seasoned, aggressive individual who understood and pushed the appropriate balance between "making money day to day and week to week," improving support services such as warehousing and advertising, and strategic and category planning.

While the company struggled with lower-level planning, the corporate level continued to set annual strategic priorities, programs, and action plans in a process that now operated smoothly.

Year Four

The merchandising vice presidents developed plans at their level while category-level planning continued under that umbrella. Although some of the first-pass plans were rough and creating them was a difficult learning experience, the vice presidents owned and pushed the process, and it became firmly imbedded.

Western's personnel facilitated their own meetings, including their annual retreat. The process and its documentation were, for the most part, in their hands; outside consultants played only a minor role at category-manager conferences and in fine-tuning activities.

Merchandising group and category planning finally became smoothly integrated into Western's annual strategic and operating planning and budgeting, as was proper. A handful of new, high-priority merchandise categories were selected each year for detailed planning, as were the corporate strategic priority issues and programs.

Year Five

With the phasing out of external consultants, Western revamped its family-dominated board of directors to include high-level food and retail executives to get more outside input on its strategic efforts.

Significantly, over five years and in a stagnant market, Western's market penetration increased slightly and its profitability improved by over 50 percent, thus achieving its original strategic objectives. In addition, Western's major competitor for the upscale market was weakened, its announced aggressive expansion program was rescinded, and significant ground was lost to Western.

Some problems still remained. Operating results at problem expansion stores improved significantly, but they were still not up to corporate standards. And some internal operations were not as efficient as desired. Western still needed to deal with aggressive new discount competition in its highly competitive markets and to continue work on geographic expansion and major categories in need of strategic planning.

Finally, Western discovered that the financial hurdle had been raised. Though the company had achieved its first objective—above-average profitability for the industry—it discovered that similar chains in other parts of the country were significantly more profitable. It vowed to achieve profitability equivalent to those regional leaders during its next planning period. Fortunately, the management and systems were in place to plan changes needed to meet the new profit goals and deal with the rapidly changing marketplace and category-competitive situations.

Turning Around a Small Entrepreneurial Company: So Much to Do, So Little Time: Issue-Focused Planning

PHW, a small, family-owned company that specializes in selling fire and casualty insurance to banks to cover repossessed or uncovered mortgaged properties, had an excellent product and good market position. Nonetheless, it was losing money and was in danger of bankruptcy. Both supported and pressed by a nonfamily officer, who wanted to retire, and his son, who was running the largest division, the CEO sought "strategic planning" to cure PHW's ills. He brought in a professional facilitator/planner to help develop a strategic plan.

The consultant began with an internal audit. Interviews with fifteen key management and support people and twenty customers revealed how well the company was perceived in the marketplace. Respondents gave superior ratings to its policies, service, and the computer systems that interfaced with the customer. The company's market penetration varied significantly from city to city and state to state, however, and there was no systematic selling and market penetration effort.

Internally, the company was in costly turmoil. Over the years, a kind and paternalistic chief executive had concentrated on sales and had spent very little time fixing problems, installing budgets or controls, developing people, or dealing with internal inefficiencies. A major computer system upgrade had stalled, and to keep up without it the company was pouring immense expenditures into internal and external personnel. Overhead and selling expenses were way out of line with industry standards. One business unit, a retail agency, was poorly managed and bleeding heavily; an underperforming, sick acquisition had diluted capital and losses were sapping the bottom line. In many areas staff was underqualified, overpaid, unproductive, and certainly not held accountable. Fortunately, the competition was not aggressive.

The situation dictated an issue-oriented approach. In fact, the company did no formal planning. Instead, in three heated, highly interactive sessions, two consultants, the CEO, his son, and the CFO/treasurer identified six do-or-die issues that acknowledged the need to (1) cut overhead and expenses; (2) evaluate personnel to identify and cut deadwood and surplus; (3) reorganize into a more efficient and market-oriented structure; (4) increase market penetration; (5) quickly complete the new computer system, which formed the core of effective customer service and internal cost efficiencies; and (6) quickly sell the losing agency. They determined that a spending cut of $800,000, or 10 percent of revenue, would bring them to the break-even point. An additional $800,000 in profit would bring them to their minimum objective of 13 percent pretax profit, the ultimate objective being 20 percent (a leadership position for their industry). Given the company's internal fat and inefficiencies and its underpenetration of the market, this objective looked reasonable and in fact was exceeded.

The company acted quickly. First, it put the sick brokerage business, only an adjunct to the main business, up for sale. Second, it cut 30 percent of staff, including several ineffective officers and managers in key positions. Third, it developed rigorous job descriptions for key top managers and defined objectives and accountabilities, including the company's first detailed cost budget, department by department. Fourth, it stopped its stifling habit of management by committee, which had slowed or stopped strategic innovation and progress and had brought decision making to a virtual standstill. In addition, the son took over as CEO and ran the company on a very short, taut directive leash while using team input where appropriate to make key decisions and run critical projects.

The company also made key personnel changes. The CEO turned sales management over to a highly aggressive former regional sales manager who oversaw the revamping of the sales force and the development of a computer system that tracked sales force performance and fed back competitive information to headquarters. A new chief information officer was appointed and a new CFO brought in from the outside.

Finally, PHW developed systems to locate the geographical areas in which the company was not adequately penetrating the market and the accounts that were not delivering profitable, desirable business. It also started a pilot prospecting program to qualify and sell to desirable unpenetrated accounts.

At the end of the first year of issue-oriented planning, the company was running at break-even, efficiencies were up despite a 30 percent decrease in personnel, and the program to increase market penetration was under way.

Focus groups and a telephone survey revealed that PHW's existing and targeted customers judged its products and customer service to be excellent and, for the most part, superior to those of the competition. That result confirmed management's conviction that internal problems were driving the company's lack of profitability and that there was time to fix them before competition took its toll.

During the second year of its planning process, PHW continued to reduce staff, improve its marketing, and upgrade its computer systems. It was profitable, earning a 15 percent return on pretax income, very close to its strategic objective.

PHW entered its third year, it felt, well positioned to grow. To gain complete control, the son of the founder purchased the company from his father through a leveraged buyout.

PHW found that while it had addressed many of its operational issues, it still faced a number of additional problems. First, a suitable buyer for the agency could not be found. The CEO decided that the agency could become profitable if revenue grew rapidly enough to reach a prescribed critical mass, if it had a pro to run it, and if it added more standard insurance lines to its portfolio. He also decided that keeping the agency and its stable property and casualty business would offset the cyclical turns of the blanket-fire insurance business. He accomplished his objectives through acquisition of another agency and its book of business, chief executive, and complementary insurance lines.

Second, PHW's new environmental product line, which insures purchasers of real estate against claims for prior environmental damage and necessary cleanup, was not faring well; it was losing money and had to be repositioned and shored up—or dropped. Subsequent negotiations yielded a contract with a major carrier to market and administer PHW's environmental insurance program nationally. Third, the system for identifying and directing the sales force to underpenetrated accounts was foundering and a year late. Finally, the market had softened, leading to a deterioration of prices and the loss of a key account.

These factors, coupled with investment in diversification projects, reduced third-year profitability to 8 percent of sales before tax. In addition, the CEO found that he had relinquished too much control over day-to-day operations while he was cleaning up and repositioning the company. Although he remained confident that PHW would achieve its 20 percent return on income, he felt that he had to spend more time concentrating on operations. This was necessary to ensure that targeted market penetration took place, core product lines were enhanced in time to bolster PHW's basic market position, new products were developed and tested that took advantage of its systems and distribution strengths, profit objectives were met, and finally, that remaining personnel were forged into a team with the necessary skills to handle further growth.

DO'S AND DON'TS

DO

- *Recognize that planning takes years* to develop a complete and effective process and to get strategic results.
- *Plot where you expect to get to in the first three to four years,* both in the process and in tangible results, so that your expectations are realistic. Use the change model (see Chapters 3 and 15) as your guide.

DON'T

- *Assume a straight path to success.* The road is littered with detours and unexpected successes as you drive toward your goal. Use planning to react effectively to these unpredictable, sometimes welcome and sometimes not, distortions of your game plan.

Part Four

Team Processes

Chapter 16

Effective Teams and Productive Team Members

Grant ran his staff as a sort of barbershop meeting, where those with a place round the spittoon were as free to air their views as they were to spit tobacco juice or—depending how late the evening had drawn—take a pull at the friendly bottle.

—John Keegan, British military historian

At the core of the strategic planning process in this book is the team. Teams provide the coordination that makes the process work, not only in the planning phase, but during implementation.

Essentially, teams do what line managers do. They:

▲ *Plan*, determining their mission, objectives, strategies, programs, and action plans.
▲ *Organize* their efforts by finding the needed human, physical, and capital resources and putting them into action.
▲ *Assign tasks* to team members who have the power and resources to get them done or take the responsibility for persuading non-team members to do the necessary work.
▲ *Accept accountability* for accomplishing results.

If the role of the team parallels that of the traditional manager, why not just use the existing management hierarchy to plan and implement strategy? Because teams are better than the traditional line organization at implementing complex, multifunctional, multilayer projects that require high involvement and have high economic impact.

Made up of empowered representatives of the key functions involved, a cross-functional implementation team has the knowledge and resources to determine the right course of action and the best sequence of steps. It can function efficiently, breaking through bottlenecks with the least expenditure of time and money and the least disruption of the existing business.

Companies that implement through teams reap a wealth of other benefits, including:

▲ *Collaboration.* Team members help one another achieve the objectives of the team and support each individual's contribution to those objectives.
▲ *Communication.* Within teams, members get early warnings of potential problems and early news of upcoming opportunities.
▲ *Commitment,* which results from wrestling with an issue until the team achieves consensus on the best solution to a problem.
▲ *Realism.* Thrashing out implementation details kills pie-in-the-sky and wishful thinking and results in realistically sequenced multifunctional events. A new product launch, for example, calls for a well-thought-out sequence of tasks, progressing, sometimes consecutively and sometimes concurrently, from engineering to manufacturing to marketing.
▲ *A doable pace* that accommodates the resource demands made by both the existing business and programs for strategic change so that both get accomplished.
▲ *Accountability.* Through peer pressure, teams are self-policing. In plotting success and avoiding failure, members hold one another accountable and are far tougher on themselves than their superiors are likely to be. They are also faster at getting rid of noncontributors.

What Team Members Gain

As teams mature, their members acquire characteristics and attributes that serve them well in both their team and their individual activities. Through their involvement in teams, people develop:

▲ *Trust.* Team members learn that they won't get hurt if they are direct, honest, and willing to deal positively with conflict and controversy. They discover that others will understand and help them overcome their own functional and managerial shortcomings and that they can provide the same support for their teammates.
▲ *Creativity.* Teams push and energize their members to generate creative ideas and solutions.
▲ *Strategic thinking.* Most teams have to take the corporate perspec-

tive, exposing them to overall strategy and its implications for diverse functions and multiple layers.

▲ *A broader perspective.* Teams pull people out of their functional boxes, expose them to other functions, and teach them to be sensitive to others' needs. Team members are also often exposed to senior management and therefore have the chance to observe the skills they themselves will need for promotion.

Types of Teams

There are five types of teams that contribute to developing and implementing strategic plans. In most companies there is a place for all five: business teams, functional teams, formal program teams, informal temporary teams, and ongoing work teams. Although the team dynamics are similar in each, their purpose, makeup, and life span vary widely.

1. *Business and functional management teams.* Business teams and functional management teams literally run businesses or functional areas, respectively. Epitomized by the top corporate management team, they can also operate at other levels of the organization, such as strategic business units, or in functional areas such as human resources or marketing. A management team usually exists for the life of the business or for as long as its unit is an effective form within the organizational structure.

At the highest level, the top management team usually has representatives from all important functions in the company and often includes people from levels below those that report directly to the president or chairman. Its strategic role is to see that inputs from both the outside world and the internal organization are integrated into the strategic plan. It also reviews plan commitments, allocates resources, and monitors implementation to ensure that the organization gets its planned strategic results. At the same time, the top management team runs the company's day-to-day and short-term business and oversees the development and implementation of the annual plan.

Top-level functional management teams usually consist of the functional vice president or manager and his or her direct reports. A team led by the vice president of manufacturing in a moderate-size company would typically include several plant managers and the managers of engineering, maintenance, and quality.

The right teams can turn around a floundering business. CORNING ELECTRONICS, a division of Corning, Inc., was a small, unprofitable manufacturer of electronic components in the mid-1960s and early

1970s. In order to grow and become profitable in that heyday of electronics, the division faced complex tasks. It had to decide which technologies to pursue, build new manufacturing facilities, rebuild an organization rife with conflict and separated by geography, develop new products and enter new markets, acquire other companies and technologies, and develop a cost-effective manufacturing organization.

The struggling division formed a top management team charged with planning and running the business. To run each of its three SBUs, the division installed business teams with representatives from all major functions: marketing, manufacturing, finance, sales, and technology. It used project teams to manage major new product development, marketing, and manufacturing projects.

Although making team management work was not without struggles and conflicts, as it ironed out its problems, Corning Electronics grew from an $18 million operation in 1964 to a profitable $150 million business in the mid-1980s, when it was sold.

2. *Formal program teams.* Formal program teams are created to carry out important strategic programs that involve multiple functions, cross several levels, and require high effort and high coordination. They typically tackle weighty programs such as cost reduction, new product development, customer service improvements, design and installation of MIS systems, or organization restructuring. Formal teams exist for the life of the program, no longer. During that time, however, their members and the functions they represent should expect to devote considerable work and substantial resources to the program.

Thanks largely to its first trained formal new product development team, the UNITED STATES TOBACCO COMPANY was able to launch a new product in ten months instead of the originally estimated two years. In the past, product development at USTC had been a vertical and compartmentalized process: Project coordination took place at the most senior level, and each function took its orders from the top. When key issues surfaced or disputes occurred, they had to work their way up the ladder to the highest levels for resolution. Replacing that cumbersome process, the new product development team:

▲ Defined its own goals and timetable in an attempt to meet the nine-month product launch constraint decreed by top management.
▲ Coordinated all of the technical efforts in various departments: R&D, product development, QA/QC, manufacturing, and sales.
▲ Consolidated responsibility for the program into one place, assigning co-leadership to marketing and engineering.
▲ Brought marketing into product development on an ongoing basis for the first time. As one senior vice president put it, "We

lifted the veil between them." In prior product developments, marketing's input had been sporadic and sometimes disruptive.

USTC ultimately developed a team management training program and made it available to the entire organization.

3. *Informal program teams.* When one or two functions have primary responsibility for a task, informal program teams work well for getting input from other functions when necessary. Such teams are task-focused and short-lived. A typical example is the development and launch of a marketing program to promote and expand the market for existing products. The marketing department and marketing communications carry the brunt of the assignment; when they need advice from manufacturing, engineering, and information systems, they pull together a temporary, informal team.

4. *Ongoing work teams.* Sometimes called self-empowered or self-managed work teams, ongoing work teams are charged with carrying out and improving ongoing operations. They are important to strategy implementation when they become "point" or key implementors of strategic projects or if they perform one of the leverage functions critical to continuing execution of strategy.

When ONTARIO CHEMICALS identified superior customer service as a key strategy, its service department, along with a consultant, was charged with diagnosing its deficiencies and developing and installing new computer and customer service systems to meet customer needs. In addition, the department constituted itself as an ongoing work team to monitor service quality and to make continuous improvements in service and the methods used to deliver it.

Characteristics of Effective Teams

While line management frequently puts a premium on quick, individual decision making, effective teams take a different approach, characterized by:

▲ Considerable discussion
▲ Open communication
▲ Debate, even conflict, on key issues
▲ Decision by consensus whenever possible
▲ Monitoring, measuring, and correcting of their own team behaviors

This doesn't mean that team members are joined at the hip, jointly managing the day-to-day execution of projects and talking every minor

Figure 16-1. Characteristics of effective teams.

▼ The task or objective of the group is well understood.

▼ The atmosphere is informal/relaxed.

▼ There is a lot of pertinent discussion.

▼ Members listen to each other.

▼ There is disagreement/conflict.

▼ Criticism is constructive, frank, frequent, and relatively comfortable.

▼ People discuss feelings as well as ideas.

▼ The chairman does not dominate.

▼ The leadership role is flexible.

▼ The group examines its own operations.

▼ Clear assignments are made and accepted.

▼ Decisions are generally reached by consensus.

▼ The team follows good meeting rules/behaviors.

▼ The team coordinates its work with other units.

▼ The group holds itself and its members accountable for results.

Source: Adapted from Douglas McGregor, *The Human Side of Enterprise,* pp. 232–235. Copyright ©
by McGraw-Hill Book Company. Used with permission of McGraw-Hill Book Company.

issue through to consensus (or exhaustion). Once the team has set objectives and made key decisions, team members take individual responsibility for executing their assignments and for making the decisions
necessary to keep the project on track.

Figure 16-1 lists the characteristics of effective teams described by
Douglas McGregor and others.

Qualities of Effective Team Members

Teams require members who listen well, participate and contribute,
represent their own areas of expertise but give up turf issues for the
sake of the whole, take a multifunctional perspective on issues, and can
set aside their own egos and who are flexible, secure, competent, and

Figure 16-2. Helping and hindering factors.

Helping	Hindering
Being open	Holding back
Being honest	Negative attitude
Being direct	Not honest/open
Contributing ideas	Protecting your turf
Riding on ideas	Hidden agendas/games
Supporting	Not contributing your ideas/perspective
Supportive conflict	Angry conflict
Clarifying — restating issues	"Taking my tin dishes" behavior
Keeping to the subject/task at hand	Playing the power/authority game
Listening to understand	Silence
Willingness to be influenced/change	Unwillingness to compromise
Willingness to give up your interest	Won't admit to problems or that you're wrong
	Won't take personal risks in being direct/honest

Source: Adapted from Michael Beer, *Organization Change By Development*, p. 145. Copyright © 1980 by Goodyear Publishers, Santa Monica, California.

inclusive. Figure 16-2 summarizes the helping and hindering behaviors of team members observed by organization psychologists.

Besides personal qualities and team-oriented behaviors, team members need some particular skills to be effective in team meetings. These seminal skills are best learned through a combination of formal training and extensive observation and experience. They include:

▲ Stand-up meeting facilitation
▲ Consensus building
▲ Probing and questioning for information and clarification
▲ Restating and clarifying issues
▲ Summarizing concepts and meeting segments
▲ Framing concepts and issues
▲ Identifying issues and solving problems
▲ Giving and receiving feedback supportively

▲ Generating ideas
▲ Observing and processing team effectiveness

Getting Teams Started

Putting a group of people together, calling them a team, and telling them to get on with the job using teamwork is a certain recipe for failure. To set a team up for success, you must pick the right members, give them a clear charter, train them in team skills, and start them off with professional facilitation.

Pick the Right Team

The Team Leader

Team leaders need to be capable of handling a variety of tasks, including:

▲ *Facilitating the team*—preparing agendas, performing administrative tasks, facilitating meetings, building consensus, and making decisions in cases of "consensus lock."
▲ *Developing the team and building the team culture*—ensuring that the team has members with the right functional and team skills, getting training for the team, motivating team members and encouraging positive behaviors, counseling members who don't pull their weight, replacing team members as necessary, and ensuring that the team critiques its own actions and effectiveness and controls the quality of its own operations.
▲ *Managing the company hierarchy*—keeping top management informed of the team's progress and managing functional conflict, turf protection, and jealousies both inside and outside the team—a sometimes prickly task.
▲ *Coordinating team member efforts outside of meetings*—handling executional issues one-on-one or in small groups.
▲ *Performing functional tasks*—related to both the team assignment and the leader's regular job.
▲ *Sharing leadership*—both for relief from the burden and to develop members' leadership skills. Some teams have formal co-leaders, especially if two functions are equally critical to project success. All teams benefit if members share facilitation tasks. Sometimes a team member with specific expertise takes over team leadership when that expertise is most needed. It may be

time for someone from manufacturing to assume team leadership, for example, when a new product moves out of development and into pilot production.

When you pick a team leader, you need a person who can handle all these responsibilities. Look for someone with all the characteristics of good team members, plus:

▲ *Experience in leading teams or the capability to learn.* Such people exhibit both the helping behaviors listed in Figure 16-2 and traditional managerial skills. They are communicative, articulate, supportive, results-oriented, and used to dealing in a collaborative environment. They know how to motivate, set objectives, and keep a program on track. They are emphatically not egotistical autocrats.

▲ *Functional expertise in one or more areas important to the project,* preferably the area most important to project success, for example, marketing in the case of new product development.

▲ *Respect from peers.* Potential team leaders earn respect for their technical skills, accomplishments, and leadership ability.

Team Members

Over their life span, strategy implementation teams usually comprise a cadre of permanent members, along with some temporary members who serve for shorter time periods and, occasionally, visiting experts.

Permanent team members—those who are expected to serve on the team from its formation to program completion—should possess four important qualifications. They need:

1. Functional and technical expertise that contributes to the program.
2. Time taken from their regular jobs to devote to the team.
3. Authority to commit resources from their functional areas or the ability to get them quickly.
4. Potential to be team players and to develop team skills. Look for people who have good communication skills and who are collegial, open to questions and conflict, willing to work out compromises with other functions, honest, and direct.

Temporary team members may be brought in for brief periods of time when their focused expertise is needed. For example, a new product launch team may include a member from R&D for the time it takes to complete development of the product technology and transfer it to product development and engineering. At that point the R&D person leaves the team. Although their tenure is shorter, temporary team members need the same skills as permanent ones if the team is to thrive while they are on board.

Finally, the team may bring nonmember experts to meetings occasionally to answer questions and to deal with specific issues as needed. For example, USTC product development teams bring in market research at three stages: when product specifications are being developed, during consumer testing of the product and of the marketing campaign, and postlaunch to determine how the product is faring in the marketplace and to get feedback on refinements needed.

Give the Team a Clear Charter

Explain the team's mission and objectives, the scope of the project, how it fits the vision, and how team members will be measured and rewarded. Of course, the team members should have latitude to modify these points, but they need to know the top team's expectations.

Train Team Members

Management by teams is alien to our frontier heritage of individual achievement and contrary to the authoritarian corporate regimes of the 1950s through 1980s in the United States. For many organizations, therefore, working in teams is new. For this technique to succeed, people need training in how to manage teams, facilitate meetings, deal with conflict, arrive at consensus, be good team members, and operate in the fluid and flexible team environment. Expecting a team to perform without training not only invites failure for the team's project but could cause a permanent setback to team management in your organization.

Every implementation team can benefit from a good one- or two-day course in which members learn and practice basic team and facilitation skills. At the same time, the facilitator/trainer leading the course can facilitate the team to agreement on its mission, roles, objectives, action plans, and operating rules. (A typical course in team management skills is outlined in Chapter 6, Figure 6-1.)

Provide Professional Facilitation

For its first few meetings, provide each team with a professional facilitator. If the team did not come to agreement on its mission and on other important points during training, it will need to do so now, led by an expert. The facilitator should also give members on-the-job training in team and facilitation skills and intervene when the program or the team process gets off the track. After about three facilitated meetings, the team should be ready to go it alone, but it's a good idea to make the facilitator's services available to the team should it get bogged down or need a tune-up later.

The Pitfalls of Teams and How to Cope With Them

Implementing a strategic plan through teams isn't all clear sailing. Teams, particularly new ones, have some predictable problems, most of which emanate from three root causes: impatience, conflicting job demands, and the frustration of working in a new environment.

Many companies that embrace teams are simply unprepared for the amount of time it takes for teams to become noticeably more effective than individuals. Teams don't form, acquire new skills, and mesh as effective working units overnight. They need training, nurturing, and a long lead time for members to gain experience working together. Changing to teams from a long-standing culture of rugged individualism is an investment in the future effectiveness of your organization that takes both time and money. Ultimately, operating in teams should improve efficiency by removing organizational friction and barriers to progress, quickening the pace of change, and reducing costs.

The second root cause of problems is the conflicting demands imposed by each member's team job and that member's regular job. It is a lose-lose proposition to expect a team member to devote fifty to sixty hours a week to his or her regular job and still take on demanding team tasks. There is bound to be conflict when a person tries to satisfy three bosses—the team, the team's boss, and the functional boss back at the regular job. Avoiding that conflict requires:

▲ Agreement up-front on the time period during which the team will operate and on how much time will be required of each team member
▲ Back-filling the team member's regular job if the team and regular jobs together require more time than one person reasonably has available
▲ Rewarding team results separately from regular job performance but including both in each team member's performance appraisal
▲ Making functional bosses responsible for their subordinates' team performance by including effective team performance by the subordinate in the boss's performance objectives

Expect a high level of frustration in the early stages of team development. While team members are dealing with new, important, and

Figure 16-3. Typical team problems and conflicts.

▼ Bosses or nonteam members meddle.

▼ The boss is on the team.

▼ Some team members don't or won't contribute.

▼ A team member is incompetent.

▼ There are time conflicts with "other" jobs.

▼ The team lacks control over resources needed.

▼ Members lack team and facilitation skills.

▼ There are personality/style conflicts.

▼ Members carry negative baggage from prior jobs.

---

often innovative and complicated tasks, there is often an initial lack of clarity around what those tasks are. Individual roles and how the team will function are usually equally unclear. Newcomers to teams often miss the degree of comfort and the sense of being in control they experience in their regular jobs. The best defenses against debilitating frustration are establishing realistic expectations at the outset and providing training, professional facilitation, and team building.

Ignoring these needs sets a team up for sure failure. One company created a multifunctional business team and charged it with planning the future of an SBU that was struggling to service a rapidly changing market for retail automotive parts. The company chose a team leader who was convinced he could do the job faster alone and demanded that the team do everything his way, and the other team members were marginally competent at best. The company provided no team training or professional facilitation. The team floundered for about a year, buried in paperwork and struggling to get organized, then collapsed—and the team leader was fired from the team and from the company.

There are a number of predictable problems and conflicts, including those listed in Figure 16-3, that teams should be able resolve internally. Here are some of the most common, along with advice for handling them:

▲ *Meddling by bosses or other nonmembers.* When members' bosses or other interested bystanders ask to sit in on meetings "for information," the team must say no—with no exceptions. This kind of meddling disrupts team effectiveness and stifles the normal flow of information.

If someone from outside the team wants a briefing, have a team

Figure 16-4. Team rules.

Desired Management Behavior Changes	**Team Responsibility**
▼ Involvement in details: Level of comfort relates to executive commitment to detail. If not involved, then do not second-guess. Always the right to ask questions but start at co-leader level. ▼ Leave delegation in place. Don't take the monkey back. ▼ Don't interfere (hold us responsible). ▼ Leave project reporting structure in place.	▼ Meeting overall project (corporate) objectives ▼ Reviewing activity vs. plan schedule and results ▼ Making decisions related to additions, modifications, deletions of tasks not affecting overall scope ▼ Being accountable for project/one another

Project Accountability	**Project Authorization Levels**	
Team will present project status review on set schedule: ▼ Activity vs. plan schedule, deliverables, expense. ▼ Achieved results. ▼ Open issues. ▼ Resolution. ▼ Review of planned tasks assignments. ▼ Team submits bimonthly status report.	Executive Committee	▼ Project schedule, resource (personnel or budget $) change ▼ Policy or major procedure modification ▼ Impact store costs/ bottom line (+ or – 10%)
	Project Management Team	▼ Everything else

member brief the person or schedule a special update meeting outside of regular team meetings. But hold team meetings sacrosanct. Allow no one to attend who is not either a team member or a guest invited by the team to provide input.

▲ *Inclusion of the boss on the team.* Many teams have members from two or more organizational levels, and occasionally two members may have a boss-subordinate direct reporting relationship. To make this situation work, both need to practice extraordinary openness on the one hand and restraint on the other. The boss must be careful not to dominate or play a power game; the subordinate may find it difficult to confront and give feedback, not only to the boss, but also to other team members when the boss is present. In a supportive environment, the subordinate can learn to overcome this hesitation.

▲ *Lack of contribution by some team members.* Deal quickly and directly with incompetents and laggards. Most teams try to get recalcitrant individuals on board by confronting their lack of effort or accomplishment during team meetings. If that doesn't work, the leader usually counsels the lagging member privately. If that too fails, advise the member's boss of your problem, get a replacement, and then ask the person to leave.

The best way for teams to avoid getting bogged down in problems is to decide up-front how to deal with the predictable ones. One project team at a major uniform manufacturer got the top team to agree to the set of rules shown in Figure 16-4.

Getting Organizational Buy-In

Your first team can seed the widespread use of teams in your organization. Let members know they are the explorers and leaders in the team realm. Give your first team a critical task. From your best people, pick those with the right personalities and experience to staff it. Choose team members who have the potential to lead and train other teams, and then train them well and ensure their success by providing all the process help they need. Herald their successes to the entire organization; reward teams publicly, and keep team rewards separate from the normal individual and corporate compensation system.

But don't get impatient if the whole organization doesn't immediately embrace teams. Because of the cultural and behavioral changes involved, it takes at least three years for teams to become effective and for companies to imbed them as a way of life for creating strategic change. And organizational buy-in doesn't happen until teams have proven their effectiveness, team members have been rewarded for their accomplishments, and it is clear even to the skeptics that the company is serious about using teams to drive change.

For Those Who Can't Adapt

There will be people who can't function within the team environment. Most companies find places for such people as individual contributors or managers in more traditionally structured parts of the organization.

Unfortunately, as companies convert to team management, there may be no fall-back places for individuals, particularly those at the highest levels or in leverage positions, who can't adapt. One business initiated a companywide conversion from vertical autocracy to team culture by managing its strategy and business through a top-level business team. The company eventually replaced five of its top eight officers because they couldn't deal with the team culture or weren't functionally competent to handle the company's new, more demanding performance requirements. Personnel changes are an unfortunate but often necessary by-product of cultural change.

Who Supervises Teams?

Teams usually report to a single line manager or to a business team. It's common, for example, for a team handling a key strategic program such as corporatewide overhead reduction to be accountable to the entire top management team; a team responsible for bringing a new product to market may be responsible solely to the vice president of marketing.

In either event, the single or collective body to which the team reports has four primary roles: (1) to resolve conflicts that cannot be resolved by the team; (2) to give direction and functional expertise to the team and to members needing help; (3) to find needed resources, including team members and human skills; and (4) through oversight and review, to judge the performance of the team and of its individual contributors.

Team Building:
When Critical Teams Don't or Won't Function

Some teams simply don't jell. Others wallow and are only moderately effective, even with occasional professional facilitation. Ineffective, dysfunctional, or start-up teams, particularly those that will be ongoing and that are expected to perform over the long pull, frequently benefit from a formal team-building program.

Team building is a process by which a group of individuals, such as members of the top management team or of a project team, learn to work together more effectively and efficiently. Under the guidance of a skilled organization psychologist and facilitator, members:

▲ Discuss how well the team does or does not function in accomplishing its job.
▲ Identify barriers to the team's effective functioning.

▲ Decide how to change team behavior, structure, and process to make the team function more effectively in the future.

▲ Critique the style and contributions of team members and suggest ways for individuals to improve how they serve the team.

▲ Learn team management and process skills to be more effective personally and to train their subordinates in those skills.

Dimensions of Effective Teams

While there are many models of team building, all provide a framework against which to judge team effectiveness. Typical factors include:

▲ *Coordination.* Members collaborate, share information, and coordinate efforts within the team. They coordinate effectively with the rest of the organization outside the team.

▲ *Communication.* Members state their positions clearly and engage in direct, constructive dialogue.

▲ *Probing and listening.* Members probe and encourage others to present their views. They listen carefully, using active listening skills.

▲ *Conflict and disagreement.* Members freely voice disagreement and systematically explore all sides of an issue before resolution. They use consensus to determine the "best" solution, which they accept willingly.

▲ *Meeting quality.* Members are involved, present constructive ideas, listen attentively, and engage others' interest. The team runs efficient meetings according to good meeting rules such as those presented in Chapter 17 (Figure 17-2).

▲ *Participation.* Members participate in team activities, contribute useful ideas, and don't dominate.

▲ *Planning.* The team plans its joint work, partitions tasks, and delegates them to the individuals responsible for carrying them out.

▲ *Objectives and expectations.* The team establishes objectives that are realistic and achievable but sets leadership standards for the organization and the industry. It manages to these mutually agreed upon objectives and holds team members accountable.

▲ *Decision making/problem solving.* The team systematically analyzes alternatives before selecting the best one. It gets appropriate inputs and data from insiders and outsiders who should be involved. It stays objective and factual.

▲ *Facilitation.* Members use good facilitation skills, share the facilitation role, and cooperate with and support other facilitators.

▲ *Representation of the team to the organization.* Members delegate team objectives, integrate organization inputs into the team's planning and action, and develop teamwork within their own units.

▲ *Candor/feedback.* Members are appropriately direct, open, objective, specific, and honest in interchanges.

▲ *Execution/follow-up.* The team achieves its objectives consistently. Members follow through, take initiative, and ensure effective execution by involving others, obtaining their understanding and commitment. They accept responsibility for accomplishing accepted objectives and tasks.[1]

Models for Team Building

One very effective model for team building involves four steps.

1. Team members do pre-session work prior to attending a team-building session with the entire team. They read material and/or attend a brief seminar where they learn the team-building process and positive and negative behaviors related to the team-effectiveness dimensions. They privately rate both team and individual behavior on each of the dimensions just described.

2. Members attend a one- to three-day, professionally facilitated team-building meeting where they share their ratings of the team, give examples supporting their ratings, and then, as a team, agree on team strengths and weaknesses and on a plan to improve the team's effectiveness.

3. Members of the team then share their ratings of team members on each dimension. Again, they identify strengths and weaknesses and develop action plans to improve individual performance.

4. The team agrees on a continuing process to be used after the initial meeting. Successful team building takes place over months and even years, with the team frequently critiquing its process and effectiveness as a whole and the effectiveness of each individual.[2]

Team building has the most impact when it is used across the organization, throughout successive layers and in every function. Some companies ultimately build teams, teach facilitation and team leadership skills, and install team management throughout the organization, starting at the top and going right down to the factory floor and the admin-

1. Adapted from *Dimensional Management Training* (St. Louis, Mo.: Psychological Associates, 1988).
2. Ibid.

istrative workplace. Depending on the size, culture, and complexity of your organization, expect to spend from two to six years installing effective total team management.

If your key managers don't function effectively as a team now and you can't wait for months of team building before you begin strategic planning, your company might consider an alternate team-building model, one that is task-oriented and that forms a part of the strategic planning process itself. Under this model, the planning team is asked to develop the company's strengths, weaknesses, opportunities, threats, and mission statement during a long conference. During the process, all of the team-building elements we have mentioned are addressed, using behavior at the conference as examples.

By the way, holding a retreat where people set objectives, socialize, and play golf together is not team building. While communications and understanding are often improved by such meetings, these sessions do not give the team or individuals an operational framework within which to judge team or individual behavior, don't give direct and focused feedback, and, above all, don't result in team and individual process improvement action plans.

DO'S AND DON'TS

DO

- *Use teams for complex tasks* that involve various functions and multiple organizational levels.
- *Train first-time teams* and team members, and give them professional facilitation.
- *Go slow.* When your first one or two teams are effective, then start more.
- *Give team members time* away from their ongoing jobs to perform team functions.
- *Give the team time* to get organized, coalesce, and function effectively.
- *Reward members as a team* for team performance.

DON'T

- *Follow fads.* Don't use teams just because they are hot in the 1990s.
- *Use teams everywhere.* They are for select circumstances only.
- *Get "teamitis."* Resist tendencies to make all decisions with the entire team, insist on 100 percent consensus on every issue, or call the team together to deal with minor issues or to transmit nice-to-have information. Teams should facilitate forward motion, not inhibit it through overdependency on the process.
- *Force-fit teams* into your organization. Don't try teams if you really don't have people who can become effective team members.

Chapter 17

Facilitator's Guide III: Techniques for Team Tasks

It has been said that the difference between the major and minor leagues is just a matter of inches and consistency. That is essentially true of the difference between excellence and mere adequacy in poetry or surgery or anything else.

—George F. Will, newspaper columnist

The harder you work, the luckier you get.

—Gary Player, professional golfer

Every facilitator needs a repertoire of standard techniques to use during team meetings and throughout the planning and implementation process. An excellent facilitator is skilled in all of the techniques and knows when to use each one or more than one to help the group achieve its objectives.

Using the classic facilitation techniques listed in Figure 17-1 and summarized and expanded in the form of "cue cards" in Figure 17-2, you can:

▲ Get information from the group.
▲ Boil it down to key issues and problems to be addressed.
▲ Lead discussions to debate, further define, and clarify issues.
▲ Develop solutions to problems and conflicts.
▲ Gain consensus on issues and actions to be taken.
▲ Ensure that critical decisions are made even when there is conflict or no consensus.
▲ Test to see if the group process is working.

This chapter details how to use the twelve classic team facilitation techniques.

Figure 17-1. Key facilitation and meeting management techniques: meeting rules.

▼ **T-1** Meeting rules

▼ **T-2** Round-robin idea generation

▼ **T-3** Brainstorming

▼ **T-4** Consensus

▼ **T-5** Storyboarding

▼ **T-6** Open discussion

▼ **T-7** Problem solving

▼ **T-8** Small groups

▼ **T-9** Solution development

▼ **T-10** Fishbowling

▼ **T-11** Process meeting/feedback

▼ **T-12** Personal intervention

Meeting Rules (T-1)

Good meeting rules make for good meetings. Agree on them before every meeting. Some teams establish a set of rules that they will use to govern all of their meetings and then post them on conference room walls. While it is the facilitator's job to see that the rules are developed, agreed on, and adhered to, in practice, groups quickly become self-policing, making the facilitator's job easier.

Figure 17-2 contains a set of rules that work well for strategic planning (and most other) meetings.

Round-Robin Ideas (T-2)

A round-robin is a technique for listing and condensing ideas that the team members may have developed as part of the meeting prework and brought to the meeting on worksheets. Alternatively, the facilitator may allow members to spend a few minutes during the meeting to privately develop their lists of ideas before discussion. Or the facilitator may ask members to give their ideas spontaneously. The objective of the round-robin is to get all ideas aired without duplication or discussion, regardless of the quality, and then boil them down to the most relevant and important few.

Depending upon the topic, a round-robin can take anywhere from twenty-five minutes (for airing threats to the organization) to sixty minutes (not uncommon for identifying weaknesses).

When to Use a Round-Robin

Aside from open discussion, the round-robin is probably the most widely used team facilitation technique. It's an effective way to list and condense SWOTs, priority issues, and program selections, and strategic planning facilitators use it whenever there are ideas, issues, new product suggestions, or problems that need to be identified, discussed, prioritized, and acted upon.

Basic Rules of the Round-Robin

▲ Everyone must participate. Going around the group in order ensures that this happens.
▲ No criticism or evaluation of ideas is allowed during this part of the process. That will come later.
▲ Brief explanations, twenty seconds or so, are allowed for clarification of what is meant by the idea or why it is being introduced.
▲ Brief questions for clarification are allowed if a team member doesn't understand what is meant by an input.
▲ No one should duplicate an input already given.

Detailed Procedure

1. Prepare the team or group. Review the rules just given. Be prepared to list ideas on a flipchart, or appoint a recorder to do so. The recorder should:

    a. Write down ideas in the order in which they are suggested.
    b. Tape filled pages to the wall, keeping them in order.

2. Assign prework. If the team did prework prior to this meeting, go to Step 3. If not, give the group five to seven minutes to develop individual lists of ideas.

3. Solicit ideas. Ask someone to supply one idea from prework. Ask the next person to do the same. Do not allow duplicates. Tell team members to go on to their next suggestions if their favorite idea has

(text continues on page 277)

Figure 17-2. Key facilitation and meeting management techniques: cue cards.

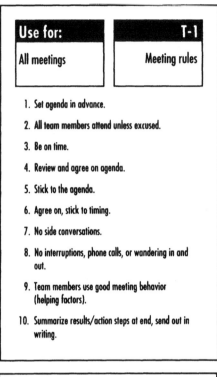

Use for: **T-1**

All meetings   Meeting rules

1. Set agenda in advance.

2. All team members attend unless excused.

3. Be on time.

4. Review and agree on agenda.

5. Stick to the agenda.

6. Agree on, stick to timing.

7. No side conversations.

8. No interruptions, phone calls, or wandering in and out.

9. Team members use good meeting behavior (helping factors).

10. Summarize results/action steps at end, send out in writing.

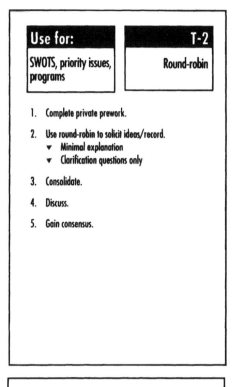

Use for: **T-2**

SWOTS, priority issues,   Round-robin
programs

1. Complete private prework.

2. Use round-robin to solicit ideas/record.
    ▼ Minimal explanation
    ▼ Clarification questions only

3. Consolidate.

4. Discuss.

5. Gain consensus.

Use for: **T-3**

Ideas for programs to   Brainstorming
address priority issues

1. Review brainstorming rules.

2. Frame the task.

3. Random idea generation—list ideas.

4. Cull the list/combine.

5. Discuss/challenge/explain.

6. Rank.

7. Assign.

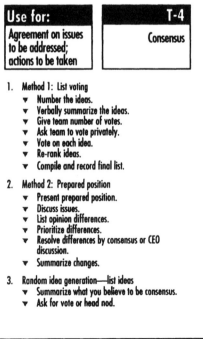

Use for: **T-4**

Agreement on issues   Consensus
to be addressed;
actions to be taken

1. Method 1: List voting
    ▼ Number the ideas.
    ▼ Verbally summarize the ideas.
    ▼ Give team number of votes.
    ▼ Ask team to vote privately.
    ▼ Vote on each idea.
    ▼ Re-rank ideas.
    ▼ Compile and record final list.

2. Method 2: Prepared position
    ▼ Present prepared position.
    ▼ Discuss issues.
    ▼ List opinion differences.
    ▼ Prioritize differences.
    ▼ Resolve differences by consensus or CEO discussion.
    ▼ Summarize changes.

3. Random idea generation—list ideas
    ▼ Summarize what you believe to be consensus.
    ▼ Ask for vote or head nod.

Use for:	T-5
Vision/mission, values, strategy statements	Storyboarding

1. Frame the issue or concept.

2. Do private prework—one card/phrase or word.

3. Serially:
   - ▼ "Wall" the cards.
   - ▼ Allow open observation.
   - ▼ Facilitate consensus areas, divergences.
   - ▼ Resolve divergences or assign/defer.

4. Summarize.

5. Flesh out key words into statements.
   - ▼ Small groups
   - ▼ Assigned for later buy-in

Use for:	T-6
Whenever want unstructured inputs on analyses, key topics	Open group discussion

1. Establish the subject or range of subjects that will and won't be discussed.

2. Define the discussion's purpose. For example:
   - ▼ Explain/expand on an idea.
   - ▼ Define pluses/minuses of a concept.
   - ▼ Define a problem's underlying causes.

3. Establish time available.

4. Open discussion by soliciting inputs at random.

5. Facilitate discussion by:
   - ▼ Keeping it on the subject
   - ▼ Limiting air time
   - ▼ Sticking to the timing
   - ▼ Getting widespread participation
   - ▼ Summarizing frequently
   - ▼ Listing key points on a flipchart
   - ▼ Summarizing the overall discussion

6. Synthesize the discussion into conclusions/actions.

7. Close by getting agreement/consensus.

Use for:	T-7
Developing solutions to any complex problem	Problem solving

1. Frame the problem; write it down.

2. Brainstorm root causes.

3. Discuss.

4. Assign impact—major, moderate, minor.

5. Identify solutions.
   - ▼ Brainstorm, discuss, or round-robin.

6. Develop implementation action plans.

7. Assign action.

Use for:	T-8
Throughout—when need ideas, energy, buy-in	Small groups

1. Frame the issue.

2. Establish:
   - ▼ Leader
   - ▼ Recorder
   - ▼ Presentation method
   - ▼ Time
   - ▼ Suggested method

3. Monitor/nudge.

4. Present.

5. Discuss/contrast.

(continues)

Figure 17-2. (*continued*).

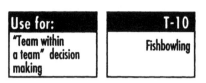

Use for:	T-9
Strategic program ideas	Solution development

1. Do prework.

2. State priority issue.

3. Create small groups.
   - ▼ Single assignment
   - ▼ Multiple assignments

4. Provide assignment:
   - ▼ Frame the issue.
   - ▼ 1-, 3-year objectives.
   - ▼ List all "how" ideas.
   - ▼ Condense/discuss.
   - ▼ Review:
     Who, what, when
     Impact
     Coordination requirements

Use for:	T-10
"Team within a team" decision making	Fishbowling

1. Present/discuss all sides of issue.

2. Summarize discussion.

3. Frame issues to be decided.

4. Put small decision-making team in front of larger group with rules:
   - ▼ Set time limit for debate.
   - ▼ No inputs from onlookers unless asked.
   - ▼ Must come out with a decision.

5. Decision-making team facilitates own "fishbowled" meeting to final decision.

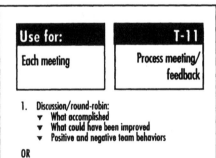

Use for:	T-11
Each meeting	Process meeting/ feedback

1. Discussion/round-robin:
   - ▼ What accomplished
   - ▼ What could have been improved
   - ▼ Positive and negative team behaviors

OR

2. QC questionnaire later.

Use for:	T-12
As needed	Personal interventions

1. Organization problems:
   - ▼ Structure.
   - ▼ Overall discontent/confusion

2. Dysfunctional teams

3. Critical unsurfaced issues

4. Bad decisions

5. CEO style

6. Managerial style/conflict

7. Performance/competence problems

8. Resourcing

already been mentioned. Continue going around the group as many times as is necessary until all ideas have been listed.

Allow each person offering an idea to say a few words to explain it and to give a few reasons why it is important, but do not let the explanation go on for more than thirty to forty seconds. Allow others to ask questions for clarification—for instance, "Is this what you mean?" or "Would you explain that please?" Do not allow argumentative or judgmental comments at this time. (These usually begin with something like "I think that . . . ," "I don't agree, but . . . ," or "How about . . . ?")

Once it is obvious that most ideas have been rendered, make a quick check for additional ideas and close the solicitation.

4. Cull and combine the list. After the ideas are listed, ask the team to combine duplicates (which creep in despite the no-duplicates rules), and eliminate any ideas that team members feel don't fit or don't make sense. Make sure there is consensus on eliminations.

In reality, the process of culling the list will merge into Step 5, discussion. Team members will need to discuss and expand on some ideas to see if they should be combined with others or remain separate.

Help members resist the temptation to overcombine, putting everything but the kitchen sink under one or two generic subjects. New and inexperienced teams, particularly, find this a tempting way to save almost all their ideas. Remember that every idea that survives the distillation process will ultimately result in an action plan, and too many action plans overburden the organization.

To test for separateness ask:

    a. Is the issue functionally separate and distinct from others? A sales issue, for example, is distinct from a manufacturing issue.

    b. How much effort does it take? Major issues requiring significant effort over sustained periods of time need to be separate.

    c. If it is in the same functional areas as other important issues, will it require different resources (including people) to accomplish the action?

    d. Will it be managed and accomplished separately from other programs?

For example, the group might be tempted to group both the need for a new manufacturing facility and the need for a cost reduction program for the existing facility under the single category "manufacturing." While both of these are manufacturing issues, they are programs of such magnitude that they require separate implementation efforts. They may share major resources, such as manufacturing engineering, but they also require separate additional resources, such as architectural design and construction engineering for the new facility. They therefore need to be separate issues, however functionally and organizationally related they may be.

5. Discuss the ideas. Now is the time to explain ideas, expand concepts, debate pluses and minuses, and home in on disagreements and differences of opinion. Team members will propose solutions to issues at this time. When that happens, acknowledge and record the proposals, but don't permit them to be discussed in detail. That will come later once the key issues are agreed upon. (See the discussion of problem solving later in this chapter.)

The culling and discussion steps usually last from fifteen to forty-five minutes or one hour, depending on the complexity of the issues.

6. Achieve consensus on priorities. To do this, follow the procedure described under Method 1 in the section on consensus in this chapter.

Brainstorming (T-3)

Brainstorming is a team technique for generating creative ideas in great quantity. The quality of the ideas is not important at the outset.

Unlike the round-robin, brainstorming relies on rapid, free-flowing inputs from any source in any order. It encourages riding on and expanding other team members' ideas. Like the round-robin, brainstorming produces a great number of ideas, which the group then culls, discusses, and distills by consensus to a few selected for action.

When to Use Brainstorming

During the strategic planning process, brainstorming is most useful for generating ideas and potential programs to address strategic priority issues.

You can also use brainstorming to generate ideas for potential new products or markets, new applications for strengths, potential causes of problems, and solutions to them.

Basic Rules of Brainstorming

▲ Everyone is expected to participate.
▲ No criticism or evaluation of anyone's ideas is allowed.
▲ No idea is labeled dumb or silly.

▲ Participants should build on one another's ideas to gain momentum, trigger new thoughts, and increase creativity.

Detailed Procedure

1. Prepare the team or group, and review the brainstorming rules. Prepare to record ideas, or appoint a recorder to do so. The recorder should:

    a. Write ideas rapidly on a flipchart in the order in which they are suggested.
    b. Tape filled pages to the wall, keeping them in order.

2. Frame the task. For example, you might say, "We want as many ideas as possible about how to reduce headquarters overhead costs." Make sure everyone understands the goal of the exercise.

3. Generate ideas. Begin the brainstorming process by asking for inputs. If the group hesitates, call on someone to supply the first idea. Do not allow discussion during this phase. Let this process run until no new ideas are offered, probably no more than ten to fifteen minutes. Do not allow it to degenerate into foolishness, but remember that some good ideas do begin as jokes. Encourage people to ride on the ideas of others.

Encourage a rapid pace of ideation with comments and questions such as "Keep it moving," "That's a good idea; what if you . . . ," "Who can expand on that idea?," and "Is there another way of doing that?" The facilitator's job is to keep the juices flowing. Don't hesitate to throw in your own ideas or to embroider on ideas of others.

4, 5, 6, and 7. Cull, discuss, achieve consensus on the rank order of ideas, and assign actions to address top-ranked ideas. To do this, follow the processes described under Round-Robin (T-2) and Consensus (T-4), Method 1.

Consensus (T-4)

Team discussions and idea-generating activities are valuable because of the diversity of ideas that surface. The objective for most sessions is a team consensus on actions to be taken, policies to be implemented, or the key issues to be addressed.

Consensus doesn't mean that everyone agrees with a conclusion or decision. It means that after a thorough discussion of the issues, most team members feel one approach is in the best interest of the organization. Those who disagree are willing to go along with the preferred plan if they have to participate in its implementation.

When to Use Consensus

Seek consensus anytime a discussion must lead to an agreement on action to be taken or issues to be addressed. In strategic planning, some form of consensus culminates every step requiring a conclusion—SWOTs, priority issues, KRAs, objectives, mission, and so on.

Detailed Procedure

Method 1

Vote to rank the ideas after the issue under consideration has been thoroughly discussed, lists of ideas have been made and culled, and the group is ready to make a decision. The process should take only about fifteen minutes.

1. **Renumber the culled list of ideas.**

2. **Give each team member three or four votes,** depending on the number of ideas and the number wanted on the final list (usually three, no more than four). Ask members to decide privately which they will vote for. Then ask for the vote on each idea.

3. **Rerank the list.** If there is a fair consensus on the top three or four ideas, stop. If there is not, continue the rating and elimination process until you have reached a consensus or there are only three or four ideas left.

4. **Compile your final list.**

Method 2

Start with a prepared position if prework on the issue has been completed and circulated. In strategic planning, this technique is commonly used for the environmental analysis, marketing analysis, marketing strategy, mission, and objectives.

1. **Have the preparer briefly review the prepared position.** Take questions for clarification only.

2. **Discuss the issues.** As the discussion proceeds, list the group's

differences with the presented position. Limit discussion time to a predetermined period.

3. List the differences of opinion in order of importance on the basis of your feel for the discussion. Make sure everyone agrees on which differences are really significant.

4. Resolve differences of opinion through discussion of each issue, testing verbally for consensus before going on to the next. If the group is polarized on an issue, clarify the major differences and vote, or have the CEO decide.

5. Summarize the changes. Wait until later to perform any detailed wordcrafting of mission, vision, values, or policy statements.

When there is a large quantity of information to be critiqued, you can apply a small-group variation of this procedure. Divide the large group into two or three work groups consisting of three to five people each, and assign to each group a section of the presentation, making sure that each group contains all the functional or organizational expertise needed to address its assignment. Have each group agree on changes in its assigned section; then bring the larger group back together, have each small group present its conclusions, and get agreement on changes from the entire team.

There is another small-group variation that works well for critical and controversial issues such as developing the vision or choosing a strategic posture for business units. Again, you divide the team into two or more small groups. In this case, however, ask all groups to critique the same issue and then have each group present its conclusions to the entire team. Identify similarities and differences among the groups' conclusions, and, after discussion, manage the team to consensus on major issues.

Method 3

A third method for achieving consensus calls on the facilitator to "test and vote" when it seems obvious where the consensus lies. The facilitator can save time by simplifying the process as follows:

1. Summarize what you believe to be the consensus.

2. Vote. Ask for head nods or a show of hands, or ask, "Is there any disagreement?" If it's a controversial topic, go around the room, asking each person for agreement or disagreement and comments. If there are strong disagreements, air them, focusing on the advantages of each point of view. Then summarize and revote.

As a variation, ask someone else to summarize what he or she thinks is the consensus. Then, as before, vote by voice or show of hands. (This is particularly helpful if the facilitator is perceived to have a vested interest in one particular option.)

Decision Making Without Consensus

[*Despite the desirability of consensus, business teams are not democracies in which the majority always rules. There are times when vetoes rule or when one person's vote carries more weight than the votes of others.*

For one thing, some opinions are better than others. When the issue is highly technical, the team has to rely on the experts. It would be foolish for a management team to sanction a new product development, for example, if the technologists thought it would be impossible or foolhardy to pursue it.

If the group cannot come to a consensus, the boss must make the decision. In organizations that use the strategic planning process outlined in this book, 90 percent or more of all key decisions are made by an obvious consensus. On the few occasions when no consensus can be reached, the buck stops with the CEO. After the team crystallizes its differences of opinion and clarifies why the differences exist, the CEO must mandate a decision. Strategy, sooner rather than later, has to be nailed in stone, implementation has to be started, and results achieved. When there are mandates after lively debate, they are usually accepted and implemented with commitment. If they aren't, those who drag their heels don't belong on the team in the long term.]

Storyboarding (T-5)

Storyboarding is an engaging team technique for developing a consensus on the key words, along with their definitions, to be used in crafting conceptual statements such as the mission, including vision, business definition, and value statements. The key words are later fleshed out, wordcrafted, and put in the plan.

When to Use Storyboarding

Storyboarding is helpful in developing the mission statement in Prework II, as well as in writing the strategy statements.

Basic Rules of Storyboarding

▲ Have people focus on a few succinct, meaningful words and phrases drawn from the gut to describe the subject or concept. Avoid prose.

▲ Quickly get each individual's key words out in front of the team for energetic group processing.

▲ Spend most of your time getting an understanding of what's meant by words, exploring differences between concepts, and then managing to consensus.

Detailed Procedure

1. Frame the issue or concept to be storyboarded. If the task is to develop a statement of "what we want our customers to say about us," for example, tell team members they are to arrive at consensus on the key words to be incorporated into the statement and on the meanings of those words.

2. Assign private prework. Have each individual list key words and phrases addressing the subject on separate 8½ × 11 cards or sheets of paper.

3. Process the team members' input as follows:

  a. Have all members tape their cards on a wall.
  b. Encourage open observation. Ask team members to comment on what they see, particularly on similarities and differences among one another's input.
  c. Identify what appear to be the three to five critical key words to express the concept under discussion. Note and record disagreements or divergences.
  d. Resolve differences. Solicit input on why team members have differing views. Facilitate to consensus on each contested area. If that's not possible and further thought or information is needed to get agreement, defer the specific issue, or assign it to someone for a recommendation.
  e. Review and summarize the consensus words. Write them on a flipchart, and go on to the next concept to be storyboarded.
  f. As an option once the words are agreed on, stimulate understanding and discussion of the job to be done by asking, "How well do we perform on each word or dimension now?" "Where should we be in the future?" and "What will we have to do to get there?" This is especially helpful when dealing with quantifiable performance concepts such as profitability, size, quality, and service.

4. Flesh out the key words by one of two methods:

Method 1: Small Groups

- Break the planning team into two or more groups to put flesh and meaning on each word or phrase. For example, ask, "What do we mean by this word?" and "Operationally, how will we turn this word or concept into action and get results?"
- You can, as an option, have the groups grade the company's performance A, B, or C in each area and give recommendations or corrective action in the C (need significant improvement) areas.
- Have each group report its results to the entire team.
- For each assigned area, give a three- to four-minute presentation of conclusions. Then spend five to ten minutes getting consensus on the key concepts and, if you choose, the operational steps to be taken in inadequate performance areas.
- Assign the wordcrafting of a completed statement to an individual.

Method 2: Individual Assignment

- Assign the drafting of the complete statement to an individual.

---

5. Finalize the statement at a later date by circulating the draft to team members for further input and buy-in. It's often helpful for team members to have their direct reports also meet and comment on the draft if its contents affect them.

Chapter 10, on Prework II, suggests typical concepts and procedures for developing a mission statement.

Open Discussion (T-6)

The ability to guide discussions productively is a critical skill for facilitators. Good discussions are characterized by:

▲ Focused, rather than rambling, discourse
▲ Participation by all group members who have valuable input
▲ Exclusion of irrelevant points, subjects, or data

When to Use Open Discussion

Open discussion is useful anytime you need to explore, clarify, and get depth and richness in a subject. Use it when there is conflict or controversy over or lack of understanding of an important subject. Almost every topic in strategic planning uses some degree of open, free-form discussion.

Detailed Procedure

1. Establish the subject or range of subjects that will (and won't) be discussed.

2. Define the purpose of the discussion. For example, the purpose might be to:

▲ Explain and/or expand on a concept or idea.
▲ Define the pluses and minuses of a concept or idea before making a decision.
▲ Define a problem's underlying issues.

3. Establish the time available for the discussion.

4. Open the discussion by soliciting inputs at random.

5. Facilitate the discussion, following these guidelines:

a. Keep to the subject of the discussion. To deflect the introduction or discussion of an irrelevant point, either state that it is irrelevant or acknowledge its importance and then move on. Or put it on a hanging-issues list for subjects to be dealt with later. Decide at the end of the meeting how and when you will deal with hanging issues.

b. Limit air time. With experience, facilitators learn to sense when a point has been made, when discussion is waning, or when people are straining for things to say. To move the discussion on, summarize and close off the subject. If one person is monopolizing the discussion, acknowledge and involve others who want to or should make points.

c. Don't inhibit discussion by cutting people off too soon. Let people take a few tangents and peripheral paths to trigger creative thinking and divergent points of view. But don't let them wander too far.

d. Stick to the preset time limit. Get the group's agreement in advance on the time to be allowed for a given subject, and make sure that that limit is adhered to.

e. Use other good "helping" facilitation techniques, including getting widespread participation, summarizing frequently, and listing key points on flipcharts.

6. Synthesize the discussion into key conclusions and actions to be taken.

7. Use consensus techniques for getting agreement on conclusions and actions.

Problem Solving (T-7)

Approaching a problem in a systematic way can eliminate a lot of wasted time, misunderstanding, and superficial analysis. Systematic problem solving is particularly useful in identifying causes and solutions to poor strategic performance in areas such as cost, service, new product development, and market penetration.

When to Use Problem Solving

Use systematic problem solving when the roots of a problem are complex and obscure and particularly when the causes and solutions to the problem are multifunctional and functionally interrelated.

Basic Rules of Problem Solving

▲ Use the technique sparingly, saving it for complex problems whose cause and solutions aren't obvious.
▲ Make sure when you are finished that you have really identified the key roots of the problem and aren't simply attacking symptoms.

Detailed Procedure

1. Identify the problem, and state the problem to be solved. This prevents group members from working at cross-purposes. If the root problem is not obvious, brainstorm all of the possible problems, facilitate the group to consensus on a single problem to be solved at this time, and write a problem statement to define the problem for the group.

2. Analyze the problem. Brainstorm all possible underlying causes of the problem, and consolidate and group obvious duplicates and related thoughts.

Apply the 80/20 rule (20 percent of all causes account for 80 percent of the problem), and agree on a measure of impact (such as money or time) for measuring the impact of the causes you detect.

Discuss ideas in order, agreeing on whether each is a major, moderate, or minor cause.

3. Develop solutions. Once the causes are identified and ranked, seek solutions for the most critical. To do this, brainstorm all possible solutions to the causes you have identified, then narrow the list with consensus decision making.

4. Develop implementation plans. After isolating the best ideas by consensus, develop action plans to solve the problem, assigning programs or action steps and making sure team members are accountable for completing their assigned activities and that they accept the responsibility for their tasks.

During implementation, review the plan results regularly.

Small-Group Techniques (T-8)

Facilitators often divide meeting participants into small groups of three to seven people when they want intense, interactive discussion of an issue or need a wide range of inputs before guiding the team toward making a decision. The groups are usually formed so that members come from diverse functional and experiential backgrounds relevant to the issue being addressed.

When to Use Small Groups

Small groups are the best vehicle for:

▲ Debating and resolving critical corporatewide issues, such as the content of the mission statement.
▲ Tackling more issues than the team as a whole can handle expeditiously.
▲ Meeting the top team's need for a lot of input on a subject before making a key decision. For example, small groups can provide a wealth of responses to the question "What are the organization barriers to achieving our strategic objectives?"
▲ Re-energizing the group and getting a productive output when a meeting loses energy and is bogging down.
▲ Generating a better understanding of problems, points of view, and coordination issues in members of a group that has never worked together before. Small groups are particularly useful

when different functional areas and organization levels are being asked to work together for the first time.

During strategic planning, when top planning teams typically include six to thirteen people, small groups are usually used to debate and contrast differing opinions on the mission statement and to generate ideas for ways to address priority issues. At large retreats with fifteen to thirty-five participants, small groups permit detailed and meaningful discussion of issues important to the entire group. The large group can confirm, consolidate, or modify the small group's output.

Basic Rules of Small-Group Techniques

▲ Make sure that each small group has the technical skills in its member mix to address the issue assigned.
▲ Appoint a skilled facilitator to lead each group. Facilitators should be respected and have good team and people management skills; they should also have facilitation expertise and carry little or no political baggage.
▲ Don't succumb to the temptation to use small groups for every task. One to two small groups per day is plenty. And remember, small-group output has to be presented to the entire team for information and consensus.

Detailed Procedure

1. Frame the issue and the job to be done. Configure the small groups so that the expertise and leadership needed to address the assigned subject are present in each group; for example, all groups addressing new product development issues need members with marketing and production know-how.

Assign a good facilitator and recorder to each group and make sure groups understand how to report their output (e.g., flipcharts, handwritten transparencies).

Set time limits, and suggest techniques groups can use to complete their tasks (e.g., round-robin, problem solving).

2. Keep the groups on track. Monitor their progress by wandering and watching. Suggest how they can proceed faster and better if they're bogged down, give content suggestions on solutions to problems where appropriate, and ask provocative questions to get the groups moving, but intervene as little as possible and avoid taking over a small group's meeting. Your job is only to facilitate the groups' accomplishment of desired outcomes. If all is going well with the groups, stay out of their hair.

It damages participants' concentration and pace if one group finishes its work long before another. Therefore, if the groups are moving at significantly different rates, speed up the slower group, give the faster group additional work, or adjust the schedule.

3. Facilitate reporting of results. Bring the groups back to report results to the entire team. If the groups are working on the same issue, have each present its findings, allowing questions for clarification only. Put each group's conclusions on a flipchart and post the display on a wall. After all groups have presented their work, summarize common conclusions and significant differences. Through open discussion, explore the differences and why they exist. If appropriate, resolve differences on the spot; otherwise, decide how and when they will be resolved.

Solution Development (T-9)

Solution development, an important variation of problem solving (T-7), is a technique for generating ideas on how to attack an identified issue and then condensing the ideas presented into solutions that will have the greatest impact and that are practicable.

When to Use Solution Development

Solution development can generally be used to develop action plans to address any issue, problem, or opportunity arising in strategic planning or day-to-day operations. It is particularly useful during your priority-setting meeting to develop tentative action plans to address your priority issues.

Basic Rules of Solution Development

▲ Use small groups consisting of individuals representing the functions that will likely have to implement the resulting action plan.
▲ The small-group facilitator should be the person who will lead execution of the action plan.

Detailed Procedure

1. Prework is accomplished prior to developing solutions to an issue. In strategic planning, the prework usually is the consensus on other instances, people may be asked to come to a meeting with the issue already defined and, often, with ideas on how to address it.

2. The team facilitator restates the issues to be addressed and ensures that participants understand the meaning of each issue.

3. The facilitator forms groups of three or more using the technique described in the section on small groups (T-8). Groups may be given one or more issues to deal with; for very important or controversial issues, you may have two or more groups address the same issue and later contrast and reconcile their results.

4. Each team facilitator completes the following assignment:

▲ The small-group facilitator frames the priority issue, restating what the issue is and why it's important.
▲ Private work: The facilitator asks team members to write down what they think the objectives should be for the priority issue and what actions might be taken to address them. Some highly verbal teams prefer to skip this step and jump right in, soliciting ideas from the floor.
▲ The facilitator solicits one- and three-year objectives from the group. These objectives are discussed thoroughly to make sure that they are measurable or that objective measures can soon be found (one of the biggest impediments to program implementation is fuzzy or unmeasurable objectives). The facilitator then brings the group to consensus by:
  —Brainstorming all ideas for attacking the issue, using the procedure discussed in the section on brainstorming (T-3)
  —Applying the 80/20 rule to condense the ideas to the vital few that will have the most impact. Be sure to agree on how you will measure impact (on money, time, morale, etc.)
  —Listing the key "who, what, and when" for all key "hows"
  —Ballparking the impact of the program strategically and financially
  —Listing coordination requirements (the key departments or outside resources that must contribute to the program)

5. Have each small group present its conclusions to the entire planning team. Allow plenty of discussion, and lead the entire team to consensus.

6. Assign a leader and team members to work out detailed action plans, usually for presentation at the strategic planning meeting.

Fishbowling (T-10)

Fishbowling is a decision-making tool that is exceptionally useful for team-within-a-team decision making, such as occurs when an executive committee makes final decisions in front of a larger planning group after getting that group's inputs and presentations. The advantages of fishbowling are that it forces on-the-spot decision making and builds understanding of and commitment to the decisions by allowing the larger group of implementors to hear the considerations that went into the decisions.

When to Use Fishbowling

Fishbowling is useful when there are significant decisions to be made and there is no obvious consensus from a larger group with self-interested factions; when the decisions recommended by the larger group are of such moment that the smaller decision-making group feels that it must further debate the issue; and when the decision-making team disagrees with the larger group's consensus. The technique is often used in resource allocation decisions when there are excessive and competing claims on limited resources and the larger planning group cannot agree on their allocation.

Basic Rules of Fishbowling

▲ Use the technique sparingly, saving it for the resolution of key issues on which a larger planning team is gridlocked or in conflict with the top decision makers.
▲ Position the technique as an open method of involving an expanded planning team in the final decision-making process.

Detailed Procedure

1. **Through presentations and/or open discussions, air all sides of the issue before the entire planning team.** Frame and post the alternatives on flipcharts.
2. **Summarize the discussions, and frame the issues to be decided.**
3. **Place the decision-making team in front of or in the center of a larger planning group.** Give the small team a specified length of time, perhaps ten or fifteen minutes, to debate and decide the issue. The peripheral team is not allowed to participate in the discussions, but they may be questioned in their role as "experts" by the decision-making team as deliberations proceed.

Process Check (T-11)

The process check is a technique for getting people's reactions to meetings and other aspects of the strategic planning process. It uncovers how people feel about the meeting or process, what could be improved, and what, if any, barriers to the meeting's success were observed.

When to Use Process Checks

Feedback on the overall planning process is particularly important during the first year. Do process checks shortly after initiation of the process, after the priority-setting and strategy meetings, and after the plan has been in motion for three to four months. To get feedback on meetings, do process checks during and after each one.

Detailed Procedure

1. During meetings. At the midpoint of each meeting, ask the group for random and open inputs on whether the meeting is on track; if it is not, ask what should be changed. Anytime you sense that the group is not involved and engaged or that the meeting is bogging down, ask the same questions. Be prepared to reorder the meeting or deal with simmering unanticipated items when you make this intervention.

2. At the end of meetings. In a round-robin, ask participants how they felt about the meeting—its pluses, its minuses, and what they felt it accomplished. Have the CEO speak last.

Particularly at early team meetings, it's helpful to have team members complete a questionnaire probing the extent to which the team believes that it is adhering to good team behaviors, getting results, and taking corrective action when it isn't obtaining the results it wants. Ask the members to complete a form similar to the one shown in Figure 17-3, and tabulate the answers after the meeting. Address the negatives and reinforce the positives at a future meeting.

3. During and after the process. When you are installing a first complete planning process, it is critical that you meet face to face periodically with a sampling of participants. This allows you to see examples of their work, answer questions, and ensure that the process is proceeding well and has been correctly communicated. It also lets you change and improve the process as needed. Every planning process gets changed significantly after its first year; some are partially restructured during their first implementation.

Figure 17-3. Team member questionnaire.

1. Facilitative Behavior

   Positive: Check facilitative behaviors that were used by members of the team:

   __Clarifying/restating issues
   __Keeping to subject at hand
   __Contributing ideas
   __Being open and honest
   __Riding on others' ideas
   __Demonstrating positive attitudes/ involvement

   __Exhibiting willingness to confront tough issues
   __Following good meeting rules
   __Engaging in supportive conflict
   __Being willing to compromise
   __Demonstrating high levels of participation

   Absent or negative: Check the behaviors that weren't used and should have been:

   __Clarifying/restating issues
   __Keeping to subject at hand
   __Contributing ideas
   __Being open and honest
   __Riding on others' ideas
   __Demonstrating positive attitudes/ involvement

   __Exhibiting willingness to confront tough issues
   __Following good meeting rules
   __Engaging in supportive conflict
   __Being willing to compromise
   __Demonstrating high levels of participation

2. Accomplishments

   Write the three major things that the meeting accomplished:

   1. _____
   _____
   _____
   _____
   _____

   2. _____
   _____
   _____
   _____
   _____

   3. _____
   _____
   _____
   _____
   _____

(continues)

Figure 17-3. *(continued).*

3. Lack of Accomplishment
   List three items that we should have accomplished and didn't:

   1. _____
   2. _____
   3. _____

4. Overall Assessment

   Circle the number that best represents your feelings about this meeting and the overall progress of the team:

   1 = Strongly disagree   4 = Agree
   2 = Disagree   5 = Strongly agree
   3 = Agree more than disagree

   Quality of meeting: The team used
   good meeting rules. Facilitative behavior on team members' part was
   high.   1———2———3———4———5

   Accomplishments: We accom-
   plished the meeting's objectives.   1———2———3———4———5

   Commitment: The team is commit-
   ted to accomplishing its objectives.   1———2———3———4———5

   Direction: What needs to be done
   next is clear and correct.   1———2———3———4———5

   Progress: I am satisfied with the
   progress of the team to date in
   moving toward its objectives.   1———2———3———4———5

   Satisfaction: The team is challeng-
   ing and fun to work with.   1———2———3———4———5

   Facilitation: The quality of facilita-
   tion is high.   1———2———3———4———5

   Skills: We have the right skills, personalities, and motivated team
   members.   1———2———3———4———5

   Mission: The mission, objectives,
   and measures for judging success
   are clear.   1———2———3———4———5

In addition, you should send out quality control questionnaires several times during the process, including after the priority-setting meeting and the final strategic planning meeting. These questionnaires should ask respondents to rate the quality, responsiveness, impact, and innovation of the planning process, as well as the quality of the relationship with the facilitator. They should also elicit comments on what went well and suggestions for improvement.

Finally, before your final meeting, send out a questionnaire asking for a critique of your planning manuals and materials so you can improve and clarify them during your second year of planning.

Personal Interventions (T-12)

In a personal intervention, the facilitator identifies a significant flaw—or a blockage in or opportunity to expedite the planning process—and consciously and personally sets out to change the course of that process. Personal interventions require the facilitator to meet in person with individuals or teams to crystallize and resolve the intervention issue. As pointed out in Chapter 4, personal interventions by the facilitator in the strategic planning process are critical to its success and can significantly compress the change process.

The ability to make effective personal interventions is the most sophisticated and valuable personal skill a facilitator can possess. Intervention requires extensive experience with the planning process, sensitivity to people, good personal relationships, credibility, an extensive bag of solutions to various process problems, and an exquisite sense of timing as to when to intervene. Therefore, there is no simple cookbook that mechanically teaches how and when to make an intervention. It's a matter of experience, formal and on-the-job training in organization intervention techniques, and inherent skill. While more a personal skill than a technical facilitation skill, intervention ability is included in the cue cards because it is so important and serves as a quick reminder of the most common intervention situations as you implement a planning process.

The most common interventions, covered in more depth in Chapter 4 and elsewhere throughout the book, are summarized here:

1. **Organization problems.**
   ▲ *Structure.* Reorganizing functions and personnel to fit new strategies and overcome organizational blockages to strategic progress
   ▲ *Discontent/confusion.* Identification of the causes and solutions to overall attitude and morale problems or organization confusion about new directions and their role in implementing them
2. **Dysfunctional teams.** From the top team on down, diagnosing and correcting problems in team processes; redirecting team

meetings that are off track; counseling individuals or teams when their behaviors are counterproductive
3. **Critical unsurfaced issues.** Pointing out key business, process, or interpersonal issues identified in private conversations, sensed in individual or team meetings or seen, based on experience, before anyone else
4. **Bad decisions.** Challenging poor decisions and offering alternatives
5. **CEO style.** Counseling with the CEO or head of the organization to make his or her personal managerial style more effective, particularly when the organization is in transition from an authoritarian to a team-based culture
6. **Managerial style/conflicts.** Counseling and recommending ways of resolving style conflicts between teams and individuals when cultures and managerial styles clash—for example in cases of cultural clashes between technical and marketing cultures or authoritarian, old-line styles and open team styles
7. **Performance/competence problems.** Helping management decide how to deal with poor performers, people whose skills don't fit the new job or culture; counseling individuals unhappy with or incapable of handling the change process
8. **Resourcing.** Suggesting resources to deal with special problems outside of the organization's expertise, such as where to obtain or how to provide personal counseling, communications training, team building, benchmarking studies, market research, technical and managerial skill training, and specialized consultants

===

DO'S AND DON'TS

DO

- *Learn all the techniques.* You'll need them all, and then some.
- *Fit the technique to the situation* as it develops. What you planned to do may not fit the needs and mood of the group as your agenda unfolds.
- *Invent new techniques* on the spot. Use combinations of the techniques listed here or invent something new and effective. Don't be afraid to experiment. Most groups are very forgiving if you make a mistake and very appreciative when you use a unique technique that energizes them and gets the job done.
- *Train the team* to use the facilitation techniques as you go along so that they can apply them independently. Let them practice by leading segments of your meetings and the process.

DON'T

- *Get so bound up in process* and technique so that the objectives aren't accomplished. Go for what works.
- *Hesitate to confront* the situation if meetings and the process get off track. Find out what's not working, and move on.
- *Force people into a spotlight role* if it is clear they are uncomfortable and ineffective as on-their-feet facilitators.

Chapter 18

Unstopping Typical Blockages

If you have made a mistake, cut your losses as quickly as possible.
—Bernard Baruch, financier and adviser to U.S. presidents

No change goes smoothly. Somewhere along the line, your planning process will stall, swerve, or even grind to a dead stop. A savvy manager or facilitator will detect both obvious and subtle signs of blockage and, like a good doctor, dole out the medicine before the disease becomes fatal. This chapter describes the classic blockages and what you can do about them (typical blockages are summarized in Figure 18-1).

Common Blockages to Plan Success

Lack of CEO Commitment

This is the most serious blockage and the most difficult one to unstop. The very people who should be spearheading planning—CEOs—do occasionally resist or simply give lip service to planning. Their reasons are many. Like other people, they may fear change, feel intimidated by planning because they don't know how, or think it's too much work, or they may be satisfied with the status quo. Some refuse to share power with others, and a few are shackled by egos so big they are convinced they can lead the organization to glory on their own instincts.

There are several ways, however, to shake recalcitrant CEOs loose from their negativism or inaction. Although corporate boards have recently shown themselves more and more willing to apply the ultimate solution—removal—the approaches listed here fall short of that. They

Figure 18-1. Typical planning blockages.

▼ Lack of CEO commitment

▼ Lack of time and resources

▼ Changing corporate direction and priorities

▼ Stalled teams

▼ Reluctant or incompetent team members

▼ Lack of lower-level execution

▼ Lack of lower-level leadership and competence

▼ Poor coordination between functions

▼ Incompetent incumbents

▼ Unsuccessful plan

▼ General organization malaise and cultural inertia

▼ Temporary crises

▼ Competitive threats

▼ Failure of a major program

are aimed more at other senior managers who may be able to influence CEO action.

1. *Demonstrate the need.* Enlist the support of top-team members, board members, or even outsiders who have the CEO's ear to get permission to run an organization diagnostic. If you can confront your CEO with objective evidence that the organization or markets are in trouble, the competition is winning, and the company is missing significant opportunities, you may convince the chief executive to act. It helps if the CEO's own staff strongly supports planning and participates in the discussion of diagnostic results and remedies.

2. *Take it one step at a time.* A CEO who balks at full-scale strategic planning will probably accede to a suggestion to develop the organization's priority issues. It is a rare and foolish CEO who won't authorize this simple and inexpensive step.

3. *Settle for tacit approval* if you can't get the chief's participation. One indifferent officer of a Fortune 500 company let his staff plan for

the organization, rubber-stamped their output, and let them run with it. The best way? No. Better than nothing? Yes, even if your CEO only approves portions of your plan.

4. *Plan strategically at the SBU and the functional level,* even if the top won't have anything to do with the process. In one Fortune 500 company led by a chairman who would not plan, two key line officers developed plans for their own units. They made assumptions about what the corporate direction would be and confirmed them with top management. Their results over several years were so far superior to those of other parts of the company that the chairman finally followed their lead and began planning for the entire corporation.

Lack of Time and Resources

Any organization that uses lack of time and resources as an excuse not to plan is doing itself a tremendous disservice. Planning shows you how best to deploy what resources your organization does have available and often results in increased resources. It's up to the CEO to schedule the process sufficiently in advance and to insist that people find the time to do it.

Changing Corporate Direction and Priorities

Corporate direction and priorities do change, and for good reasons, including changes in the outside world, changes in inside performance, needed changes in strategy, and changes in resources available. Shifting direction and priorities, however, can cause tremendous confusion at lower levels and block progress toward strategic objectives.

When direction changes, top management must communicate those changes throughout the organization and ensure that lower-level plans are quickly realigned with new priorities.

Stalled Teams

When top or lower-level teams lose momentum, it is usually the result of lack of leadership, the press of ordinary business, or lack of commitment. A professional facilitator will usually detect the dysfunction and get the team moving again after diagnosing and removing the blockages. If the team is not using a professional facilitator, bring one in to help the team diagnose its operations and propose and implement its own solutions.

Reluctant or Incompetent Team Members

If confronting and counseling a poorly performing team member doesn't work, the person has to be replaced. It is the team's responsibility to reject laggards and ask for a replacement from the top team or the functional boss to whom the poor performer reports.

Lack of Lower-Level Execution

Poor execution of plans at lower levels is a significant problem, particularly in the early stages of implementing change. The key to solving it is diagnosing it early enough to get the plan back on track. Keep your antenna up to detect missed objectives, consistently late performance, or constantly revised action plans. Quarterly strategic reviews, normal operating and functional reviews, and personal performance reviews should flag poor execution and spur immediate remedial action.

Rather than wait for problems to reveal themselves, you may want to use a professional facilitator to identify systemic problems, such as confused delegation of corporate objectives, lack of understanding of what's expected to support the corporate strategy, inadequate training in setting objectives and planning at lower levels, and reward systems that thwart planning. The facilitator should also audit action plans in leverage areas to point out where competence, resource, coordination, or other problems stand in the way of success. Expect such a facilitator to offer solutions both to those implementing the plan and to general management.

Lack of Lower-Level Leadership and Competence

If the lower levels of your organization lack the leadership, managerial skills, and functional competence needed to implement your plan, get training and counseling help fast for the underskilled. If you don't have time to change behaviors, you will have to change the people.

Poor Coordination Between Functions

Poor interdepartmental coordination is one of the most common and insidious of problems. Prevention is better than cure, so pay attention to intergroup coordination requirements during planning, and make sure that the importance of coordinating major strategic tasks is understood by all and is systematically required by your planning process.

Despite your best efforts, some coordination problems and conflicts are bound to occur. Surface them through strategic reviews. In addition, your facilitator should be able to spot potential problems before they erupt by conducting informal and confidential interviews with key strategic executors.

Ask your facilitator to recommend solutions or to bring the affected parties together to develop their own solutions. Finally, make sure your performance appraisal and compensation systems reward good teamwork and coordination.

Incompetent Incumbents

Unfortunately, people who can't function in the new order are casualties of the change process. You will have to remove them, particularly if they occupy leverage positions. Be kind but quick, and change them sooner rather than later.

The Plan Isn't Working

Sometimes, even when the plan execution effort is high, you don't get the results you want. Perhaps, despite all your internal efforts, you are not seeing cost reductions; perhaps, after all your analysis and targeted marketing, you are still disappointed in your market share. If so, it's time to stop, sit back, diagnose what's wrong, and redirect your efforts. Take your cue from one company that engaged in a little detective work when it was unable to get consistently high results in customer service. The cause turned out to be a hairy snarl of interrelated problems—poor production scheduling, inadequate documentation of orders, supervisory incompetence, and lack of adherence to procedures. It took some regrouping to solve the problem, which had been misdiagnosed as resulting from production inefficiencies and poor order forecasting and scheduling.

General Organization Malaise and Cultural Inertia

It's not uncommon that, in the first year of planning, people just don't get the message and continue to be uncomfortable with planning and unsure whether the organization is serious or whether this is just the latest snake oil. As a result, planning is done reluctantly and perfunctorily, and plans, programs, and objectives aren't accomplished.

You can resolve this only through leadership, communication, persistence, and accountability. The CEO should continually emphasize the importance of planning and drive it home by holding people accountable for results, publicly acknowledging positive achievements, recognizing people who get results, and showing disappointment in those who don't. In addition, signal actions such as chopping losing or strategically unimportant businesses, replacing incompetent incumbents, and giving extraordinary rewards to those who succeed get the message across quickly.

One billion-dollar corporation got only tepid results during its first year of plan execution. It had never held its people accountable for anything other than budget; the corporate culture rewarded people for getting along with everybody, avoiding tough issues, and taking orders from above, rather than for independent thinking and action. Consequently, most people dismissed planning as unimportant; execution and coordination of plans were poor, and business went on as usual. That year the company accomplished only 65 percent of its objectives and strategic action steps. The message got across at year's end, however, when key individuals were denied significant portions of their bonuses because they hadn't achieved promised results. Implementation improved considerably in the second year, reaching a more acceptable 85 percent.

Dysfunctional Organizations and Management Teams: The Chain-Saw Solution

Self-interested managers and old-line, bureaucratic cultures whose dogged purpose is to maintain the status quo or to keep a favored group in power can and will sabotage change. Their strategies include passive resistance to progress, inaction, and, sometimes, Byzantine plotting, scheming, and outright collusion in power plays and coups d'état.

There are sick and unchangeable cultures where the leadership and the culture are truly dysfunctional and unchangeable. There is no solution but to replace key leadership throughout the organization and then ask the new leadership quickly to remove subordinate players who don't have the motivation or the ability to implement needed changes. One Fortune 500 chairman tried to invoke change over a four-year period by instituting moderate organization structure changes and minimal changes in the management ranks. Management, particularly at the middle and lower levels, thwarted his plans at every turn, leading to two major subsequent reorganizations. Interviewed ten years later, the chairman said simply that if he had it to do over again, he'd go through the organization with a chain saw on day one, cutting out the deadwood and bringing in competence and "his own type." Not a pretty solution, but often necessary.

Temporary Crises

Sometimes unforeseen crises do intervene and force organizations to set aside plan implementation temporarily. It's better to postpone action plans until a clearly established date than to frustrate the organization and dilute operating and strategic results by insisting people perform the impossible. Reaching your strategic objectives is important; doing so on an exact day is less so.

Competitive Threats

When you face new external threats, don't just sit there; redo the plan. When club stores and food discounters such as Sams and Costco moved into their market, conventional supermarkets had to redo their plans quickly. They had only three choices: Lose significant market share and money, open their own discount outlets, or compete selectively in specific merchandise categories and for targeted customers. Most supermarket chains revised their plans in favor of the third alternative. In a similar vein, Compaq Computer belatedly but effectively switched gears to take on the clone computer manufacturers in 1992. The company quickly gained a significant share of the low-price personal computer market.

Failure of a Major Program

When a major program flops, regroup and figure out why it failed—then don't repeat your mistake. One large manufacturer of packaged goods, for example, rushed a new product to market to access a new, strategically important market segment. Because it was in a hurry, the company bypassed even minimal market research and testing. The product bombed. Big time and big bucks—lost. Next time around, the company did the research and testing and pulled a new product before it cost them a bundle.

Identifying Blockages Through Organizational Feedback

Many companies use a facilitator or organization behavior consultant during the first several years of planning to conduct periodic confidential interviews with the people who are responsible for plan execution at all levels. Such interventions once or twice a year are not expensive and provide important feedback as the interviewer finds out what's working and what's not, counsels and suggests solutions on the spot, and brings serious or systemic problems to the attention of the top team or the CEO.

During such an audit, for example, one large company discovered that a recently implemented incentive scheme emphasized short-term earnings and functional objectives, thereby acting as a strong disincentive to long-term strategic progress and intergroup coordination. The company quickly revised its incentive and performance appraisal program to put more emphasis on corporate results, accomplishment of strategic programs, and longer-term results.

Another organization found that top-level plans and objectives were being incorporated into lower-level plans inaccurately and too late. This changed when the company required officers to meet with their own organizations immediately after each year's planning meetings. Under the new system, as officers got lower-level input for fleshing out top-level plans, they ensured that those plans were reflected in objectives and programs at all levels. If any downstream problems surfaced, they reported them back to the top team before the entire plan was put in motion.

DO'S AND DON'TS

DO

- *Be a diagnostician.* Detect and jump on problems fast, particularly in the early years of planning when they tend to pop up all over. You can't manage the details, but you can find out where the blockages are and use organizational Drāno to unstop them.
- *Be somewhat patient.* It takes time to remove resistance and blockages and get results.
- *But don't wait too long.* If people are the problem, change their behavior fast or change them.

DON'T

- *Expect things to go smoothly* once you have developed the plan and sent it out to the troops. You're only on square one. Making the plan work is the tough and time-consuming part.

Chapter 19

Summary:
Lessons for Success

You have to play this game right. You have to think right. . . .
You've got to take it one game at a time, one hitter at a time. You've
got to go on doing the things you've talked about and agreed about
beforehand. You can't get three outs at a time or five runs at a time.
You've got to concentrate on each play, each hitter, each pitch. All
this makes the game much slower and much clearer. It breaks it
down to its smallest part. If you take the game like that—one pitch,
one hitter, one inning at a time, and then one *game* at a time—the
next thing you know, you look up and you've won.

—Rick Dempsey, 1988 Los Angeles Dodger

From all the lessons in this book, what can we extract that succinctly
defines good planning, superior plans, and productive implementation?
What qualities ensure successful planning or point down the road to
failure? Comparing successful and futile planning experiences reveals
the following lists of benchmarks for excellence and predictors of
failure.

Successful planning processes:

▲ Have a top-level driver/visionary at the helm.
▲ Are spare, lean, simple, and well understood.
▲ Are light on paperwork, long on thinking and doing.
▲ Develop out of what the organization needs and its culture and
  strategic situation, not from a textbook process.
▲ Are championed by people in the organization who can identify
  how planning helps them move forward and obtain needed re-
  sources.
▲ Involve those who must implement at all levels.
▲ Dynamically and continually allocate resources.

▲ Allow for quick change when the outside world or inside priorities change.
▲ Depend on teams to do the job.
▲ Use top-notch facilitators, whether external or internal.
▲ Tie naturally into the company's operations planning and financial and budgeting systems.
▲ Allow for annual tune-ups and redos.

Successful plans:

▲ Are market-based.
▲ Have doable objectives.
▲ Set priorities for businesses, strategic issues, programs, and activities.
▲ Allocate resources on the basis of those priorities.
▲ Select only a few strategic priorities on which to act.
▲ Address both external strategy and internal support strategies.
▲ Establish clearly understood, written, and publicized accountabilities for objectives, programs, and actions.

Successful implementations:

▲ Work because the driver/visionary constantly reinforces the vision and plan and pushes, shoves, nudges, and cajoles the implementors to keep them on track.
▲ Have good leaders/managers strategically placed in leverage managerial positions.
▲ Place the right doers in leverage jobs throughout the organization.
▲ Use teams from the top down to develop and implement plans.
▲ Utilize facilitators to start and keep the ball rolling.
▲ Enforce accountability through personal objectives and performance reviews.
▲ Include scheduled plan review and rework.
▲ Reward success financially and psychologically.
▲ Are flexible, cutting and fitting programs and reallocating resources as progress occurs and the outside world changes.

Failures happen when:

▲ Organizations pay lip service to planning, going through the motions and paperwork, because common wisdom says every good company must have a plan.
▲ The planning team is process-bound, rather than oriented to-

ward setting priorities, establishing accountabilities, and pursuing end results.

▲ The CEO is not a visionary and is not committed to planning and strategy.

▲ The people who must execute the plan are not involved in planning, not committed, and not held accountable for strategic results.

▲ The plan is not reviewed.

▲ The current business is not "put to bed"; barriers to progress are not removed.

▲ The wrong people are in the wrong places, and the organization is unwilling to deal with problem people.

▲ The organization and the culture are unwilling to change.

▲ Planners ignore marketplace realities. They use incorrect facts, assumptions, and strategies and believe too much in their internal wisdom.

▲ Management is not tough enough.

▲ The plan includes too many objectives, programs, and activities.

▲ The organization lets day-to-day crises intervene.

▲ Existing resources are inadequate or improperly allocated to do the job.

Those are the keys to being a success or a failure. Which are you now? Which are you going to be?

Appendix

Mission Statements and Strategic Plan Summaries

1. Henning Packaging, Inc.
2. Sterling Bancshares
3. UST Human Resources Department

Henning Packaging, Inc.: Strategic Plan Summary

MISSION

Henning Packaging, Inc., will be a niche marketer and a superior supplier of value-added packaging, directing its efforts toward servicing those market segments where customers are willing to pay for exceptional quality, service, and technical assistance.

Business Definition

HPI is a printer and converter of paper and plastic packaging.

We market our products in the United States and Canada and, if opportunities arise, in Mexico.

We will seek market segments where there is a need for exceptional graphics, printing, other special characteristics, and superior service.

Our current end-market focus is primarily in packaging for pet food, flour and meal, agricultural commodities, lawn and garden products, salt, and human food; we also sell high-density sheeting for various industrial uses, including sales to paper packaging companies for use as a barrier ply.

Strategies

Our strategic thrusts (competitive advantages) will be:

1. Superior service—being highly responsive to customer needs; being on time all the time; making complete shipments all the time; and helping our customers solve packaging problems

2. Quality—putting out 100 percent defect-free packaging all the time and protecting a total-quality image
3. Technical support—providing the market and our customers with alternatives to meet their emerging packaging needs and with solutions to their printing and packaging problems.

Our product-market strategies will be:

1. *Grow:* To grow in sales of _____ packaging (especially to _____ producers), _____ packaging to _____ companies.
2. *Hold:* At least for now, to hold our position in sales of _____ packaging to the _____ and _____.
3. *Study:* To study the _____ markets with a view to reconfiguring our marketing mix in the _____ division for increased profitability.

Our pricing strategy will be to seek less price-sensitive customers and market segments so that, where price is equal, the advantages we will build in quality, service, and technical assistance will win the business.

We will strive to be a leader in developing new and innovative packaging solutions and offering them to our customers and to the market. We will creatively and effectively use the best of the current state-of-the-art materials and equipment to provide innovative packaging.

We will be competitive in cost; we will work together vigorously and constantly to reduce costs, contain overhead expense, improve productivity, and reduce waste.

Objectives

Financial: 1993: Sales of $___ million.
                       Net income of $___ million.
                1994: Sales of $___ million.
                       Net income of $___ million.
                1995: Sales of $___ million.
                       Net income of $___ million.

Quality: 1993: (1) ___% gross returns and allowances.
                       (2) Have improved internal quality. Satisfaction survey in place by 1/1/93.
                1994: Have customer quality satisfaction survey in place.

	By 1995:	No more than one unit rejected per ____ shipped.
On-time Delivery:	1993:	99% of all units shipped on time, meaning (a) within the time frames to which we have committed, and (b) at least as quickly as any of our competitors could respond.
Product Development:	By 1995:	7.5% of sales are of products new to Henning. A new product will be considered "new" for three years.
Cleanliness and Housekeeping:		Reach levels of cleanliness and housekeeping required for us to be a certified supplier for each customer or targeted customer that has a vendor-certification program, according to each such customer's timetable.

Values

A. Internal

▲ At all times, we will conduct our business in a legal, moral, and ethical manner.
▲ In all activities, safety will come first.
▲ We will treat employees fairly.
▲ All employees will have a chance to develop their skills, abilities, and opportunities for personal and financial reward, within our policies, according to their potential and without discrimination on the basis of race, religion, sex, age, or national origin.
▲ As the company succeeds, we will share the fruits of our success with our employees by providing good jobs and through annual increases and profit sharing or incentive bonuses.

B. External

▲ We will be driven by an obsession for customer satisfaction, and we will gear our entire operation to that end.
▲ We will deliver what we promise, when we promise it.
▲ We will strive to provide pleasant surprises, and no unpleasant surprises, to our customers.
▲ We will do our part to protect the environment and to support the communities in which we operate.

Priority Issues

There are seven priority strategic issues on which we will focus our efforts in the coming year (at least):

1. Quality
2. Manufacturing cost (further reduction in waste and increase in efficiency)
3. Service (quick turnarounds, on-time delivery, complete shipments, full and effective communication with customers)
4. Developmental projects (offering a steady stream of new packaging products on a regular basis)
5. Human resources (training, morale, etc.)
6. Management information systems—provide better information systems, including real-time information
7. _____ division: restructuring the marketing and product mix of the _____ division for significantly improved productivity

Sterling Bancshares: Mission Statement

MISSION

The strategic, highly profitable objective of Sterling Bancshares Corporation is the building of a high-performance, full-service community bank where people matter.

We offer and deliver competitive product lines that meet targeted customer needs and expectations while maintaining asset quality, capital strength, and earnings performance. We provide these products only when we are able to deliver them with the service and quality our customers deserve. For the Corporation to continue to fulfill these goals, we must be able to guarantee that the four cornerstones of our success—our customers, our employees, our communities, and our shareholders—are always firmly in place.

We must respond to:

Our customers:	They are our business. We will provide them with the products they want and need.
Our employees:	They are The Bank. Our customers know them as The Bank. We will provide them with the training, the working environment, and the recognition that encourage and promote growth.
Our communities:	Their success is our success. We will meet the financial and public service needs of our communities, as a corporation and personally as individuals.
Our shareholders:	They are the owners of the Corporation, and, as our shareholders, they are entitled to a fair return on their investment.

Vision

▲ Return on equity of:
    _____ by 1995
    _____ by 1997
▲ Maintain an equity-to-asset ratio of 6 percent.
▲ Take advantage of unique market opportunities to grow to:
    $_____ billion by 1995
    $_____ billion by 1997
▲ Raise additional capital of $_____ million.

Business Definitions and Scope

▲ Our customers will be diverse, depending upon product line and local demographics. Our focus will be a geographical market concentration within Middlesex County and, should strategic market opportunities present themselves, elsewhere in Metropolitan Boston.
▲ Our products will emphasize:
—Increasing the commercial loan portfolio, while maintaining asset quality and expanded fee income.
—Increasing home equity production by leveraging the branch network and broadening the product line.
—Increasing residential mortgage production and loan servicing volume.
—Selectively increasing commercial real estate lending, while maintaining asset quality in a continually difficult market.
—Increasing core deposits (non-time) by emphasizing relationships, providing quality customer service, and leveraging the branches into full banking service operations.
—Our product line will be enlarged and, as a community bank, we will provide most (98 percent) customer needs. We will not be all things to all people.

Strategic Emphasis

▲ Community bank
▲ Responsiveness
▲ High level of quality customer service

▲ Professionalism
▲ Financial stability/strength

Values

For Our Customers

▲ Responsive/flexible
▲ Service-oriented
▲ Well-trained and profes-
   sional

▲ Broad product line
▲ Competitive
▲ Convenience

For Our Employees

▲ Rewarded for performance
   and teamwork
▲ Well-managed
▲ Staff treated fairly

▲ Good benefits
▲ Management cares
▲ Community participation

For Our Community

▲ Being a community leader
▲ Caring about the com-
   munity

▲ Investing in the community

For Our Shareholders

▲ Profitable
▲ Well-managed

▲ Growth-oriented
▲ Communication/credibility

Sterling Bank and Sterling Bancshares Corporation will be ethical in all
their external and internal business.

We must have the capital strength, the human resources, the
strong customer base, and the healthy communities for the Corporation
to succeed.

UST Human Resources Department: Mission Statement

MISSION

What We Are . . .

HR is a professional services team that supports the corporation's objectives and facilitates strategic change within UST, Inc.

Our Overall Purpose . . .

We are dedicated to helping the corporation, its business units, departments, and individuals to change, where appropriate, from their current state of skill, performance, and work satisfaction to their preferred future states as defined in their strategic, operational, and personal development plans.

Measures of Success . . .

Our key measure of success will be our customers' satisfaction with our performance in accomplishing mutually established objectives.

Vision

Our vision is to be perceived:

Internally as a major factor in the strategic and long-term success of UST, its business units, and its functions and of individuals within those entities

Internally and *externally* among targeted peer companies as a leader in HR management and in the development and application of modern, effective HR techniques

Roles

▲ *Proactive roles.* Develop, initiate, and proactively implement processes to help customers change their culture, behaviors, and performance from the current state to the preferred state as defined by the corporate strategic plan and value statement and other customers.

▲ *Corporate support roles.* Support human resources elements or corporate-directed strategies, policies, and programs, as well as other corporatewide HR programs.

▲ *Customer support.* At their request, meet the unique needs of customers.

▲ *Internal development.* Be outstanding with the highest level of competency—develop HR skills and be a leader in technical competence in our field. To be committed to continuous improvement in sustaining our standards of excellence.

Scope of Business

Target Customers

Companywide: individuals, functions, subsidiaries, and management.

Products and Services (see Figure A-1)

▲ Audit/trend analysis
▲ Benefits

Figure A-1. Human resources products and services.

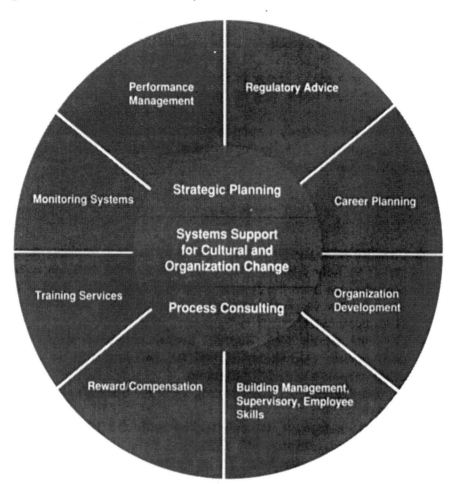

▲ Change processes
▲ Compensation
▲ Employee relations/counseling
▲ Facilitation of strategic planning
▲ Government/regulatory compliance
▲ Health programs
▲ HR data analysis and maintenance
▲ HR/people planning/career development
▲ Information systems
▲ Labor relations
▲ Organizational consulting
▲ Recruitment, selection, and retention of employees
▲ Safety/environmental practices
▲ Support staff services
▲ Training/management development

Stakeholders

Shareholders, employees, internal and external customers, and government communities.

Values

HR Employees

Within HR we value:

▲ An environment that yields satisfied employees committed to their team and its accomplishments; high morale; and a balance between challenge, growth, security, and personal satisfaction
▲ Participation
▲ Achievement of rigorous objectives
▲ Teamwork within the department and with customers
▲ Growth in each individual's technical and personal skills

Our Customers

For our customers we will:

▲ Be responsive
▲ Be timely in meeting their needs
▲ Foster superior working and personal relationships

We will strive for them to see us as:

▲ Having significant impact
▲ A highly competent, professional, and hard-working team
▲ Valued counselors, listeners, and resourceful facilitators

The Corporation

The corporation will see us as:

▲ Visionary catalysts of strategic change
▲ Understanding UST's businesses

▲ Having high impact with doers and thinkers who add significant value and make measurable and innovative contributions to the achievement of overall corporate objectives

Shareholders

To our shareholders we will:

▲ Provide stable, consistent, competitive, and equitable HR policies, procedures, and programs
▲ Be cost-effective in supporting business's needs
▲ Be fiscally responsible fiduciaries of UST resources; fair to both employees and shareholders

Government, Legislative, Regulatory

With an overall reputation for integrity, we will be proactive in:

▲ Responsibly complying with regulations
▲ Serving as a partner in developing and interpreting regulatory guidelines in the companywide environment
▲ Maintaining a safe and healthy workplace
▲ Remaining an environmentally responsible corporate citizen
▲ Nondiscriminatory practices and programs

Communities

We will be an excellent corporate citizen through:

▲ Leadership in our communities: supporting education, charities, and the development and maintenance of high community standards
▲ Active involvement: generously giving time and money

Vendors

We will seek partnership with our vendors to:

▲ Provide the best possible, cost-effective service to the company
▲ Establish long-term, dedicated, win-win relationships that are enjoyable and rewarding and add value to both parties
▲ Define clear, mutual objectives, direction, and expectations

Glossary

Strategy Terms

operational/tactical Plans, programs, actions, or objectives with short-term (usually one year or less) time frames for completion. Operational plans usually call for "making the numbers" and involve tactics in sales, pricing, production, and short-term costs.

strategic Matters that are long term and structural in nature; the fundamental ways that you will conduct business in the future. For example, strategic changes often involve target markets, product categories offered, geography served, organization structure, manufacturing processes, distribution channels, and financial structure.

strategic business unit (SBU) An organization unit that is responsible for the bottom-line financial performance of the business. It usually has under its control or influence the resources needed to compete successfully in a specified target market. SBUs within the same company usually serve different markets and often have distinct products, services, operations, marketing methods, and support functions. They sometimes share resources, such as manufacturing, product development, and sales, with other SBUs.

strategy How you will achieve your objectives. Usually refers to broad, long-term, and significant structural methods and actions. Strategies are taken at many levels within companies. The line between strategies and tactics is blurred.

Overall Strategies

postures Real (unit) sales and investment posture for key business units, markets, products, and customers. Generally defined as grow (invest, grow sales and share), hold (maintain position, maintenance investment), milk (manage for cash generation), and divest (sell/shut down for cash generation or to stop losses). Note that a business can be high-priority (because it's big and important and is the core of the enterprise) but be in a hold or milk posture.

priorities Rank order for resource allocation of key markets, prod-

323

ucts, and customers. Sometimes classified as core (most important), secondary, and tertiary.

routes The methods of change or growth open to a business or a market. Possibilities include acquisition, internal growth, licensing, joint venture, and restructuring and divestiture.

External Strategy

competitive advantage One of the three basic and broad methods of achieving a competitive advantage: cost-price, value, and differentiation.

strategic fixes Means of fixing performance in important customer need areas in which you're judged deficient. For example, a deficiency in customer service (defined as percentage of orders delivered on time and complete) has to be fixed through a focused strategic fix program.

strategic thrusts The top one to four overall external strategies used to gain a competitive advantage and to beat the competition within the chosen area of competitive advantage. They must meet one or more high-priority customer needs better than the strategies of the competition and are usually expressed in broad terms such as quality, service, and technical innovation. These broad thrusts are then fleshed out with implementation details. For example, a goal of quality may refer to achieving a specified percentage of rejects; reaching this level in turn requires an internal quality program that will produce the desired strategic results and advantage.

subsidiary external strategies Other important external strategies that are of secondary importance to the customer or are "customer invisible," such as media and point of sale advertising.

Internal Strategy

executional details The many detailed actions that must be undertaken to implement a strategic thrust or strategy. For example, a "quality" strategic thrust for a produce distributor will require myriad actions and dedicated resources in the areas of purchasing, computer systems, distribution facilities, specialized trucks, and handling systems.

strategic thrusts The two to four key internal strategies that are most important in implementing the external strategic thrusts. For example, an external thrust of customer service may require internal strategic thrusts of advanced information systems in order entry, processing, and manufacturing to produce the service demanded by the customer.

marketing strategy External strategies in the areas of the four P's: Product/Services, Price, Place, and Promotion. Some elements of the marketing strategy may be important enough to be strategic thrusts; the rest are simply executional details.

subsidiary internal strategies Other key internal strategies that, while important to success, do not support the external strategic thrust. For example, a company whose strategic thrusts are product innovation and customer service may have a subsidiary internal strategy of manufacturing cost reduction through process automation.

Other Strategic Terms

action plans Forms that summarize program objectives and key action steps—the "who, what, and when's"—needed to accomplish the program. Action plans include the expected impact, cost and gain, required nondollar resources such as people and skills, and any necessary coordination requirements between departments.

assumptions Those few external trends that will significantly affect the plan's results and that are the foundation on which the plan rests. Their validity must be monitored throughout the plan; if actual events deviate from expectation, it may be necessary to review or adjust the plan.

core competencies Those few internal competencies at which you are very, very good, better than your competitors, and that you will build on and use to beat the competition and to achieve your strategic objectives.

corporate Issues and matters that (1) require commitment of resources from throughout the organization, (2) are so critical to the future of the corporation that management by the top team is required, (3) need top-team involvement to coordinate and resolve actions between several functions or divisions, or (4) are assigned exclusively to top corporate management, such as the treasury function.

critical success factors Those activities that must be done well to excel in the marketplace.

external assessment A strategic assessment of external trends that can help or hurt the company in the future, leading to definition of opportunities and threats. Trends are usually examined in the seven key areas of markets/customers, competition, sociodemographics, technology, factors of production, government/legislative, and economy. Sometimes called environmental analysis.

functional/departmental Issues and matters that affect and can usually be resolved within a particular department or functional area, such as sales, quality assurance, manufacturing, and human resources. Significant functional issues may become corporate issues if they have a major impact on the business. For example, while the sales division may spearhead a program to revamp the customer service delivery system, the activity may be so important that it "makes the corporate list."

internal assessment   A strategic assessment of internal capabilities and performance leading to definition of strengths and weaknesses. Typical areas examined include the organization structure and people competence, capital assets, systems, technology, financial structure and performance, service, quality, and product and service performance; these areas are often benchmarked against the competition.

internal linkages   Horizontal (between peer functions) and vertical (between organization layers) linkages between organization units that have a part in executing strategic programs and objectives. The linkages usually consist of jointly held or delegated objectives, committing functions and departments to specific actions supporting corporate strategy. For example, to implement an external strategy of providing products with superior performance, a linkage must be made to R&D that specifies what products are required, when, and at what performance levels as well as the resources and time that will be devoted to producing them. R&D must accept responsibility for the assignments in order for the linkage to be complete.

key result area (KRA)   An area of business activity in which the business must excel to meet customer needs, beat the competition, and meet stakeholder/shareholder expectations. For each area, the company must decide how success will be measured and then set specific objectives.

leverage functions   Functional areas whose performance is key to strategic success and implementation of the plan.

leverage managers   Managers who have a critical role in implementing strategy.

market segment   A group of customers within a broad market whose needs and wants are similar and who tend to purchase similar goods and services. Because market segments respond in the same way to a given offer and have some needs that are distinctly different from those of other segments of the market, each segment can be targeted with differentiated product, service, and promotional offerings. Most markets can be divided into a number of segments.

mission   A broad articulation of the corporation's purpose (why do we exist?), direction (where do we want to go? what do we want to become?), and how it will reach its objectives (what strategies and routes will we use to get there?). Technically, it has three parts:

1. *The vision*—a succinct statement that defines (a) the purpose of the corporation (why do we exist?), (b) its desired future state (what does the company want to become in the future?), (c) its key strategic thrusts and strategies (how will it get there?), and

(d) its core values (what are the pivotal values that drive our behaviors and culture?).
2. *The business definition*—the range of markets, customers, products and services, distribution means, and technologies that the company will consider in fulfilling its mission.
3. *Values*—The complete set of values that the company and its employees stand for and that, if embraced, will lead to the desired future. Values are divided into (a) internal values, directed toward fellow employees and (b) external values, directed toward customers, suppliers, the business community, the general community, and the government.

There are almost as many definitions of what missions, visions, business definitions, and value statements are as there are CEOs and strategists. This definition has worked for me and for many companies over the years and is the one used throughout this book. It doesn't matter, however, what you call the elements in and information required under the mission, nor is it important where you put it in your strategic plan, what its written length is, or how you communicate it to your employees.

What does count is that you address all of the mission elements, communicate them effectively to your employees and stakeholders, and put them into action using terminology and a format that works for your business and culture. The mission becomes a founding document, like the Declaration of Independence and the Bill of Rights, that is used day to day to ensure that key decisions are in line with the mission's direction and within its constraints.

objectives Your goals, what you want to accomplish. They are measurable in terms of time, quality, quantity, and/or dollars.

opportunities Trends, events, and ideas that can be capitalized on to increase future profits and market share. Common opportunities include emerging market segments, new technologies, new products or services, geographic expansion, acquisitions, divestitures, a faltering competitor, and cost reductions.

priority issues Those select strengths, weaknesses, opportunities, or threats that must be dealt with because:

▲ They have high, long-term impact on profitability or competitive advantage.
▲ Timing is critical, and quick action is essential to take advantage of fleeting or rapidly developing situations.

programs Coordinated actions that will lead to the accomplishment of the objectives of the specific program and, indirectly, to the accomplishment of the higher-level objectives of the priority issue the program relates to and of the business overall. Programs are summarized in program action plans.

situation analysis An evaluation of the company's strategic situation, including internal performance and competencies and external trends that can significantly affect the company.

strengths Current capabilities that are superior to those of the competition and that help meet a top-ranked customer need or give a significant advantage over the competition in the marketplace. Companies need to maintain or improve key strengths over time.

SWOTs Acronym for strengths, weaknesses, opportunities, and threats.

threats Possible events outside of your control that you need to plan for or decide how to mitigate. Typical threats include the entrance of a new competitor, competitor's actions, legislation, or regulations that will increase costs or eliminate a product, or a declining core product or market.

values Qualities that you want your employees to hold and use to guide their behaviors and spending in conducting business. Usually broken down into (1) internal values, held toward internal stakeholders, such as employees, and (2) external values, held toward external groups, such as suppliers and the community.

weaknesses Areas in current capabilities that prevent the company from achieving advantage and/or meeting top-ranked customer needs or strategic objectives. Weaknesses need to be fixed quickly before irretrievable losses in market share or profits occur.

Index